THE SIMON & SCHUSTER
POCKET GUIDE TO BEER

MICHAEL JACKSON

REVISED AND UPDATED
THIRD EDITION

A Fireside Book
Published by Simon & Schuster Inc.
New York London Toronto
Sydney Tokyo Singapore

Dedication

To my late father, Jack Jackson
born Isaac Jakowitz, Yorkshire, 1909–84.

Acknowledgments

Brewers and importers of beer all over the world, and their trade
organizations, have gone to trouble and expense far beyond their
self-interest to help me research this book. My heartfelt thanks to
them. Many friends and professional colleagues have also helped,
and I am indebted to all of them. For their help specifically on this
most recent edition, my thanks to Erich Vogt, in Germany; Derek
Walsh, in The Netherlands; Gary and Libby Gillman, Alan Stokell,
John Maxwell, Andrew Ferguson and others in Canada; and
especially to the brewing consultants Alan Dikty (of BRD, Evanston,
Illinois) and Vince Cottone (of Seattle) and Bret Nickels, of *The
California Celebrator*. My further thanks to Steven Slesar, Bill
Miller, Nancy Noonan, Blair Potts, Michael Lovelette, Bryan
Holberton, David Hull, Ben Pearson, Dave Heidrich, Mike Allen,
Greg Walz, Tom Burns, Tom Brandel, Tom Kristianson, Frank
Morris, Charlie Papazian, Jeff Lebesch, The Dukes of Ale, Harold
and Audre Gee, Reg Brice, Denise Dillon, Peter Lincoln, Hubert
Smith, Bert Grant; to Four Seasons Hotels, The City of Cleveland,
and the countless others who helped me on my way.

Editor Alison Franks
Art Editor Paul Drayson
Proofreader Martin Noble
Production Sarah Schuman
Maps John Hutchinson

Managing Editor Chris Foulkes
Senior Art Editor Nigel O'Gorman

The Simon & Schuster Pocket Guide to Beer
Edited and designed by
Mitchell Beazley International Limited, Artists House,
14–15 Manette Street, London W1V 5LB

CONTENTS

MAPS

INTRODUCTION

THE NEW APPRECIATION OF BEER

The *hauteur* that rightly attends wine has for too long overshadowed beer, but that is changing. It is increasingly being appreciated that the two are companions of honour as the principal types of fermented drink: part of the gastronomic heritage of the warm and cool climates that grow the grape and the grain respectively.

The spread in travel and leisure has made for a more universal interest in wine, and the same is true in respect of beer. There is an international wave of serious interest in beer, from Italy (where it is the most chic of drinks), through Germany and Belgium (where speciality styles are in ever-greater demand) to Britain (first came the "real ale" renaissance; now the surge of "designer" lagers) and to the United States (where imported beers arrive in bewildering profusion). In all of these countries, there has been in recent years a blossoming of "boutique" beers.

As in the case of boutique wines, some are the vanities of people from outside the industry. It is possible to hire a technical consultant, create a beer, and have it produced under contract by an existent brewery. Some of the "contract brews" have proven very commercially successful, others less so.

Another way of making beer on a boutique scale is to establish a tiny brewery in the back-room of a pub. There are now hundreds of new "brewpubs". The British sometimes call them "homebrew houses". The German term is *Hausbrauerei*. The earliest brewers worked on this scale, and now the tradition is being revived.

There are also scores of new free-standing, "pint-sized" micro-breweries. These are usually much smaller than the traditional local brewery.

Many of these new breweries concentrate on specialities, rather than producing everyday beers. Some of the older breweries have also begun to see the sense of this.

Most varieties of wine are understood outside their traditional region of production, but the stylistic diversity of beer is only now beginning to confront the consumer. A tart, fruity *Berliner Weisse* is not meant to be full-bodied and strong. Nor will a *Trappist Triple* or a *barley wine* quench the thirst, though it might be a delight with a late-night movie or a book at bedtime. The wrong beer for the occasion will at best disappoint and at worst confuse. The same is true if the beer is not served in the manner, or at the temperature, at which it best expresses its qualities of aroma, palate and character.

Whether the beer-fancier carries out his (or her) explorations in the local pub or restaurant, or by trains and boats and planes, this Pocket Guide may be of assistance.

WHAT MAKES A GREAT BEER

Wine is more vulnerable to the mercies of soil and weather, but beer is the more complicated drink to make. The barley must first be malted and made into an infusion or decoction, the enigmatic (and none too hardy) hop added as a seasoning, and the whole brewed before it can be fermented, matured and conditioned.

In carrying out these procedures, the brewer is seeking to impart (in aroma, palate and finish) his own balance between the sweetness of the barley malt, the herby dryness of the hop, and the background fruitiness of the yeast used in fermentation. These characteristics are immediately evident in a fresh beer, especially one that has not been pasteurized (this process, unless it is carried out with the greatest of care, may merely deaden the beer to the ravages of travel and time).

The balance will be weighted differently according to the style of the beer, but it must always be achieved. A chef may intend one dish to be delicate, another to be robust, but each must have its own balance. After balance comes complexity. A wine-maker knows that each style is expected to have certain features, but beyond those there should be the individuality of its own character. Each time the drinker raises a glass of fine wine, new dimensions of aroma and palate should become apparent. So it is with a fine beer.

Any fine food or drink is enjoyed with the eyes and nose as well as the palate. The more individualistic beers, especially of the darker styles, can have a great subtlety of colour; most styles will present a dense, uneven "rocky" head if they have been naturally carbonated in fermentation, rather than having been injected with carbon dioxide; a properly carbonated beer will leave "Brussels lace" down the sides of the glass after each swallow. A good beer should be poured gently down the side of a tilted glass. A final, upright, flourish may contribute to its appearance, but the formation of a good head should not rest on the beer's being dumped violently into the glass.

Conventional beers are intended to be clear though excessive refrigeration can cause a "chill haze" in a good-quality, all-malt brew. The haze should subside once the beer reaches about 7°C (45°F). Conventional beers are also at risk of general deterioration (though they will not necessarily succumb to it) from the moment they leave the brewery. They are intended for immediate drinking, and not for keeping.

Brews indicated to be conditioned in the cask or bottle will contain living yeast. Unless the beer is poured carefully, the palate will have a "yeast bite", but the sediment is not harmful (in fact, its health benefits are quickly apparent). Very strong bottle-conditioned brews will improve with age.

Bottle-conditioned ales naturally have a very fruity aroma. In any beer, an unpleasant aroma reminiscent of damp paper or cardboard indicates oxidation (quite simply, the beer has gone stale). A cabbagey or skunky aroma means that the beer has been damaged by supermarket lighting or by being left in the sun. Beer is a natural product, and does not enjoy rough treatment.

Strength

This is not a measure of quality. The ideal strength for a beer depends upon the purpose for which it is intended. A beer that is meant to be quenching, and to be consumed in quantity, should not be high in alcohol. The classic example, the *Berliner Weisse* style, has around 3 percent alcohol by volume. A typical premium beer, whether in Germany, Britain or the United States, might have between 4 and 5 percent by volume. A strong "winter warmer" may typically have between 6 and 8 percent. Although there are specialities exceeding 13 percent, beers of this strength are hard to brew, and to drink in any quantity. At these levels, alcohol stuns beer yeasts to a point where they can no longer work, and the residual sugars make for heavy, cloying brews. There are, of course, wines of this strength, but they are not drunk by the half-pint.

Alcohol by volume is the system most commonly used to describe the strength of wine, and it is the simplest rating to understand. The European Community now uses this system, so does Canada, but American brewers usually quote alcohol by weight. Since water is heavier than alcohol, this produces lower figures. In several brewing nations, the authorities were traditionally more concerned to tax what goes into the beer: the malt, wheat or other fermentable sugars. This is variously described as density or original gravity. Each of the older brewing nations developed its own scale for measuring this, the German Plato and similar Czechoslovakian Balling systems being the most commonly used. In those countries, drinkers are inclined to be less familiar with alcohol content than with gravity.

The two do not have a direct relationship, since alcohol content is also a function of the degree of fermentation. The more thorough the fermentation, the higher the level of alcohol produced from a given gravity. The less thorough the fermentation, the fuller the body. Alcohol content and body are quite different, and in this respect opposed, elements of a beer.

The Malts

As grapes are to wine, so barley malt is to beer the classic source of fermentable sugars. The barley is malted (steeped in water until it partially germinates, then dried in a kiln) to release the starches that are then turned into fermentable sugars by infusion or decoction in water in a mashing vessel. This process is parallel to that carried out in the first stages of production of malt whiskies.

In addition to deciding the proportion of malts to be used to achieve the desired density, the brewer is also concerned with their origin.

Certain varieties of barley are grown especially to be malted for the brewing industry. Among them, those that are grown in summer are held to produce cleaner-tasting, sweeter malts, though there is some debate on this. Some brewers also feel that inland, "continental" barleys produce better results than those grown in maritime climates. With varying harvests, there are differences in the quality and availability of barley, and the brewer has to account for this in the fine detail of his mashing procedure, its durations and temperatures. He will also adjust these according to the precise character he is seeking in his beer. They are among the hundreds of variables, and thousands of permutations, that contribute to the final character of every beer.

The traditional malting barleys are of varieties that have two rows of grain in each ear. Six-rowed barley is also used, though it produces a huskier, sharper character in the beer. Traditionalists stick to two-row barley but some brewers claim to seek the character they find in six-row varieties.

To the consumer, the more immediately obvious influence is the way in which the barley has been malted. There are many different standard malting specifications, each intended to produce a different result in terms of both colour and palate. As to colour, the more intense the kilning of the malt, the darker the beer. In palate, the character of the barley and the way in which it is malted can impart tones that are reminiscent, for example, of nuts, caramel, chocolate, espresso or licorice. These variations in malting differ in the moisture of the grains at the time of the kilning, as well as in the cycles of temperature and duration.

Depending upon the style of beer being produced, the brewer may use only one or two different types of malt, or as many as seven or eight. He may also use a proportion of unmalted barley, sometimes highly roasted, as in the case of dry stouts like Guinness. German and Belgian "white" beers are made with a proportion of malted wheat. So, naturally enough, are *Weizen* beers (it means wheat, after all). Belgian *lambic* beers use a proportion of unmalted wheat. One or two highly specialized beers use other grains. Less traditional grains include proportions of rice and corn, both used to lighten beers, and the latter especially for its low cost. Also for reasons of cost, and to boost alcohol in expensive strong beers like American malt liquors, cane sugar may be used. In Belgium, candy sugar is used in strong Trappist monastery beers. In Britain, milk sugars are used in sweet stouts.

In a cheap beer, barley malt may represent 60 percent of the mash, and corn or other adjuncts the rest. In Bavaria, barley malt and wheat are the only fermentable materials allowed. Elsewhere in West Germany, the same goes for domestic beers but not for exports. One or two other countries have similar laws, the closest being those of Norway and Greece. Within the European Community, a country may insist that its own breweries work within a "Pure Beer" law, but it cannot block imports for failing to conform.

The Hops

Early wine-makers lacked the knowledge to produce by fermentation alone products of the quality they sought, so they employed seasonings of herbs and spices, creating the forerunners of today's vermouths and of patent aperitifs like Campari. Distillers, faced with similar difficulties, used a spicing of juniper and coriander to dry the palate of their product, thus creating gin. Liqueurs like Chartreuse have a similar history of development. In the same tradition, early brewers used tree-barks, herbs and berries.

Juniper and coriander are still used in a handful of highly specialized beers, but the hop eventually became the normal choice. The hop is a climbing plant, a vine, that is a member of the same family as cannabis. In ancient times, its shoots were eaten as a salad, and in Belgium they still are. Its cone-like blossoms can have a sedative effect, and are used in hop pillows. The cones also produce tannins that help clarify and preserve beer, and resins and essential oils that are the principal sources of aroma and dryness.

This dryness, or bitterness, is a part of the flavour balance of beer. An especially hoppy beer is a marvellous apéritif because its bitterness arouses the gastric juices. Brewers have their own scale of Units of Bitterness. Some very bland beers have as few as 12 Units of Bitterness; one or two tasty classics have more than 50. A very hoppy beer will be full of earthy, aromatic, herbal, flavour notes.

Since all hops contain elements of both bitterness and aroma, the same variety may be used for both purposes, but this is not generally done. Each variety of hop is usually identified as being ideal either for bitterness or aroma. A brewer may, indeed, use just one variety, but he is more likely to use two or three, occasionally even seven or eight. He may put hops into the kettle once, twice or three times. The early additions are to provide bitterness, the later ones to confer aroma. To heighten aroma, he may even add blossoms to the hop strainer, or to the conditioning vessel. This last technique is known as "dry hopping". At each addition, he may use only one variety, or a different blend of several. He may use hop oils or extracts, or the whole blossom, in its natural form or compacted into pellets.

There are many varieties of bittering hop, but few that enjoy special renown. Aroma hops are the aristocrats.

In continental Europe, the classic is the Saaz hop, grown in the area around the small town of Žatec, in Bohemia, Czechoslovakia. In Germany, considerable reputations are enjoyed by the Hallertau Mittelfrüh and Tettnang aroma hops, named after areas near Munich and Lake Constance respectively.

In Britain, the delightfully named Fuggles are often used for their gentle, rounded, bitterness, though they are also regarded as aroma hops. The counties of Hereford and Kent are known for their hops, and the latter especially for a slightly more bitter and hugely aromatic variety called Goldings. These are at their finest in east Kent, near Faversham, allegedly in a strip of countryside a mile wide.

In North America, the Cascade is the classic aroma hop, grown especially in the Yakima Valley of Washington State. There are hop-growing areas in British Columbia, Canada, too, and in not dissimilar latitudes of the southern hemisphere, in Tasmania.

The Yeast

Among wines, it might be argued – perhaps simplistically – that there is a central division along lines of colour, between the reds and the whites. Among beers such a division concerns not colour but the type of yeast used. For centuries, all brewing employed what we now know as top-fermenting, or "ale", yeasts. In those days yeast was barely understood, except as the foam which, when scooped from the top of one brew, acted as a "starter" for the fermentation of the next. In this primitive method of brewing, the yeasts naturally rose to the top of the vessel, and were able to cross-breed with wild micro-organisms in the atmosphere. In the summer, they did so to a degree where beer spoilage made brewing impossible.

Brewers in the Bavarian Alps discovered, empirically, that beer stabilized if it was stored (in German, *lagered*) in icy, mountain caves during the summer. Not only was it less vulnerable to cross-breeding; the yeast sank to the bottom of the vessel, out of harm's way. As scientists began to understand the behaviour of yeast in the 19th century, "bottom-fermenting" strains were methodically bred.

Today, all of the older brewing styles – ales, porters, stouts, German *Altbier* and *Kölsch* and all wheat beers – are (or should be) made with top-fermenting yeasts. All of the *lager* styles – Pilseners, Muncheners, Dortmunders, *Märzen*, Bock and double Bock and American malt liquors – are made with bottom-fermenting yeasts.

"Top" yeasts ferment at warm temperatures (classically 15–25°C/59–77°F), after which the beer may be matured for only a few days, or a couple of weeks, at warm temperatures. With modern means of temperature control, brewing in summer no longer poses a problem. A beer that has been "warm conditioned" will most fully express its palate if it is served at a natural cellar temperature, ideally not less than 12°C (55°F). This is why a well-run British pub will serve ales at such a temperature. British ale can be rendered worthless by refrigeration.

"Bottom" yeasts ferment at cooler temperatures (classically 5–12°C/41–54°F), and the beer is then matured by being stored (*lagered*) at around 0°C (32°F). Many mass-market beers are lagered for barely three weeks. Even in Germany, many brewers are content with four weeks, but traditionalists argue for three months. Bottom-fermenting beers taste best if they are chilled to between 7°C (45°F) and 10°C (50°F), the lighter their body, the lower the temperature and vice-versa.

In both techniques, very strong ales and lagers are matured for longer periods, sometimes for nine, or even 12 months. For whatever duration, this is a period in which the remaining yeast settles, harsh flavour compounds mellow out, and the beer gains its natural texture and carbonation (its "condition").

In top-fermenting ales that have a short period of maturation, the yeast may be settled with the aid of finings, usually isinglass. In Britain the classic ales are delivered to the pub with some working yeast still in the cask, so that they may reach the prime of condition in the cellar. This is known as *cask-conditioning*. Some speciality ales are bottled without filtration, or with an added dosage of yeast, as in the *méthode champenoise*. This is known as *bottle-conditioning*.

Because they pre-date the true understanding of yeasts, some top-fermenting strains are hybrids. Others have picked up some "house character" from the micro-organisms resident in the brewery. Some brewers of top-fermenting specialities intentionally use a blend of yeast, or employ different strains at different stages. Many, of course, use single-cell pure cultures, as do almost all brewers of bottom-fermenting beers. Bottom-fermenting has its origins in a more methodical, scientific, approach to brewing.

Beers made with top-fermenting yeasts are inclined to have more individualistic and expressive palates, often with elements of fruitiness and acidity. Bottom-fermenting beers tend to be cleaner and rounder but the trade-off is that they may be less individualistic.

The Water

Claims about the water used in brewing were probably the most common feature of beer advertizing in the Victorian and Edwardian periods, and they are still to be heard.

In the 18th and 19th centuries, sources of pure water were not always easy to find. That is why towns or cities with good sources – among them, Pilsen and Munich in continental Europe; Burton and Tadcaster in England – became centres of brewing.

Even today, a source of water that requires little or no treatment is an asset to a brewery. A great many breweries have their own springs or wells (this may not be the rule, but it is by no means the exception). In a good few instances, the town supply is adequate once the chlorine has been removed. Only in isolated cases is a water supply a problem. There is at least one island brewery that has to de-salinate sea water.

Even if the water does come from the brewery's own spring or well, natural salts may have to be added or removed for the production of different types of beer. As environmental concerns grow, sources of pure water may once again be an asset about which to boast, but that time has not yet come.

"It's the water!" boast some breweries. "It's the beer!" would be a more convincing claim.

THE LANGUAGE OF THE LABEL

Abbey, Abbaye, Abdij Bier Not necessarily made in an abbey, or by monks, but imitating the Trappist style. Sometimes licensed by an abbey. See Trappist.

Ale The English-language term for a brew made with a top-fermenting yeast, which should impart to it a distinctive fruitiness. Ales are produced to a wide variety of colours, palates and strengths (see also Bitter, Brown Ale, India Pale Ale, Light Ale, Mild, Old Ale, Scotch Ale, etc). Only in some American states is the term determined by law (wrongly) to indicate a brew of more than 4 percent weight (5 by volume).

Alt German word for "old". See **Altbier.**

Altbier A German term for a top-fermenting brew. The classic examples, copper in colour, mashed only from barley malt, fermented from a single-cell yeast and cold-conditioned, with an alcohol content of 4.5–4.7 by volume, are made in Düsseldorf.

Barley Wine An English term for an extra-strong ale (implied to be as potent as wine). Usually more than 6 percent by volume and classically closer to 11. Most often bottled. Both pale and dark versions can be found.

Bayrische German word for Bavarian.

"Beer" Confusingly, the Americans use the term "beer" to mean only lager. The British employ it to mean only ale. Neither is correct. Both lager and ale – as well as porter, stout, and all the Belgian and German specialities – are embraced by the general term "beer". It is all beer, so long as it is a fermented drink made from grain and seasoned with hops.

Berliner Weisse Berlin's classic "white" (cloudy), sedimented, top-fermenting wheat beer, with the quenching sourness of a lactic fermentation, the sparkle of a high carbonation, and a low alcohol content of around 3 percent by volume.

Bière de Garde French term originally applied to strong, copper-coloured, top-fermenting brews, bottle-conditioned for laying down. Today's examples have an alcohol content in the range of 4.4–7.5 by volume, and may be bottom-fermented and filtered.

Bitter English term for a well-hopped ale, most often on draught. Although examples vary widely, the name implies a depth of hop bitterness. There is usually some acidity in the finish, and colour varies from bronze to deep copper. Basic bitters usually have an alcohol content of around 3.75–4 percent by volume, "Best" or "Special" bitters come in at 4–4.75; the odd "Extra Special" at about 5.5.

Bo(c)k The German term for a strong beer. If unqualified, it indicates a bottom-fermenting brew from barley malt. In Germany, a bock beer usually has more than 6.25 percent alcohol by volume, and may be golden, tawny or dark brown. Outside Germany, strengths vary, and a bock is usually dark. Bock beers are served in autumn, late winter or spring, depending upon the country. (See also Maibock, Doppelbock, Weizenbier.)

Brown Ale In the south of England, a dark-brown ale, sweet in palate, low in alcohol (3–3.5 by volume). In the northeast, a reddish-brown ale, drier, of 4.4–5. The slightly sour, brown brews of Flanders are also ales, though they do not generally use the designation.

Cream Ale An American designation, implying a very pale (usually golden), mild, light-bodied ale that may actually have been blended with a lager. Around 4.75 by volume.

"Dark beer" There are many, quite unrelated, styles of dark brew. If this vague term is used without qualification, it usually means a dark lager of the Munich type.

Diät Pils This has nothing to do with slimming, but was originally intended for diabetics. A German style so popular in Britain that many drinkers think there is no other kind of "Pils". Carbohydrates are diminished by a very thorough fermentation, creating a relatively high content of alcohol (about 6 percent by volume) and therefore lots of calories. In German law, the alcohol now has to be reduced back to a normal Pilsner level (5 percent by volume).

Doppelbock "Double" bock. German extra-strong bottom-fermenting beer, tawny or dark brown. Around 7.5 by volume or stronger. Southern speciality, seasonal to March and April. Names usually end in *-ator*.

Dort Abbreviation used in Belgium and The Netherlands to indicate a beer in the Dortmunder Export style.

Dortmunder This indicates merely a beer brewed in Dortmund, but the city's classic style is Export (see **Export**).

Dry Beer Originally a milder adaptation of the German Diät Pils, re-named Dry Beer by the Japanese. After its great marketing success in Japan, the term Dry Beer was taken up in North America. There, the style was made milder still. American Dry Beer has a conventional alcohol and calorie content but is notable for having scarcely any taste, and no finish.

Dunkel German word for "dark".

Eisbock An extra-strong (*Doppel*) bock beer in which potency has been heightened by a process of freezing. Because water freezes before alcohol, the removal of ice (*eis*) concentrates the beer.

Export In Germany, a pale, Dortmund-style bottom-fermenting beer that is bigger in body than a Pilsner, and less dry, but not as sweet as a Munich pale beer, It is stronger than either, at 5.25–5.5 by volume. Elsewhere, Export usually indicates a premium beer.

Faro Once Brussels' local style, a version of a *lambic* sweetened by candy sugar. 4.5–5.5 by volume.

Festbier In Germany, any beer made for a festival. Styles vary, but such beers are usually above average strength, often around 5.5–6 volume.

Framboise/frambozen Raspberry beer, usually based on *lambic*. Alcohol content varies.

Gueuze A blend of old and young *lambic* beers. Around 4.4–5.5 by volume.

Haute fermentation French for top fermentation.

Hefe- The German word for yeast, indicating that a beer is bottle-conditioned and sedimented.

Hell German word for "pale", indicating an everyday beer that is golden in colour. Ordered as a *Helles (hell-es)*.

Imperial Stout See **Stout**.

India Pale Ale A reminder of the days when the Indian Empire was supplied with ales (high in gravity, and well hopped, to stand the voyage) by the British. Today, the term implies a super-premium pale ale.

Kellerbier German term indicating an unfiltered lager, in which there is usually a high hop content and a low carbonation. Strengths vary according to the original style.

Kloster Bier "Cloister beer". German term for a beer that is, or formerly was, produced in a monastery or convent.

Kölsch Cologne's distinctive style of golden, top-fermenting brew. 4.3–5 by volume.

Kräusen In German custom, a traditional technique of carbonation is to add a small dosage of unfermented malt sugars (in English, wort) to the conditioning tank. In a normally *kräusened* beer, the wort ferments out and the beer is conventionally filtered. An unfiltered beer based on this technique is known as *Kräusenbier*.

Kriek Cherry beer, usually based on *lambic*. 5–6 by volume.

Kruidenbier Flemish term for spiced beer.

Lager Any beer made by bottom-fermentation. In Britain, lagers are usually golden in colour, but in continental Europe they can also be dark. In Germany and The Netherlands, the term may be used to indicate the most basic beer of the house, the *bièr ordinaire*.

Lambic Spontaneously fermenting style of wheat beer unique to Belgium, notably the Senne Valley. About 4.4.

Light Ale English term describing the bottled counterpart of a basic bitter. In Scotland, "Light" indicates the lowest gravity draught beer (usually dark in colour), neither term implies a low-calorie beer.

Light Beer American term, indicating a watery Pilsener-style beer. 2.75–4 by volume. Low in calories, and in interest. In some other countries, "Light" means lower in alcohol than a conventional beer.

Maibock A bock beer of super-premium quality. Usually pale. Made for the end of April and beginning of May to celebrate spring.

Malt Liquor Not especially malty, though they are usually low in hop character. Certainly not liquors, though they are usually the strongest beers in an American brewer's range. Malt liquor is the American term for a strong, pale lager, at anything from 5–7.5 by volume, often cheaply made. Regrettably, laws in some states encourage the term to be used on imported strong lagers of far greater character.

Märzen From "March" in German. Originally a beer brewed in March and laid down in caves before the summer weather rendered brewing impossible. Stocks would be drawn upon during the summer, and finally exhausted in October. In Germany, this tradition has come to be associated with one specific style. *Märzenbier* has a malty aroma, and is a medium-strong version (classically, more than 5.5 percent alcohol by volume) of the amber-red Vienna style. It is seasonal to the *Oktoberfest*, where it is offered as a traditional speciality alongside paler beers of a similar strength. Confusingly, in Austria the term refers not to style but to gravity.

Mild English term indicating an ale that is only lightly hopped. Some milds are copper in colour, but most are dark brown. These beers were devised to be drunk in large quantities by manual workers, and have in recent years suffered from their blue-collar image. Around 3 by volume, but often relatively full in body.

Munchener/Münchner Means "Munich-style". In international brewing terminology, this indicates a dark-brown lager, a style that was developed in Munich (although another Bavarian town, Kulmbach, also has a long tradition of – very – dark lagers). In Munich, such a brew is clearly identified by the word *Dunkel* ("dark"), and classic examples have an alcohol content of around, or just over, 5 percent by volume. The brewers of Munich, and Bavaria in general, also impart their own distinctively malty accent to their everyday, lower-gravity (alcohol content around 3.7) pale beers. These are sometimes identified as *Münchner Hell*, to distinguish them from the same brewers' Pilsener-style product.

Obegärig German for top-fermenting.

Oktoberfest beers See **Märzen**.

Old (Ale) In Australia, "Old" simply means dark ale. In Britain, it is most commonly used to indicate a medium-strong dark ale like Old Peculier, which has just under 6 percent by volume. However, by no means all ales describing themselves as "old" are in this style.

Pale Ale Pale in this instance means bronze or copper-coloured, as opposed to dark brown. Pale ale is a term used by some English brewers to identify their premium bitters, especially in bottled form.

Pilsener/Pilsner/Pils Loosely, any golden-coloured, dry, bottom-fermenting beer of conventional strength might be described as being of this style (in its various spellings and abbreviations), though this most famous designation properly belongs only to a product of "super-premium" quality. Too many brewers take it lightly, in more senses than one. In their all-round interpretation, it is the German brewers who take the style most seriously, inspired by the *Urquell* (original) brew from the town of Pilsen, in the province of Bohemia, Czechoslovakia. A classic Pilsner, has a gravity of around 12 Balling and is characterized by the hoppiness of its flowery aroma and dry finish.

Porter A London style that became extinct, though it has recently been revived. It was a lighter-bodied companion to stout, and the most accurate revivals are probably the porters made by American micro-brewers like Sierra Nevada. Around 5 percent by volume. In some countries, the porter tradition remains in roasty-tasting dark brews that are bottom-fermented, and often of a greater strength.

Rauchbier Smoked malts are used in the production of this dark, bottom-fermented speciality, principally made in and around Bamberg, Franconia. Produced at around 5 percent by volume and in *Märzen* and *Bock* versions. Serve with Bavarian smoked ham, or bagels and lox.

Saison Seasonal summer style in the French-speaking part of Belgium. A sharply refreshing, faintly sour, top-fermenting brew, usually dry-hopped, often bottle-conditioned, 5.5–8 by volume.

Scotch Ale The ales of Scotland generally have a malt accent. In their home country, a single brewery's products may be identified in ascending order of gravity and strength as Light, Heavy, Export and Strong. Or by a system based on the old currency of shillings, probably once a reference to tax ratings: 60/-, 70/-, 80/-, 90/-. Alcohol content by volume might rise through 3, 4, 4.5 and 7–10. The term "Scotch ale" is something used specifically to identify a very strong, and often extremely dark, malt-accented speciality from that country.

Steam Beer A name trademarked by the Anchor Steam Beer brewery of San Francisco. This brewery's principal product is made by a distinctive method of bottom-fermentation at high temperatures and in unusually wide, shallow vessels. This technique, producing a beer with elements of both lager and ale in its character (though also distinctive in its own right), is said to have been common in California when, in the absence of supplies of ice, early brewers tried to make bottom-fermenting beers.

Although there are more romantic explanations, the term "Steam" probably derives from the brewery's original source of power. In the days when it represented advanced technology, many breweries proclaimed "Steam" (in Germany, *Dampf-*) in their names, and some still do. In Germany, one brewery has trade-marked a product called *Dampfbier*, but this is not in the Californian style.

Stout An extra-dark, almost black, top-fermenting brew, made with highly roasted malts. *Sweet stout*, an English style, is typified by Mackeson, which has only about 3.75 percent alcohol by volume in its domestic market but more than 5 in the Americas. Sweet stout usually contains milk sugars (lactose), and is a soothing restorative. *Dry stout*, the Irish style, is typified by Guinness, which comes in at around 4 percent in the British Isles, a little more in North America and as much as 8 in tropical countries. Dry stouts sometimes contain roasted unmalted barley. *Imperial Stout*, originally brewed as a winter warmer, for sale in the Tsarist Russian Empire, is medium dry and distinguished by its great strength: anything from 7 to more than 10.

Trappist This order of monks has five breweries in Belgium and one in The Netherlands. By law, only they are entitled to use the term Trappist in describing their products. Each of them produces strong (6–9 percent by volume), top-fermenting brews, characteristically employing candy sugar in the kettle, and always bottle-conditioned. Colour varies from bronze to deep brown.

In their daily life, the monks will drink their least-strong product, and may refer to their more potent variations (for religious holidays and commercial sale) as Double and Triple. The latter is usually palest in colour.

Trub German term for sediment.

Vienna Amber-red, or only medium-dark, lager. This was the style originally produced in Vienna. Brewers still talk of a "Vienna malt" to indicate a kilning to this amber-red colour, but the beer-style itself is no longer especially associated with the city.

Ur-/Urquell "Original"/"-source of", in German. Justifiable when applied to, for example, Einbecker Ur-Bock or Pilsner Urquell, but often more loosely used.

Weisse/Weissbier, Weizenbier The German term for "white" beer, implying a pale beer made from wheat. In the north, a special renown is enjoyed by *Berliner Weisse*, a style in its own right (see separate entry). A different style of *Weissbier* is made in the south, with a more conventional alcohol content (usually a little over 5 percent by volume), a higher proportion of wheat (at least 50 percent) and a yeast (again top-fermenting) that produces a tart, fruity, spicy palate, sometimes with notes of cooking apples and cloves. Often, instead of *Weissbier*, the southerners prefer the term *Weizen* (a similar-sounding word but it means, quite simply "wheat"). If the beer is sedimented with yeast, it may be prefixed *Hefe-*. Southern wheat beers are also produced in dark versions (these *Dunkel Weizen* brews have a delicious complex of fruitiness and maltiness), and in Export and Bock strengths. *Weizenbock* is sometimes served as a Christmas beer.

White A term once used in several parts of Europe to describe wheat beers. Apart from those of German-speaking countries, Belgium's white beers (*Witbier*, *Bière Blanche*) are of considerable interest.

Wiesen/Wies'n Among several words that are confusingly similar to the non-German speaker, this one means "meadow". It implies a beer brewed for a carnival or festival (an *Oktoberfest* beer may be described as a Wies'n Märzen) or a rustic speciality (such as Kuppers' unfiltered *Wiess*).

Zwickelbier German term for an unfiltered beer without the distinguishing features of either a *Kellerbier* or a *Kräusenbier*.

THE WORLD'S
BEERS REVIEWED

The appreciation of beer having been contemplated, its qualities having been studied, the language of the label having been decoded, and the time for a sampling determined, where is the brew to be found? What follows is the most comprehensive review ever compiled of the world's beers. It deals separately with each of the countries in which beer-brewing is an important tradition. Among them, it divides the most complex brewing nations into regions. These divisions are intended to be convenient for the traveller, but they also reflect style differences in the local beers. An overview of the local beer types is included in concise introductions to each major brewing nation or region. Each of these is followed by a *Where to drink* section introducing some of the most interesting establishments in which beer is available, including a number of specialist shops.

In the later sections, the less traditional brewing nations are grouped together under regional or continental headings. Throughout, this review attempts to highlight the most interesting and distinctive beers, often from very small breweries, as well as the better-known names. The figures mentioned in the text and appearing after a beer indicate its strength; however, they are not a measure of its quality. For example, **Briljant** (12; 1048; 5.2; 6.3) has a density of 12; an original gravity of 1048; a percent alcohol by weight of 5.2; and a percent alcohol by volume of 6.3. The figures always appear in that order. See Introduction, page 6, on Strength. In the traditional homes of the craft, every other brewery has interesting products, and the properly briefed traveller will be well rewarded. In more exotic parts of the world, the overwhelming majority of beers are in the "international" derivation of the Pilsener style, and there is not a great deal to distinguish one from another.

In this review, the description of each beer deals with what is salient and distinctive about its palate, and attempts to relate it to a classic style. Star-ratings are offered, but merely as a guide. They assess beers according to the standards of each region.

      * Typical of its country and style
    ** Above average
  *** Worth seeking out
**** World Classic

An Index at the back of the book acts as a quick reference guide to breweries and their beers.

CZECHOSLOVAKIA

The world's most widely known style of beer originates from the town of Pilsen, in Bohemia: the kingdom of Wenceslas in the Middle Ages and the province around which the modern state of Czechoslovakia was created.

Czechoslovakia's brewing traditions date back at least to the beginning of this millenium. Its present President, Vaclav Havel, once worked in a brewery.

The international fixation with the term *Pilsener* can be dated, precisely, to 1842. Until that time, all of the world's beers had been dark, or at least reddish in colour, or murky. Dark malts can make for tasty beers but they were, in those days, also a way of covering up the haziness of yeasty instability.

In 1842, Pilsen's local brewery, which was then owned by the town, produced the world's first golden-coloured, clear, stable, beer by bottom-fermentation, thus "inventing" pale lager. This "invention" came at a time when opaque drinking vessels of stoneware or pewter were giving way to mass-produced glass.

At this time, the German-speaking Austrian Empire ruled Bohemia. "Pilsener-style" beer soon became chic throughout the German-speaking world and beyond. By the time steps were taken to protect the name, the drayhorse had bolted.

When the American brewer Adolphus Busch toured Europe in the late 19th century to study the lagering technique, he was particularly taken with the beers of a town called, in German, Budweis (in Czech, Ceské Budějovice), once the home of the Bohemian royal court brewery. He decided upon this allusion when he set about launching his "King of Beers" in the USA in 1876, but he had the sense to protect the name Budweiser. Busch's "super-premium" trademark Michelob (from a town now known as Michalovce) is also protected.

Czechoslovakia has excellent malting barley – sweet and clean, grown in a protected, temperate "continental" climate. The Bohemians have been famous for their hops since the earliest days, and still are. These are exclusively of the variety known as Bohemian Red, or as Saaz from the German-language name for Žatec, centre of the growing area. The fresh fragrance of these hops is nurtured not only by the climate, with its gentle rainfall, but also by the soil, rich in clay and iron.

Most Czechoslovakian breweries have an everyday beer at 7–10 Plato (3–4 percent alcohol by volume); a premium product in the range of 11–12 Plato (4–5); sometimes a dark lager at 10 Plato and occasionally a speciality of 13–20 Plato (5.5–7.5). Look out for the intense hop bitterness of Krušovice, the hop flavour of Velké Popovice and, from the East, the strong dark lagers like Ondráš and Martinský Porter.

Where to drink

Almost every town in Czechoslovakia offers its own beers locally. The capital, Prague, has 20-odd beer taverns. The most famous, U Fleků (11 Křemencova) in the "New Town" (the city centre), is the world's oldest brewpub, dating from 1499. It offers just one beer: a famous dark lager of 13 Plato, with a soft, spicy palate. U Fleků has a burlesque show. In the "Old Town", U Zlatého Tygra (17 Husova) is a famous literary tavern selling Pilsner Urquell. For the outstanding keeping of the beer, again Pilsner Urquell, some drinkers prefer U Kocoura, in the "Lesser Town" (2 Nerudova). Also in the "Lesser Town", U Svatého Tomáse (12 Letenska) serves beer from the small Braník brewery, of Prague; a lovely, firm, aromatic pale brew and a rather thin dark one. Prague's two larger breweries make the malty Staropramen and yeasty Prazanka beers.

Budweiser Budvar

Although it has a definite hop nose and finish, **Budweiser Budvar**★★★ → ★★★★ is sweet by Czechoslovakian standards, clean and rounded, with a hint of fruitiness. (Units of bitterness around 20; lagered for two or three months.) The Budvar brewery was not founded until 1895, so it must have been the similar beers from the older Samson brewery that inspired Busch. Even today, with all the changes in barley, hops, technology and market fashion, there seems to survive a vestigial resemblance between their beers and his.

Pilsner Urquell

The original **Pilsner Urquell**★★★★ has a slightly fuller colour than some of its latter-day derivatives. The local water imparts a softness, and a faintly salty tang; the use exclusively of Žatec hops ensures a big, fresh bouquet (diminished by excessive pasteurization in export shipments) and a bitterness (40 units) that is balanced by softness of body (the yeast does not attenuate very far); together with a house character imparted by wooden fermenters and pitched lagering vessels. An immensely complex beer. Pilsen also has the Gambrinus brewery, producing hop-accented (32 units of bitterness) beers which evince the cleanliness of Bohemian malt.

EASTERN EUROPE

Every Eastern European country has at least one brewery. There is a Bohemian character to Poland's dry Zywiec Krakus and the softer (but still hoppy) Okocim, both in the Pilsener style. The same is true of Russia's Zhiguli Beer, which has a slightly chewy texture and some faintly smoky notes. All of these beers can be found in the West.

In volume, the Soviet Union is a huge brewing nation. The Viennese Anton Dreher founded the Kobánya Brewery, of Budapest, which proudly produces a full range of lager beers. Porters, usually bottom-fermenting, can also be found in Eastern Europe. Hungary has a number of new brewpubs.

AUSTRIA

As an imperial capital, Vienna was a major brewing centre, famous for the reddish, malty style of lager first produced there by Anton Dreher in 1841. This style was revived in 1987 by Ottakringer, the city's sizable local brewery, to celebrate the jubilee of the enterprise. **Ottakringer 150 Jahr★★★** (13–13.5 Balling) has a full, reddish-bronze colour (25 EBC units); a malty aroma, a lightly sweet, soft start and a dry, rounded finish. Previously, Ottakringer had regarded its paler **Gold Fassl★★** (13), sweetly malty, with some house roundness, as being its most "Viennese" beer.

After a dull period, Austria is now beginning to offer a great variety of styles. The Fischer Gasthaus brewpub (Billroth Strasse 17, Vienna) offers a soft, sweetish *Hell*, in the Munich pale style and seasonal specialities. Baron Henrik Bachofen von Echt has a more colourful range, all top-fermenting, in a brewpub in the wine-cellars of his *Schloss* (Nüssdorf, Vienna ☎372652). These include the chocolatey, fruity-dry **Sir Henry's Stout★★★** (13.75; 6 by volume); the copper, chewy **St. Thomas Bräu★★→★★★** (12.25; 5.6); the deep bronze, drier, complex **Doppelhopfen Hell★★→★★★** (30 percent wheat malt, 11 Balling); and a seasonal brew made with some whisky-malt. Austria also has several *Zwickelbiers* and *Weizenbiers*, and the odd *Altbier*. The Eggenberg brewery, between Linz and Salzburg, is known for its beautifully balanced, fresh-tasting **Urbock★★★**.

Brau A.G.

This anonymous-sounding group owns the famous Schwechat brewery where Anton Dreher created the Vienna style of lager. That brewery has a premium **Hopfenperle★→★★**, relatively light in body and dry in finish, and a super-premium **Steffl★**, with a light-to-medium body and a hoppy finish. The group, which has its headquarters in Linz, also has a number of breweries producing the fruity **Kaiser★** beers, which are a national brand. Near Salzburg, Brau A.G. has a regional brewery known for its very pale **Zipfer Urtyp★→★★**, with a hoppy aroma and sherberty dryness.

Steirische (Styrian Breweries)

Second-biggest grouping, based in Graz, embracing the local Reininghaus-Puntigam brewery and a larger company that takes its name from its Styrian home-town of Leoben-Göss. The **Reininghaus-Puntigam★→★★** beers are generally malty and fruity. Gösser has a hearty **Spezial★★**, with a full, bronze colour, a smooth, malty palate and some hop bitterness in the finish. Its **Export★★** is slightly fuller-bodied, with a cleaner palate. Its new **Gösser Gold★** is lighter and relatively bland. **Gösser Stiftsbräu★→★★** is a dark, malty, sweet beer of 12.2 Plato but only 3.6 percent alcohol by volume.

SWITZERLAND

The world's strongest bottom-fermenting beer, called **Samichlaus★★★★** ("Santa Claus"), is produced in Switzerland. This relatively new label has led lovers of individualistic brews to take a fresh look at Switzerland, which has more speciality beers than is suggested by a reputation for products that are well-made but not distinctive. Swiss beer-making tradition, at least in the German-speaking part of the country, is evidenced by monastic brewery ruins in St Gallen that date from the 9th century.

Samichlaus is brewed only once a year, on December 6, the day when the Swiss celebrate St Nicolas (Santa Claus). It is matured throughout the following year and released next December 6. Its starting gravity is 27.6 Plato (around 1110) and it emerges with 11.1–2 percent alcohol by weight; 13.7–14 by volume. Although it has a predictably malty nose and full body, its long maturation and high alcohol make for a surprising firmness and a brandyish finish. A *Hell* ("pale", but actually reddish) version is available in some markets, but Switzerland has only the dark original.

These beers are produced by Hürlimann, of Zürich, Hürlimann's more conventional beers tend to be clean, light and dry, with a spritzy finish. The company also has an interest in the city's Löwenbräu brewery (unconnected with the Munich namesake). Swiss Löwenbräu's beers are characteristically mild and dry. Among the other major products, those of Cardinal are perhaps more flowery, those of Haldengut slightly smoky, and those of Feldschlöschen have a fruity bitterness; these are, however, only slight shades of difference.

A Swiss brewery's range might embrace a basic lager (at more than 11.5; 1046; around 3.8; 4.75); a deluxe beer (12; 1048; 4.1; 5.12); a "special" (12.5–6; 1050; 4.3; 5.37); a dark special (13.5; 1054; 4; 5); a "festival" brew of similar strength; a "strong" beer of 16; 1064; 5.4; 6.75; and perhaps a dark strong beer of 19; 1076; 5.9; 7.3.

Cardinal and Warteck both have *Altbiers* in their ranges. *Weizenbiers* are produced by Calanda, Frauenfeld and the Ueli brewery at the Fischerstube "brewpub" (Rheingasse 45, Basel. ☎061-329495).

The strangest speciality from Switzerland's 30-odd breweries is a beer that is intended to taste of corn (maize) – and does. It is called **Maisgold**, contains 30 percent corn (which would hardly be unusual in the United States) and is produced by the Rosengarten brewery, of Einsiedeln.

GERMANY

As northern Europe is the home of brewing in the modern world, so Germany remains its hearth. Among Germany's many claims to this central position, the strongest is that it has far more breweries than any other country. Their number is astonishing. Almost 40 percent of the world's breweries are in Germany; there are in total more than 1,200 covering the whole of the newly reunited country. The total in the past was far greater – there has been huge erosion in recent years – but there are also new breweries opening. There were more than 100 newcomers during the 1980s, most of them brewpubs, often specializing in unfiltered beers.

Several of the new breweries use organically grown malting barley and hops, and some have attempted to create new speciality beers outside the classic styles.

Although now united, in history Germany has usually been a collection of separate states. The post-war division encouraged local loyalties. With Berlin sliced through, the other great cities of Germany vied with each other, not least in their brewing traditions. In general, the north has the driest beers; the southwest, especially the state of Baden-Württemberg, has softer brews, allegedly to suit palates weaned on wine; and the southeast (Bavaria) has sweeter, fuller-bodied products.

What is yet more interesting for the beer-lover is that each region has its own classic style. Berlin is known for its light, slightly sour, style of *Weisse* wheat beer, a summer quencher; Hamburg and the north in general are noted for extra-dry *Pilsner*-style beers; Dortmund, which makes more beer than any other city in Germany, has its confusingly named *Export* style, medium in both body and dryness; Düsseldorf drinks as its everyday brew a copper-coloured, top-fermenting *Altbier*. Cologne protects through *appellation contrôlée* its pale, top-fermenting *Kölschbier*. Einbeck and Munich share the strong *Bock* beer, especially in spring, though the latter city lays claim to winter's *Dopplebock*. Munich is the greatest of cities for stylistic variety. It also shares a tradition of dark or *Dunkel* beers with Kulmbach and other Bavarian towns (though Bamberg specializes in smoked-malt *Rauchbier*). Munich has a special interest in amber *Märzenbier* and various types of *Weizen* wheat beers.

Few of these varieties are wholly restricted to their own area or season, though they are always freshest at the appropriate time and taste best in their native place. Some brewers specialize in just one variety of beer, but more produce a range. Some brewers with regional roots have cross-bred with others to form semi-national groupings.

The biggest group is formed by Dortmunder Union, with Schultheiss of Berlin. The second largest is formed by Henninger of Frankfurt, with EKU of Kulmbach, Tucher of Nürnberg, and others. Further groups are built around Holsten of Hamburg, Beck's of Bremen, Wicküler and Küppers in the Rhineland, and Paulaner of Munich.

Within any varietal style, German breweries – especially the larger ones – are apt to make similar products. This is in part because clear standards are laid down by law.

There is also the separate question of the *Reinheitsgebot*, the German Pure Beer Law of 1516. This is observed only in the West. The industry there maintains that it will continue to adhere to the Purity Law despite a European Community ruling of 1987 insisting that it not be used to bar imports. There is now talk of a *Reinheitsgebot* in a united Germany, but time will tell.

HAMBURG

Around the world, imported beer from Germany often means Holsten, Beck's or St Pauli Girl. The first comes from Hamburg, the latter two from Bremen. These two cities remain the principal ports in Germany, a largely landlocked country, and they have been exporters of beer for more than 600 years. Their great importance in the brewing industry dates back to one of the early attempts at organized trade in Europe, the 15th century Hanseatic League.

The extra-dry speciality Pilseners produced in this part of Germany owe their character to the same circumstance. In the days when transport by water was easier than travel across land, Hamburg was twice blessed. Not only did it, as a seaport, have Europe's greatest sales of beer, its requirement for hops was met by trade down the river Elbe from Bohemia, the classic area of cultivation. The dryness of these Pilseners echoes Hamburg's role as a great hop market. The hops were used not only for flavour but also as a natural preservative in beer that was destined for long sea journeys.

Holsten is the best-known of Hamburg's three breweries. Next comes the confusingly named Bavaria St Pauli (nothing to do with St Pauli Girl of Bremen), then Elbschloss. All three produce generally dry beers, though with differences of emphasis. The Holsten products have an assertive dryness. Those from Bavaria St Pauli are perhaps a little fruitier. The Elbschloss beers are very clean-tasting, reserving their dryness for a long, lingering finish.

Where to drink

Dehn's Privat-Brauerei produces its unfiltered, malty, dark beer on an old brewery site, in premises grandly styled "Historischer Gasthof Anno 1750", at Ost-West Strasse 47, in the centre of Hamburg. Its beer is confusingly described as Gröninger Pils. It purports to be a "unique, dark Pilsener". This is nonsense: a Pilsener is, by definition, pale and hoppy. However, the establishment is a welcome enterprise. Dehn's was founded in 1986.

A further brewpub, called Luit-Brau was opened at Serrahn Strasse 3–5, in Bergdorf, Hamburg 80, in 1989 and a third has been announced for Eppendorfer Land Strasse 61, Hamburg 20.

Bavaria St Pauli

Names like "Bavaria" were adopted in the late 19th century by brewers who were following the south's lead in lager-brewing. The Bavaria brewery of Hamburg and the more locally named St Pauli merged in 1922. As if its name were not confusing enough, the brewery markets its products under the Astra label. The company's basic lager, **Astra Urtyp**∗, has a pleasant, light hop aroma and palate. The premium **Astra Pilsener**∗ has a very aromatic bouquet and palate. Astra also has a beer called **Exclusiv**∗, in the style the Germans call Export (like the Dortmund variety) and a dark **Urbock**∗ (again a confusing name, since this is a doppelbock).

In addition to that fairly standard range, there is a light-bodied but very dry Pilsener called **Grenzquell**∗ which was for some time heavily promoted in the USA. The company is best known for one outstanding product from its subsidiary Jever brewery, in the northern town of the same name in German Friesland.

Jever Pilsener★★★★, which is regarded as something of a Friesian speciality, is the most bitter beer in Germany, despite a slight mellowing in recent years. Jever has a big bouquet (the aroma hops are of the Tettnang variety), a yeasty palate (the brewery has had its own strain since 1936) and an intense aperitif bitterness in the finish. A smooth **Jever Export★★** and a firm-bodied **Maibock★★** are hard to find outside Friesland.

A Friesian nation once straddled what are now the borders of The Netherlands, Germany and Denmark, and its traditional drinks suggest a liking for intense and bitter flavours. In its handsome resort town, Jever is a proud and prosperous brewery, with a very modern plant.

Elbschloss

This brewery takes its name from the river Elbe which flows parallel to the road on which the brewery stands. Masked by rowan trees, hawthorns and sycamores, the brewery is in its original, 1881 brick building. The *Schloss* is in the woods behind. Elbschloss is partly owned by DUB-Schultheiss. It has a full range of products, including the very pleasant and splendidly dry **Ratsherrn Pils★★★**. there is also a good, malty Dopplebock called simply **Ratsherrn Bock★★**. None of the Elbschloss beers are pasteurized.

Holsten

In the days when the nobility controlled such matters as licenses to brew beer, the Duchy of Schleswig-Holstein held sway over Hamburg. The Duke of Holstein who granted the city the right to brew is remembered in the name of this company, and on its labels. The company's basic local beer is the firm-bodied **Holsten-Edel★**. It also has a German-style **Export★**, with a satisfying, wholesome texture and a soft, dry **Pilsener★**.

Holsten is the biggest German exporter to Britain, where one of its products has to the uninformed drinker become synonymous with the term "Pils". Ironically, the beer thus dubbed is not a regular Pilsener. It is the product that the company would prefer to be known by its full name of **Holsten Diät Pils★★→★★★**. This very dry low carbohydrate beer was originally produced for diabetics. Since it has a relatively high alcohol content, at 5.8 percent by volume, its calorie count does not suit weight-watchers. Its real virtue is that it is a genuine import, with plenty of hop character. Holsten also has a **Maibock★★**, labelled in Britain as Urbock. This strong beer has a malty dryness, with a hint of apricot. Holsten's beers are kräusened.

Like its principal local rival, Holsten also has a super-premium product from a subsidiary brewery. In this case, the brewery is in Lüneburg, a spa town of stepped-gable houses, their styles evolving from the 14th–18th centuries. A group of them form the old brewery and guest-house, now converted into a beautifully arranged beer museum and a restaurant serving local dishes.

The new brewery is very modern, and its dry, hoppy beer is called **Moravia Pils★★★**. The name Moravia must have come down the Elbe at some time. The beer is notable for its big bouquet, and has a rather light body. In addition to Moravia, which enjoys some prestige, there are a number of minor products, some under the Bergedorf name, and associated breweries in Kiel, Neumünster and Brunswick.

BREMEN

Churches and monasteries dedicated to St Paul have given their name to a good few breweries in Germany, including one in Bremen, long destroyed. This does not altogether explain how one of the city's famous export beers came to be known as St Pauli *Girl*, and the people who might know claim they can't remember. Another noted export is Beck's, while the local brewing company was called Haake-Beck.

Bremen had the first Brewer's Guild in Germany, in 1489, and such is its beery history that it still has a large number of brewery names. Most of these names are of brewing companies that were once independent and which are still separate but linked in a complicated corporate structure. Other labels to be taken into consideration are Hemelinger (nothing to do with the British brand of a similar name) and Remmer. Hemelinger produces a *Spezial*, a rather perfumy but sweetish beer. Remmer produces an interestingly malty *Altbier*. All of the linked breweries in Bremen share a single complex of modern buildings, with two brewhouses, in the town centre, close to the river Weser. Outside of this group is Dressler, once famous for its porters, which no longer has a brewery but survives as a beer brand owned by Holsten.

Where to drink

The Old Town area of Bremen, known as the Snoor, is a delight, and has some lovely taverns. Especially recommended for its local speciality beers is the narrow, wedge-shaped Kleiner Ratskeller, in an alley called Hinter dem Schütting. This is not to be confused with the Ratskeller itself, which is famous for the hearty consumption of wines from the Rhine and Mosel. There are also plans for a brewpub in Bremen, a joint venture with Prince Luitpold, of the Kaltenberg brewery, in Bavaria.

Beck's

The single product brewed by Beck's carries no description beyond a straightforward **Beck's Bier**$\star \rightarrow \star\star$. It is broadly within the Pilsener style, with a fresh aroma, a faintly fruity, firm, crisp palate and a clean, dry finish. It is light by German but heavy by international standards, and difficult to place in context. A very pale malt is used, and the hopping leans heavily toward the Hallertau aroma variety. Within the Beck's brand is a dark version, available in some markets. Beck's Bier is fermented with its own house yeast, at fairly low temperatures, and kräusened.

Haake-Beck

A traditional copper brewhouse is used to produce a full range of beers for Bremen and its hinterland, and also local specialities. Both its regular **Edel-Hell**$\star$ and its **Pils**$\star \rightarrow \star\star$ have a floral bouquet and a light, clean palate. While its cosmopolitan cousins do not make specific claims to the style, this Pils does, and properly has a little more bitterness than either in the finish. It is kräusened, and – unusually – is available locally (in the Old Town, for example) in unfiltered form. This version is identified as **Kräusen Pils**$\star\star\star$, and has living yeast in suspension. As if to emphasize the resultant cloudiness, it is served in cracked-pattern glasses. Even by the standards of a German Pilsner, it has a mountainous head, followed by a soft palate, with just a suggestion of chewy, yeast bitterness.

Haake-Beck also produces, as a summer speciality, a Bremen interpretation of a northern wheat beer. **Bremer Weisse★★★** is served in a bowl-shaped glass similar to those used in Berlin, and is a wonderful summer refresher. In its natural state, it has a palate reminiscent of under-ripe plums, though it is usually served sweetened with a dash of raspberry juice. It has a gravity of 7.5 Plato, producing 2.2 percent alcohol by weight (2.75 by volume). In addition to a top yeast, there is a controlled, pure-culture lactic fermentation.

Yet a third speciality, **Seefahrt Malz**, cannot strictly be rated as a beer, since it is not fermented. It is a heavily hopped malt extract, of a daunting 55 Plato, with a syrupy viscosity but a surprisingly pleasant taste. Seefahrt Malz was for a time on sale, but is now available only to eminent citizens who are invited to the House of Seafarers' annual dinner in Bremen. It is ceremonially served in silver or pewter chalices. Despite its size, the company itself has a taste for traditions. From among its towering buildings each morning emerges a line of drays drawn by Oldenburg horses to deliver beer to the people of the inner city area.

St Pauli Girl

This is produced in the older of Bremen's two brewhouses. Like Beck's, it has a lot of aroma hopping, though it emerges with a slightly lesser bouquet. **St Pauli Girl★→★★** has floral tones in its bouquet and palate, and is very clean. It has marginally less bitterness than Beck's, and is not kräusened. Although each of the two beers is made to its own specification, each with a different yeast background, the distinctions between them are less striking than the similarities. St Pauli Girl, too, is available in a dark version.

HANOVER AND LOWER SAXONY

Famous extra-dry Pilseners like Jever and Moravia (both becoming better known outside Germany) are brewed in the state of Lower Saxony. Neither name, though, is readily associated with the state, which sprawls for many miles across the north of Germany. Jever has its own, more localized regionality, and both beers have to a great extent been appropriated by the city-state of Hamburg.

The most important city in Lower Saxony is Hanover, noted not only for its huge spring industrial fair but also since the 16th century as a brewing centre. Its local speciality is Broyhan *Altbier*, from Lindener Gilde, one of three brewing companies in the city. Hanover's other breweries are the smaller Wülfel and the medium-sized Herrenhauser. Of the three, Herrenhauser is the best known outside Germany. This part of Germany is also well known for grain schnapps, including the gins of Steinhägen. A local trick is to hold a glass of beer and a schnapps in the same hand and drink from them simultaneously.

To the southeast, the town of Brunswick (known in German as Braunschweig) is appreciated for its rich architectural heritage and for the Nettelback brewery, which makes an esoteric speciality called *Braunschweiger Mumme*. This is a malt extract beer similar to that of Bremen. It is served in the Ratskeller and several other restaurants, either neat as a tonic or in a shandy with one of the more conventional local beers, of which there are a number. Mumme, which is named after its first brewer, was originally produced for seafarers, and was launched in the year that Columbus discovered America (1942). Between the 16th and 18th centuries "Brunswick Mumm" seems to have been well-known in England. The poet Alexander Pope referred to "mugs of mum" and the diarist Samuel Pepys to a "mum-house". A treatize of the time suggests that Brunswick Mumm should be produced in Stratford-upon-Avon, in what would presumably have been the brewing world's first licensing arrangement. Even today, a similar product, Mather's *Black Beer*, is produced in Leeds, Yorkshire (associated with the county's great seafarer Captain Cook). At this point, the story blends with those concerning beers made from molasses and flavoured with spruce or birch twigs. A similar *Schwarzbier* is produced in Bad Köstritz.

A much more important speciality is brewed to the south in the small town of Einbeck. The last syllable of Einbeck is believed to have been corrupted into *Bock*, and a good example of this style is produced in the town. The bock tradition seems to date from the local nobilty having at a very early stage given the citizens licence to brew. As a result, Einbeck became one of Germany's most productive brewing towns during the 14th century, making beers of a high gravity so that they could be transported far and wide while fermenting-out on their journey.

A high-gravity brew thus came to be known in the German-speaking world as a "bock" beer. Martin Luther is said to have been fortified with Einbecker bock beer during the Diet of Worms in the 16th century. In the 17th century, a northern Duke took several casks with him when he went to Munich to marry a southern noblewoman. Ever since, Munich has claimed bock as one of its own styles. The first bocks were probably strong, dark wheat beers, produced by top fermentation. Today, the term indicates a strong beer made with barley malt and a bottom-fermenting yeast.

Where to drink

In Hanover, the brewpub Ernst August (Schmiede Strasse 13) offers an unfiltered Pilsener with a slight wheat character. It also serves breakfast. In Brunswick, the brewpub Schadt's, Adolf Strasse 26, near Burgplatz, offers a Pilsener with or without filtration, and May and October bock beers. A newer brewpub, the Preminger Bierstätte, has opened in Karmarsch Strasse, and a third is promised.

Southwest of Hanover, at Lauenau, the Rupp family's Felsenkeller inn offers rooms and is known for dark bock beers (☎05043-2275). Between Hanover and Brunswick, at Celle, the Betz micro-brewery makes an unfiltered Pilsener and an interesting dark bock.

Einbecker Brauhaus

The only remaining brewery in Einbeck, controlled through Elbschloss of Hamburg by DUB-Schultheiss. Einbecker Brauhaus produces three types of Bock. These include the pale **Ur-Bock Hell**★→★★, the dark **Ur-Bock Dunkel**★★★→★★★★ and, between the two in colour, a **Mai-Bock**★★★. All three have a gravity of 16.7 Plato, a profound, smooth maltiness and a gentle Hallertau hop character. The Mai-Bock is available from the beginning of March to the end of May.

Herrenhäusen

Herrenhauser Pilsner★★ is the speciality of this company. It is a smooth beer with a sweetish palate and a very dry, but not bitter, finish. Because it has just over 4 percent alcohol by weight, it is labelled in some American states as a "malt liquor". While Herrenhauser has every right to feel insulted about that, it compounds the felony by labelling its beer Horsy in some markets. A sillier name is hard to imagine, even if the company's trademark is a rearing horse.

Lindener Gilde

The company takes its name from its origins as a civic brewery, operated by a guild. Today it produces a range of very well-made beers. Its speciality **Broyan Alt★★★** is named after a great Hanover brewer of the 16th century. This is a top-fermenting *Altbier* in a similar style to those of Düsseldorf but a little stronger (12.4 Plato; 4.2 percent alcohol by weight; 5.25 by volume), slightly darker, relatively light-bodied, malt-accented, with a delicate hop character and a low bitterness. The brewery also has a regular **Gilde Pilsener★→★★** and a premium **Ratskeller Edel-Pils★★**, both with a complex hop character and some Saaz delicacy, as well as a German-style **Edel-Export★**.

M U N S T E R

The university city of Münster, rich in history as the capital of Westphalia, is regarded with affection by knowledgeable beer-lovers all over Germany for the specialities produced at the Pinkus Müller brewery and restaurant. Pinkus Müller is an institution, despite it being nothing larger than a *Hausbrauerei* (small private brewery), producing fewer than 10,000hl a year. It makes some extraordinary beers and has the impudence to export to the USA.

Pinkus Müller's premises in the Old Town (what people in Münster call the "cow quarter", *Kuhviertel*) were originally nine houses. Over the years they have been integrated, with considerable rebuilding in the 1920s and some more recently. There are four dining rooms; in the main one the centrepiece is a Westphalian oven, set among Dutch tiles illustrating Bible stories. The fireplace hangs with Westphalian hams, a good indication of the style of food.

Where to drink

Apart from Pinkus Müller, the Münster area has a tiny Heinrich Jürgens brewery (Huhl Strasse 6, Beckum), producing a pale *Altbier*. Southeast of Münster, at Oelde, the Pott-Feldmann's have a brewpub with rooms (☎02522-2209). A new brewpub is promised in Münster itself.

Pinkus Müller

The brewery produces no fewer than four beers and is best known for what it describes as **Pinkus Münster Alt★★★→★★★★**. In this instance, the term *alt* indicates simply an old style, without suggesting anything on the lines of the Düsseldorf classics. Pinkus Münster Alt is a very pale, top-fermenting beer made from an unusual specification of 40 percent wheat and 60 percent barley malt, to a gravity of 11.3 Plato. It has a long (six months) maturation, including a kräusening. The maturation takes place at natural cellar temperature, but in conventional lagering tanks in which there is a resident lactic culture. The result is a very crisp beer indeed, dry, with a faint, quenching acidity in the finish. In several respects, not least its higher gravity, relative clarity and restrained acidity, this is a different product from the Bremer or Berliner Weisse. It is wheatier than any Kölsch, yet it does not qualify as a weizen; it is a unique speciality. In fact, the brewery does produce a **Pinkus Weizen**★★→★★★, which is worthy of special attention if only for its unusual lightness, though it is characteristically low on hop bitterness, and has a fruity finish. It is a rather northern-tasting *Weizen*, though it has a thoroughly southern ratio of 60–40 (wheat has the majority).

There are also two bottom-fermenting beers: **Pinkus Pils**★→★★, with a light but firm body and a hoppy dryness; and **Pinkus Spezial**★★★, a pale beer of 12.66 Plato, brewed with organically grown barley malt and hops. This clean, malty, dry beer, with a medium body, is sold in wholefood shops. Despite Pinkus Müller having all of these unusual brews, the house speciality is not a beer alone. The Müllers steep diced fresh fruit in sweetened water so that it forms its own syrup. They then add a tablespoon of the fruit and syrup to a glass of Pinkus Alt, so that its fresh flavours suffuse the beer and marry with the acidity of the wheat. The availability and contents of this confection depend upon which fruit is in season. Fruits with stones are not used, since they impart an incongruous, almondy bitterness. In summer, strawberries or peaches are favoured; in winter, oranges may be used. The fruit is steeped for a day in a pickling jar, with a kilo of sugar. When it is added to the beer, using a cylindrical glass, the result is known as an Altbier Bowl.

DORTMUND

The word "Dortmunder" features in the names of seven brewing companies, thus providing great confusion for beer-lovers who are not familiar with Germany. Some of these companies share facilities, but there are no fewer than five sizeable breweries in the city of Dortmund, plus a new *Hausbrauerei*. Since each of the seven brewing companies has its own range of products in various styles, there are about 30 beers with Dortmunder names. In this respect, "Dortmunder" is an *appellation contrôlée*, since no beer brewed outside the city may, in Germany, bear the designation. In other countries, however, brewers have over the years produced beers that they have identified as being in the Dortmunder style. There was a vogue in The Netherlands and Belgium for a beer style described as "Dort".

There is, indeed, a Dortmunder style. In the days when the great brewing cities of Europe vied for ascendency by promoting their own styles, that of Dortmund was a pale, medium-dry beer, very slightly bigger in body and higher in alcohol than its rivals from Munich or Pilsen. It was drier than a Munich pale beer, but less dry than a Pilsener.

As Dortmund's efforts were repaid with sales in other parts of Germany, and in adjoining countries, the local brewers began to refer to their characteristic beer as *Export*. That is how *Export* became a classic German style. Today a good Dortmunder Export beer has a gravity of 13 Plato, producing 4.4 percent alcohol by weight and 5.5 by volume, and with about 25 units of bitterness.

Unfortunately, the Dortmunder brewers' exposition of their classic style can be hard to find outside their city and hinterland. Although it made for a bigger local market, the industrial growth of Dortmund and the Ruhr was a mixed blessing for the city's image as a centre of fine brewing. In recent years especially, Dortmund brewers went through a phase of self-doubt: did a Dortmunder beer sound like a product for cloth-capped miners and steelworkers?

Although they have continued to make Dortmunder Export, the local brewers have in recent years neglected to promote it, preferring to concentrate on other products within their ranges, especially the Pilseners. This policy has not been a conspicuous success, nor does it deserve to be.

Dortmund is Germany's largest brewing city, and should be proud of its traditional style. Dortmund-inspired Export beers are, after all, included in the portfolios of brewers all over Germany.

Where to drink

For years, Dortmund was content to offer its beers to visitors at uninspiring bars (each representing a different brewery) set around the market square and church. Having been damaged in the war and quickly rebuilt during the recovery years of the 1950s, this area is a little lacking in colour.

In the mid 1980s, the two independents among the city's breweries separately decided to add a little romance. Both of them established brewpubs in the city-centre, each named after an early Dortmund brewer. Kronen opened Heinrich Wenker's Brauhaus on the Market Square. Wenker's is within the Zum Kronen restaurant complex.

Wenker's brewhouse stands among the drinkers in the bar area, and its speciality is an unfiltered, top-fermenting pale beer containing 15 percent wheat, called **Wenker's Urtrüb★★★** (12 Plato). It is a fresh, clean, lightly fruity beer with some yeast "bite". Other specialities are planned.

A few minutes' walk away, right outside the Thier brewery, is that company's offspring, Hövels Haus-Brauerei, at Hoher Wall 5–7. There, the brewhouse is visible through a window of the restaurant.

All the year-round, Hövels serves a filtered lager with a bronze colour and a malty aroma and palate, and which is misleadingly called **Bitterbier★★★** (13.5). This is a smooth, tasty, beer with a quite full body. Hövels has also produced some excellent specialities.

DAB (Dortmunder Actien Brauerei)

The middle name merely indicates a joint-stock company. Perhaps that is where the phrase "a piece of the action" originated. This very large brewing company is now part of a national grouping, with Binding, Berliner Kindl and others. In its modern brewery on the edge of Dortmund it produces beers that generally have a light, malty, dryness.

Its **Export★→★★** has a slight malt accent, while remaining dry, and is on the light side for the style. The brewery's **Meister Pils★** (marketed in the USA under the dismissive, lower-case name of dab beer), has a hint of malt in the nose but goes on to be dry, with some hop character in the palate and a fairly low bitterness.

There is more hop aroma, with a very clean and light palate, in the brewery's **Original Premium★**, marketed in the USA as

Special Reserve. DAB also has an **Altbier**★, again with a dry maltiness and a light body. This is marketed in the USA under the unflatteringly vague name of DAB Dark. In its local market, DAB has a pleasant **Maibock**★→★★ and **Tremanator Doppelbock**★→★★. DAB is a very marketing-orientated company, distributing its products widely in the north of Germany.

Dortmunder Hansa

This is part of the same group as DAB, and the two share the one brewery. In Germany, Hansa has been very active in the supermarket trade. Its **Export**★★ has a good malt aroma, a soft, full body, and a dry finish. Its **Pils**★ is light and crisp, with some hoppy acidity.

Dortmunder Kronen

Among their home-town beers, the people of Dortmund favour those from the Kronen brewery, one of two privately owned breweries in the city. Its beers are, in general, big and malty, with a clean, delicate sweetness. These characteristics are evident especially in its **Export**★★★★, and to a lesser degree in its super-premium **Classic**★★→★★★. **Pilskrone**★★ has a flowery hoppiness. The brewery also has an **Alt**★ with a relatively full body and a dense, rocky head. And there is a dark bock, called **Steinbock**★★, with an intense crystal-malt dryness. It is a shame that only the Classic, and not the whole range, is available in the bar at the adjoining museum (open Tuesday—Sunday, closed Monday; entrance free, through the main gates in Märkische Strasse).

Dortmunder Ritter

Partly owned by DUB-Schultheiss but having its own brewery, this company produces firm-bodied, fruity-dry beers that generally have a long finish. These robust, matter-of-fact Dortmunder brews are popular in the industrial Ruhr Valley. The fruitiness is perhaps most evident in the **Export**★→★★. The **Pils**★ has a malty start and a dry finish.

Dortmunder Thier

This is a privately owned brewery and its **Export**★★★→★★★★ is malty, smooth and full-bodied. It also has a well-made, dry, hoppy **Pils**★★. Although its beers sell well, they could benefit from a wider exposure. In its marketing, the Dortmunder Thier company kept something of a low profile until its opening of the adjoining Hövels Hausbrauerei in 1984 (see Where to Drink; page 31).

DUB (Dortmunder Union Brauerei)

The "Union" refers to the merger of ten or a dozen breweries more than 100 years ago. That union sufficed until 1973, when DUB linked with Schultheiss, of Berlin. The massive "U" of the "Union" logo, illuminated at night, is a Dortmund landmark atop the imposing brewery building which, looking rather like a 1920s power station, broods over the centre of the city. The DUB beers (all kräusened) have some malty sweetness and are generally mild in palate – perhaps on the bland side – and smooth. The **Export**★★★ is malt-accented, and medium-bodied. The **Siegel Pils**★ has an agreeably hoppy palate but not much finish. The super-premium **Brinckhoff's No I**★, named after a founder-brewer, has a character somewhere between the two.

Stifts

Most production, and a majority shareholding, moved to Kronen after a series of changes of ownership. Stifts has a strong local following in the south of the city, and a minority shareholding in the community might ensure that the seasonal, top-fermenting *Hoeder Festbier* is in future produced in the old location. This beer, which contains a proportion of dark wheat malt, is made for a local festival at the beginning of each year.

DUSSELDORF

Where a city is lucky, or sensible, enough to have retained a distinctive style of brewing, it often reserves a special beer for particular occasions or moods. Düsseldorf takes a different view and is one of those cities (like its neighbour and rival Cologne – or Dublin) that likes to serve its speciality as its daily beer.

Düsseldorf's prized beer is more instantly distinctive than that of its neighbour. It has a dark copper colour, is top-fermenting and is superficially similar to a British ale. The Düsseldorf beer has, though, a much cleaner palate, with a complex blend of malty body and hop bitterness and has little of the yeasty fruitiness and acidity of the classic British ales. Since the Düsseldorf beer is a significant style in its own right, a German might resent its being compared to British ale. Internationally, however, the Düsseldorf style is little known, although it has been taken up by a couple of brewers on the West Coast of the USA. In this context, its character can perhaps best be summed up by comparing it with ale.

The differences in the Düsseldorf product derive not only from the typically German barley malts and hops used, but also from the use of single cell, pure culture yeasts and – perhaps most significant – a period of cold conditioning in tanks, usually for several weeks. A German would no doubt argue that the Düsseldorf beer is cleaner and smoother than a British ale. The British would argue that their ales have more individuality. As always, this is to compare apples with oranges, neither is better; they are different.

A typical Düsseldorf beer has a gravity of 12 Plato, or a fraction more. It may be made with two or three malts. Some Düsseldorf brewers favour an infusion mash, but the decoction system is also widely used. Two or three hop varieties may be employed; Düsseldorf brewers have traditionally favoured Spalt. Open fermenters are sometimes used, especially in the smaller breweries. The warmer fermentation temperatures are reflected in slightly less intense cold conditioning, at between 0°C (32°F) and 8°C (47°F), for anything from three to eight weeks. Alcohol content is typically 3.6–3.8 by weight; 4–4.7 by volume. Units of bitterness vary from the lower 30s to the 50s; colour around 35 EBC.

After its period of cold-conditioning, Düsseldorf beer is often dispensed in local taverns from a barrel, by gravity, with no carbon dioxide pressure, blanket or otherwise. Although this method is practiced in several taverns and restaurants, notably in the Old Town, it is especially associated with the city's home-brew houses. Such is the joy of this city for the beer-lover: not only does it have its own style, of some character and complexity, it has no fewer than four home-brew taverns. In these establishments, the stubby, cylindrical glasses favoured in Düsseldorf are charged as quickly as they are exhausted.

The home-brew taverns are the shrines of the Düsseldorf brewing style, and as such their beers must be regarded as German classics. The beer-loving visitor to Düsseldorf will want to visit all of them – and also to sample the beers made in the local style by the city's four other breweries, and several others in neighbouring smaller towns.

Düsseldorf's brewers may well wish that a less imitable name had emerged for their style; they call their brews nothing more memorable than *Düsseldorfer Altbier*. No other city has such devotion either to the production or serving of beer in this style, but brewers in several other towns have in their portfolio something which they call *Altbier*. In most instances, though not all, it bears a great similarity to the Düsseldorf style. "*Alt*" simply means "old", and indicates a style that was produced before the widespread introduction of bottom-fermentation.

"*Altbier*" is the style of Düsseldorf and its brewers produce little else, except stronger brews variously called "*Latzenbier*" ("beer from the wood") or "*Sticke*" ("secret" beer) that appear very briefly in some places in winter, spring and autumn.

Of the Düsseldorf home-brew houses, three are in the Old Town (Altstadt seems especially appropriate in this instance). The fourth, Schumacher, is in the more modern part of the city centre. Among the bigger brewers' *Altbiers*, the popular Diebels is firm-bodied; Hannen is soft, rounded and well-balanced; Frankenheim is hoppy and light-bodied; Schlosser malty, but dry; Düssel the fruitiest; and Rhenania can be slightly thick-tasting.

Where to drink

None of the home-brew houses should be missed, and Zum Uerige is mandatory. Its beer can be sampled on draught in the chic food hall of the Carsch Haus department store. A further brewpub is promised.

Im Füchschen

"The Fox" is noted not only for its beer but also its food. This home-brew house, in Ratinger Strasse, produces a very good *Altbier*, simply called **Im Fuchschen**★★★→★★★★. It is a complex and beautifully balanced beer, its firm, fairly full body at first evincing malty notes, then yielding to lots of hop flavour from Spalt and Saaz varieties. In the end, its hop bitterness is its predominant characteristic.

The tavern's big main dining room serves hearty *Eisbein* and *Schweinhaxe*, at scrubbed tables. It can be very busy, but is a friendly place and diners are usually happy to share tables.

Zum Schlüssel

"The Key" is not to be confused with the larger Schlösser ("Locksmith") brewery, however easy that may be. Zum Schlüssel, in Bolker Strasse, is a home-brew house. The brewery is visible from its main room. **Zum Schlüssel Altbier**★★→★★★ begins with an aromatic hoppiness of palate, but its predominant characteristic is a light maltiness, with a touch of "British" acidity in the finish. It has a fairly light body and a bright clarity. The restaurant is quite light and airy, too, with something of a "coffee shop" atmosphere. It was founded in 1936 (a little late for Heinrich Heine (1797–1856), who was born in this street: the site of his home is now a roast-chicken restaurant). In 1963, the company opened a second, free-standing brewery, whose **Gatzweiler Altbier★★** is widely available in Düsseldorf.

Ferdinand Schumacher

Despite being in a modern part of the city this home-brew house in Ost Strasse, has the polite atmosphere of times past and is a quiet place at which to relax after shopping or a day at the office. Its **Schumacher Altbier★★★** is the lightest in palate and body, and the maltiest, very clean, with a lovely delicacy of aromatic, fruity hop character. The beer is also available at the Goldene Kessel, in Bolker Strasse.

Zum Uerige

This rambling tavern in Berger Strasse is named after a cranky proprietor. Cranky he may well have been, but it is a friendly enough place today – and produces the classic **Düsseldorfer Altbier**, an aromatic, tawny brew, deep in colour and flavour, with a slowly unrolling hop bitterness in its big and sustained finish. **Zum Uerige★★★★** beer is the most assertive, complex and characterful of the Alts. It is also the most bitter. Like all of the Düsseldorfer "house" beer, it is produced in traditional copper kettles, but this is the most beautiful brewery of them all. It also has a traditional copper cool-ship, and a Baudelot cooler, both still in use, and it is impeccably maintained and polished. The brewhouse can be seen from the most picaresque of the many bars. Every few minutes, barrels are rolled through Zum Uerige on their way to the various dispense points, while drinkers jink out of the way. Meals are not served, but Zum Uerige has its own sausage kitchen on the premises. Here, sausages of pork and liver, *Blutwurst* and brawn, are produced, with spiced dripping left over to serve with malodorous Mainzer cheese that has been marinated in beer. If those flavours are not sufficiently intense, robust gastronomes are encouraged to look for the "secret" *Sticke* beer usually on the third Tuesday of its designated months: January and October. This is an *Altbier* of 14 Plato, with an extra dash of roasted malt – and it is dry-hopped in the maturation tanks. Very intense indeed.

C O L O G N E

German beer-lovers greatly admire the speciality brewing style of Cologne, even if the rest of the world has not so far noticed it. It would be widely imitated, too, if it were not protected by its appellation *Kölschbier* (the beer of Cologne). Except in cases of lengthy precedent, a beer may not label itself *Kölsch* unless it is made in the Cologne metropolitan area. Imitations are thus pointless: they cannot identify their aspirations.

Happily, there are a baker's dozen breweries in Cologne and as many again in its hinterland. All of them produce *Kölschbier*, and some do nothing else. At least one has dropped other, more conventional, styles from its portfolio. *Kölschbier* dominates Cologne: it is possible to go into an ordinary bar in the city and be unable to find a Pilsener – even though it may be advertized outside. In the city's "home-brew" houses, of course, *Kölsch* is the only beer available.

Cologne has more breweries than any other city in Germany (indeed, in the world). Being so blessed, it naturally has a great many bars and taverns, including its home-brew houses. For most of the year, it is an engrossing place in which to sample beers, except during its pre-Lenten carnival, when the drinking becomes less considered. Whether its wealth of drinking places results from, or serves to attract, the tourist is a matter for conjecture. Some people apparently go to Cologne to study its history, see its huge Cathedral, or take trips down the Rhine. They should not be distracted from the city's distinctive beer by such diversions, though it is comfortably possible to enjoy both.

For all the envy it attracts, *Kölschbier* is not at first sight especially distinctive. It is a pale beer, much the same colour as a Pilsener, but – as its lightly fruity aroma and palate should reveal – it is made by top-fermentation.

A classic *Kölsch* has that fruitiness in the beginning, a notably soft palate (influenced by the local water) and a very delicate finish. Although *Kölschbier* brewers pay a lot of attention to hop character (two or three varieties are used, often with a Hallertau accent), their aim is to achieve a light dryness in the finish and nothing too assertive.

The very subtle character of this style is no doubt influenced also by the background palate imparted by the typical Cologne yeasts. These generally create a very vigorous fermentation, which is followed by two, three or four weeks of cold conditioning at $0°-5°C$ ($32°-41°F$). The gravity range of *Kölsch* beers is from just over 11 to just under 12 Plato. A typical example has 11.5 Plato and emerges at between 3.5 and 4 percent alcohol by weight. Most often, it is 4 (5 by volume). Bittering units are typically at the top end of the 20s.

Kölschbier is a lovely aperitif (not a bad digestif, either) and it is often consumed as an accompaniment to snacks. On its home ground, this may mean "half a hen" (Rhineland whimsy for a wedge of cheese with a roll) or "Cologne caviare" (blood sausage). Or *Mettwurst* of the tartare type. "With music" means garnished with onions.

Among the home-brew beers, P.J. Früh's is especially clean-tasting, that of Päffgen the hoppiest and Malzmühle, appropriately, the maltiest. Each has its own support as a local classic, though none of the three has a clear claim to be the definitive *Kölsch*. Nor among the rest of the *Kölschbiers* does one stand out, though a good claim is staked by Garde. This is a pronouncedly fruity *Kölschbier*, produced by an old-established private company at Dormagen-bei-Köln. Garde is one of the several companies in Germany with a woman brewer.

Differences between the more widely available *Kölschbiers* are so subtle as to be very open to the influence of freshness (of beer or the taster). Gaffel is perhaps the driest; Sion flowery and hoppy; Gereons fruitier, with a dry finish; Sester fruity and dry; Gilden fruity, with a rather heavy texture; Zunft creamy; Reissdorf light, soft and delicious; Küppers soft and sweetish; Kurfürsten and Dom sweet at the front, with a drier finish.

Where to drink

Visitors who go to Cologne to see the Roman museum or the Cathedral will find P.J. Früh's Kölner Hofbräu conveniently opposite, in Am Hof. Behind Früh is the Old Town, lined with bars and restaurants, especially on the *Heumarkt* (Haymarket). At the rear end of the Heumarkt, the Päffgen Kölsch brewery family has a restaurant, a couple of doors from which is the Zlata Praha bar, serving draught Urquell Pilsner and

Budvar Budweiser. At the far end of the Heumarkt is the Malzmühle home-brew cafe. Beside the Rhine, a pleasant ride on tram number 15 or 16 to stop at Schönhauser Strasse leads to the Küppers Kölsch brewery, where there is a restaurant serving local dishes and *Wiess* beer, and a very worthwhile museum of brewing (Altenburger Strasse 157 ☎ 0222-373242). The Cologne metropolitan area also embraces Bonn, where the new generation of brewpubs is represented by Brauhaus Bönnsch (Sternbrücke 4), in the city centre. This establishment has created its own specialities in a style that it describes as "Bönnsch". Its brews are cloudy-white, quenching and fruity, like a wheaty version of an unfiltered Kölsch. They are served in an arched elaboration of a Kölsch glass. This commercially minded enterprise is linked to Sieg-Rheinische Germania brewery, in nearby Hersel, Bornheim.

P.J. Früh's Gölner Hofbräu

Because it is the parent of its own beer, P.J. Fruh's is still regarded as a home-brew house. In fact, the brewery behind the restaurant became too small to cope with demand for the beer in the free trade. The Früh brewery is now away from the city centre. However, the bar and restaurant remains an institution in Cologne. **Früh Echt Kölsch★★★** is a soft beer, delicate in both its fruitiness of entrance and its hoppy dryness of finish. It is made with only barley malt – no wheat – and hopped with the Hallertau and Tettnang varieties.

Küppers

By far the biggest producer and exporter of Kölschbier despite being a newcomer. Küppers was established 20-odd years ago in Cologne to meet the rules of appellation, so that a *Kölchbier* could be added to the portfolio of the large Wicküler Pils company of Wuppertal. This move followed a court case over the appellation. Sales since, supported by hefty marketing efforts, have justified the determination behind Küppers establishment, but tradition is harder to build. No doubt this was in mind when Küppers established their excellent restaurant and museum. The soft and sweetish **Küppers Kölsch★→★★** is unexceptional, but the brewery wins bonus points for another gesture to tradition, its confusingly-named *Wiess* beer. Although *Wiess* is the Rhineland dialect pronunciation of *Weiss* ("white"), the designation perhaps has less to do with the cloudy tone of this beer than its rustic style; Bavarians talk in the same vein about a *Wiess'n* beer when they mean something that is to be served at a country fair. **Küppers Wiess★★★** is an unfiltered version of the normal Kölsch. It still has yeast in suspension, imparting the cloudiness and an astringent, refreshing, bitter-fruit quality. The name is not intended to suggest a wheat beer. Although some wheat is used, it is present only in the small proportion typical of Kölschbier.

Malzmühl

This is a home-brew cafe and restaurant with a pleasantly insouciant, relaxing atmosphere. Being at the far end of the Heumarkt, it is easily missed, but shouldn't be. Its **Mühlen Kölsch★★★→★★★★** is mild and rounded, with a warm, spicy aroma and palate, reminiscent almost of marshmallow. It is a distinctive and delicious beer, lightly hopped with Hallertau blossoms and fermented in open vessels.

Päffgen

A beautifully kept home-brew restaurant in Friesen Strasse which has a small beer garden. Its **Päffgen Kolsch★★★ → ★★★★** has a soft palate with a big, hoppy bouquet. By the standards of Kölschbier, it has a very hoppy finish, too.

Sion

Originally a home-brew, too. Its tavern, in Unter Taschenmacher, in the Old Town, offers brisk service and a very fresh glass of its pleasantly flowery beer. Since **Sion Kölsch★★ → ★★★** is now produced under contract by the brewers of Gereons Kölsch, knowing drinkers whisper that the two beers are one and the same. This is not true; each is produced to its own specifications. The flowery bouquet and dry finish of Sion Kölsch derives in part from Hersbrucker hops. **Gereons★★** is hopped exclusively with Hallertau.

RHINELAND'S
PILSENERS

Apart from those cities that are islands of their own style, the whole of the Rhine and its hinterland is dotted with well regarded breweries. The towns without a speciality style of their own have in several cases put their best efforts behind a Pilsener beer, developing, as Madison Avenue might term it, a super-premium product and in several instances producing nothing else.

Several of these products were among a selection dubbed "The Premium Beers" in an article some years ago in the influential newspaper *Die Welt*. The writer, Hans Baumann, is a journalist who frequently comments on both the business and social aspects of the brewing industry. His intention was not to say that these "premium" beers were the best, but that they were labels that seemed capable of commanding a high price. His "premium" tag was gratefully seized by the breweries and he now has mixed feelings about its continued use. There are, he points out, many other good beers, not all of them as intensively marketed.

The German consumer has, however, come to believe in recent years that a brewery concentrating on one style is likely to do a better job than those with a whole portfolio of products. This is a questionable proposition. If a chef prepares the same dish every lunchtime, he is unlikely to undercook or burn it, but are his the skills necessarily those of an Escoffier?

While the Pilseners of the far north are generally the driest, the same leaning is evident in Rhineland, perhaps with a softness and lightness emerging as the brewers enter wine country. Even in the far north, the extra-dry Pilseners represent a local accent rather than a varietal style, and it is again a broad regionality – even looser, but still noticed by the drinker – that groups these examples along and around the Rhine: products from as far north as Duisburg (König-Pilsener) and Essen (Stauder Pils), east into the Sauerland (Warsteiner; Veltins; Krombacher) and as far south as the Rheinpfalz (Bitburger).

The north and south represents extremes of the style, too. In the north, König-Pilsener is an unusually full-bodied style and in the south, Bitburger is almost as light as a German Pilsener can be.

Among the products that were not included in the "premium" listing, but might have been, Herforder Pils (taking its name from its home town) and Königsbacher (from Koblenz) are conspicuous examples. No doubt Wicküler (from Wuppertal) would like to be included, too. Among smaller, local brewers, Irle (of Siegen) is a Pilsener specialist in the Sauerland. Although its emergence as a Pilsener-brewing area owes less to history than coincidence, the Sauerland has come to be especially associated with this style. With its broad, green valleys, lakes and woods, Sauerland is a pleasant place for a leisurely beer tour.

The foreign visitor who is unfamiliar with Germany had better sort out the geography before starting to drink. It is not only some of the beers but also the places that have similar names. Sauerland is far from the river with which it shares a name, for example. Oddly enough, the river Sauer is closer to Saarland, which is a different place altogether. What they all share is a selection of interesting beers, in Pilsener and other styles. The visitor to Saarland might look out for an extremely bitter Pilsener from the Becker brewery, of St Ingbert.

Where to drink

In Stauder's home town of Essen, one of the company's shareholders established a "house brewery" in 1984. The Borbecker Dampfbier brewery, bar and restaurant is in Heinrich Brauns Strasse. The term *dampf* refers to the fact that the premises were a steam-powered brewery in the 1880s and not to the style of beer. The brew, called **Salonbier★★★**, is in the Vienna style and of Export strength. It has a clean, dry, malty palate and is available filtered or as a *Zwickelbier*. It's a long way from the Pilseners of the region – and a delightful contrast.

At the opposite end of Premium Pilsener country, across the border and into Saarland, another *Zwickelbier* can be found, also in a "house brewery". This is the brewery guesthouse Zum Stiefel, run by the Bruch family, in the town of Saarbrücken. Another Saarland speciality, though not from a house brewery, is Bier Eiche (Oak Beer). This was originally produced for a festival concerning oak trees, but is now available all year round. It is a pale, top-fermenting beer of everyday gravity, with a delicate hop aroma and dryness. It is produced in Merzig, by Saarfurst, a local subsidiary of the region's Karlsberg brewery. Karlsberg, in the Saarland town of Homburg, has – of course – nothing to do with the Danish brewery of a similar name but different spelling.

Bitburger

Taking its name from its home town of Bitburg, this is a specialist "Premium" Pilsener brewery. It is a very modern place indeed, producing a Pilsener with a low original gravity by German standards: 11.3 Plato. This is thoroughly attenuated, to produce an alcohol content of 3.9 by weight/ 4.8/9 by volume. **Bitburger Pils★★** is very pale, extremely light, and dry. It has a pronounced hop flavour but a very subtle, elegant, bitterness. A much-admired beer.

Beer-lovers who enjoy this very light interpretation of a Pilsener might also appreciate **Bernkasteler Pils★→★★**, which has an even lower gravity (11.2, producing 3.8; 4.7) but fractionally more bitterness. This is produced not far away by the Bürger brewery, of Bernkastel.

Herforder

Principally a Pilsener brewery though it does also produce beers in other styles. **Herforder Pils**★★→★★★, is full-bodied, with a clean, mild palate. Its gravity is 12.1 and its alcohol content 3.9; 4.8/9. Herforder also produces a malty but dry **Export**★→★★; a pale **Mai-Bock**★→★★ and a dark **Doppelbock**★→★★, both very malty. Herford is on the northern borders of Rhineland-Westphalia.

Irle

Another specialist Pilsener brewery. Its **Irle Edel-Pils**★→★★ has the classic combination of a 12 Plato gravity and an alcohol content of 4; 5, and it has a lovely clean palate and is very mild.

König

Known as a "Premium" Pilsener brewery but also produces other styles. Its Pilsener is very full-bodied but also clean and notably dry. **König Pilsener**★★★ has a rich aroma, a sustained, very smooth, bitterness and a perfumy finish. It has an original gravity of 12.1 but this is fermented down to an alcohol content of only 3.8; 4.6. The company also has a **König-Alt**★ that is fractionally less full-bodied, and much milder in hop character.

König-Alt has a rival in its home town of Duisburg. A beer called **Rheingold-Alt**★→★★ is the speciality of a smaller brewery in the town.

Königsbacher

A Coblenz brewery which produces several styles. It also has a number of subsidiaries, whose products include Richmodis Kölsch and Düssel Alt. The enjoyable **Königsbacher Pils**★★→★★★ is complex and satisfying, medium-bodied with a fresh, hoppy bouquet and a well-sustained bitterness in the finish.

Krombacher

Taking its name from its location in Kreutzal-Krombach, this house is a specialist "Premium" Pilsener brewery, proud to announce that its water comes from a rocky spring. **Krombacher Pils**★★ is medium-bodied, with a slight malt accent in the nose, a clean palate, and a pleasing hop bitterness in its late finish. In the American market, the beer has been promoted as having a crispness, a "hop taste", and "a noticeable lack of bitterness". It is hard to say whether the copywriter was being intentionally dishonest, or cloth-tongued.

Stauder

This is known as a "Premium" Pilsener brewery although Stauder does have other products. **Stauder Pils**★★ is marketed especially to expensive hotels and restaurants. Its advertizing in Germany emphasizes cold maturation, making a play on the verb to rest. Brewers sometimes describe their beer as "resting" in maturation, and Stauder is promoted as a product to enjoy in tranquillity. Since a long maturation also "cleans" beer, there is an implication that Stauder-drinkers are strangers to the hangover. Stauder Pils does not, however, have an unusually clean nose or palate, and there is a hint of fruitiness in its character.

Veltins

This brewery led the movement to speciality Pilsener brewing in Germany and is owed a debt of fashionability by its fellow "Premium" producers, especially its neighbours in Sauerland. It is a relatively small brewery, and its **Veltins Pilsener★★** still has something of a cult following. It is a sweetish, beer, with an elegant hop bitterness in the finish.

Warsteiner

Although it does have other styles this concern is known as a "Premium" Pilsener producer. It is a very up-to-date brewery, aggressively marketing and exporting its premium-priced product. **Warsteiner Pilsener★→★★** has a light hop bouquet, a dry palate, and a moderately bitter finish.

Wicküler

Wicküler Pilsener★★ has a delicate hop bouquet and a light but firm body, with quite a bitter finish. A well-made Pilsener by the standards of mass-market products (which, in the Rhineland, it is). The brewery has a full range of styles, and owns Küppers in Cologne.

FRANKFURT AND HESSE

In the Old Town of Frankfurt, the *Sachsenhausen*, the bars and restaurants serve *Apfelwein*, a cloudy, medium-dry alcoholic cider. If Frankfurt has a speciality for the drinker, then this is it. There is a theory that Europe once had a cider belt, separating the wine-grown and beer-brewing areas. It is a tenuous theory, but in this instance the argument could, indeed, be put that Frankfurt has wine to its south and west; beer to its north and east.

In this pivotal position, Frankfurt has no beery leaning of its own, no varietal style. Nor has the surrounding state of Hesse. In so far as a country the shape of West Germany can have a middle, Frankfurt is the city that stands there. If its beers are middle-of-the-road, that is only to be expected.

What Frankfurt lacks in style, it makes up in scale. With an output in the region of 2.5 million hectolitres, the Frankfurt brewery company of Binding is the biggest in Germany. Binding belongs to the group that also includes Dortmund's DAB and Berlin's Kindl breweries. Frankfurt's other brewing company, Henninger, is better known internationally. It has an output in the region of 1.75 million hectolitres.

Just as it is an important state in the matter of large breweries, so Hesse has some significance for small – or, at least, independent – ones. A nationwide organization of privately-owned breweries, the Bräu Ring, has its headquarters in Hesse, at Wetzlar, which is also the home of one of its members, the Euler company. Several other member-breweries are in Hesse, including Alsfeld, the Andreas Kloster brewery, Busch, Marburger and the Unionbrauerei of Fulda.

Where to drink

Zwölf Apostel (Rosenberger Strasse 1) is a brewpub offering an unfiltered Pilsener-style beer. There are two newer brewpubs: Hermannsbräu, Gr Rittergasse 79, Sachsenhausen; and Wäldches-Bräu, Waag Strasse 52, Ginnheim.

Otto Binding, once owner of the big Frankfurt brewery, has established a somewhat smaller enterprise between Wiesbaden and Mainz, at Eltville, in wine country. He brings water by tanker from the Taunus Mountains, uses organically grown malting barley and hops, and produces an unfiltered Pilsener and a full-bodied, malty, dark beer of low alcohol content (3.2 by weight). His Kleines Eltviller Brauhaus (℡6123-2706) even serves free-range pigs' knuckles.

In the artists' and philosophers' town of Darmstadt is a shop stocking around 1,200 beers, from 250 countries. The shop is named B. Maruhn, "Der Groesste Biermarkt Der Welt", and is at Pfumgstaete Strasse 174, in the district of Eberstadt, in Darmstadt (℡06151-54876). Owner Bruno Maruhn is a jolly, enthusiastic chap, and his claim to have the world's biggest beer shop is probably safe, despite earnest competition from the USA. East of Darmstadt, Gross-Umstadt has a brewpub bearing the town's name, at Zimmer Strasse 28. This serves an unfiltered Pilsener and a dark Export.

Binding

Germany's biggest brewing company producing a full range of beers and perhaps most noteworthy for its premium version of a German-style Export called **Export Privat★★**. It has a fresh, light hoppiness in the nose; a clean, malt-accented palate; and a faintly fruity dryness in the finish. A very similar beer, but fractionally less dry, marginally fuller bodied, and slightly paler, has been brewed for the American market under the name **Steinhauser Bier★★**. This has a little extra maturation, and is micro-filtered, to retain its freshness. Binding has been very successful with Clausthaler, one of the more acceptable low-alcohol beers.

Busch

A famous name in brewing. Southwest of Frankfurt is Mainz, from which Adolphus Busch emigrated to the USA to start the world's biggest brewing company. Northwest of Frankfurt is Limburg, where a family called Busch run a rather smaller brewery. American Busch make 90 million hectolitres of beer in the time it takes their German counterparts to brew 15,000hl.

The two families are not related and neither, of course, has anything to do with a product called Bush Beer (no "c"), made in Belgium. There are, on the other hand, historical connections, though distant, between the German town of Limburg and the Belgian and Dutch provinces of the same name. As to Limburger cheese, it originated in Belgium and is still made there and in The Netherlands, but its principal centre of production is Germany. The three Limburgs also share an interest in beer. The German Limburg produces a pleasant, very mild **Golden Busch Pils★→★★** and a **Limburger Export★★**.

Euler

The cathedral in Wetzlar gives its name to Euler's **Dom Pilsener★★**, which is medium-dry. The brewery is also known for its slightly fuller-bodied **Euler Landpils★★**. Other products include a deep amber, malty **Alt Wetzlar★★** (*alt* in this instance refers to tradition, not style. This is not an *Altbier* but a bottom-fermenting "dark" beer). Its basic **Euler Hell★→★★**, a pale, malty beer, has an export counterpart called **Kloster Bier**. The Landpils is served unfiltered at the Wetzlarer Braustuben, adjoining the brewery.

Henninger

This may be the smaller of the two principal breweries in Frankfurt, but it is still a sizeable concern and the better known internationally. Its principal products, within a considerable range, include **Kaiser Pilsner★** and the drier **Christian Henninger Pilsener★→★★**. The latter has not only more hops but also a second "e". Exports widely.

STUTTGART AND BADEN-WÜRTTEMBERG

This is the place for the eclectic drinker. Here, wine and fruit brandies oblige beer to share the table, even though the state of Baden-Württemberg still contrives to have more than 180 breweries.

In the Black Forest – or, at least, its greener valleys – village brewers produce tasty, sometimes slightly fruity, beers that reveal the softness of the local water. East of Stuttgart, towards the Swabian mountains, one or two maltier beers emerge. (The term "Swabian" is widely used in Germany to indicate the culture and kitchen of an imprecise region that might be considered to stretch from Stuttgart to Augsburg.)

Where to drink

Stuttgart has a new brewpub in its pedestrianized shopping area in the city centre. The Stuttgarter Lokalbrauerei (Calwer Strasse 31) serves an unfiltered, Pilsener-style beer: light, clean and soft, with a fruity start and a very dry finish. More specialities may follow.

Beer-lovers will want to have a nostalgic glass at the former Sanwald Brewery *Gasthof* in Silberburg Strasse. There is also a small beer garden round the corner in Rotebühl Strasse. The old Sanwald brewery's wheat beers are now made by Dinkelacker, in Tübinger Strasse. In front of the Dinkelacker brewery is a pleasant restaurant serving the company's beers and offering Swabian dishes like *Fladlesuppe* (clear soup with strips of pancake); *Maultaschen* (Swabia's salty retort to ravioli); and *Spätzle* (egg noodles). No one ever went to Germany to lose weight and the Swabians clearly subscribe to this view.

At the end of September and for the first two weeks in October this businesslike city lets its hair down for its annual fair on the Cannstatt meadows. This *Cannstatter Volksfest* is Stuttgart's counterpart to Munich's *Oktoberfest*. Beer is supplied by all three of the local breweries (three more than some cities have, though it is only half the number mustered by Munich). Special *Volksfest* beers are produced, in the *Märzen* style, and similar *Weihnachts* brews at Christmas.

In Heidelberg, always more swashbuckling, the old-established Café Schöneck (Steingasse 9) now houses a brewpub. Vetter's Alt-Heidelberger Brauhaus, producing a beer called 33 (denoting degrees Plato) that is one of several unratified claimants to being the world's strongest. Not far away in Weinheim, the Woinemer Hausbrauerei (Friedrich Strasse 23) produces an unfiltered Pilsener, a very dark dunkel and seasonal specialities. In nearby Hemsback, the Burgbrauerei brewpub (Hilda Strasse 3) has a similar range.

In Karlsruhe, the Vogel brewpub (Kapellen Strasse) produces a very hoppy unfiltered *Helles*, with more styles to follow. This brewery, in a modern apartment block, works in the evenings, so that drinkers can see their beer being produced. One of Karlsruhe's free-standing breweries, Hoepfner, produces what is today a rarity in Germany, a porter, albeit bottom-fermenting.

About half way between Heidelberg and Stuttgart, at the salt-water spa of Bad Rappenau, the Haffner brewery has its own resort hotel (33 rooms, ☎07264—1061). Its house beer is called *Kur* ("Cure") Pils.

South of Stuttgart, on the way to Lake Constance, is a brewery called Löwen (there are about 30 such, unrelated, "Lion" breweries in Germany). This Löwen brewery, at Tuttlingen, serves a *Kellerpils* in its restaurant. Drinkers who enjoy this excessively should be warned that there are no bedrooms. Between Tuttlingen and Ulm, at Bingen, the Lamm brewery serves a *dunkles Hefeweizenbier* and, yet more exotic, *Bierhefebrannt*, a clear spirit distilled from beer. Closer to Ulm, at Trochtelfingen, the Albquell brewery (five rooms, ☎07124-733) serves a *Kellerbier*.

Where to drink in Swabian Bavaria

South of Ulm, there are four breweries with restaurants, three with bedrooms. At Roggenburg-Biberach the Schmid brewery restaurant specializes in *Dunkel* and *Märzen* beers, but has no bedrooms. Hotel Löwenbrau (20 rooms, ☎08247-5056), at Bad Wörishofen, has a *Kurpils*, and is proud of its *Doppelbock*. The Hirsch brewery, at Ottobeuren, has several interesting specialities including a house liqueur made by Benedictine brothers in the local monastery. The brewery's kettles are visible to guests who soak away their hangover in the indoor pool at the adjoining hotel (80 rooms, ☎08332-552/3). Nearby at Irsee, a secularized monastery brewery produces some beers of outstanding interest, as well as having a very good kitchen. The Irseer Klosterbrauerei (26 rooms, ☎08341-8331) specializes in unfiltered beers, some matured for more than six months. A speciality called Abt's Trunk, conditioned and sold in handmade clay flasks, has been reported to have reached a record-shattering 15 percent alcohol by weight. This sounds unlikely and the owner reckons that 12 percent by volume is more realistic. This brewery also has a *Bierbrannt*. There is also a colourful range of home-produced beers and schnapps at the Post Brewery Hotel (22 rooms, ☎08361-238/9) in the mountain resort of Nesselwang. The hotel has a small museum of beer.

Eichbaum

A smoked wheat beer, a genuinely unusual speciality, features in the range of this Henninger Group brewery, in Mannheim. Both the smokiness and the wheat character are very evident in the surprisingly enticing **Eichbaum Rauch-Weizen★★★** (12.5). Unfortunately, there has been some doubt over the continued production of this beer.

Fürstenberg

The "Premium" ratings were perhaps something of a northern notion and Fürstenberg is the only southern brewery to have been dubbed in this way. It is also a house of some nobility, controlled by the aristocratic Fürstenbergs, who have been brewing for more than 500 years. The family are patrons of the arts and there is an impressive collection of German masters in the Fürstenberg museum, at the palace of Donauschingen, in the Black Forest. In the palace grounds, the Danube emerges from its underground source. Donauschingen is also the home of what is now a very modern brewery. A full range of styles is produced, but the brewery is especially well known for its **Fürstenberg Pilsener★★→★★★**. This has quite a full body, a sustained, lasting bead, and a nicely hoppy taste in its dry finish.

Dinkelacker

The biggest brewery in the southwest; it might just achieve this ascendancy on the basis of local sales, but exports are the decider. The brewery is best known for its **CD-Pils★★**. Although this is marketed as a prestige beer, the name stands not for *corps diplomatique* but for Carl Dinkelacker, who founded the brewery in Stuttgart in 1888. The Dinkelacker family, brewers since the mid 1700s, still control the company. The brewery, not far from the city centre, is a blend of the traditional and the modern. Copper kettles are used, and the CD-Pils is hopped four times with half a dozen varieties (the final addition being Brewers' Gold, in the lauter tun). The CD-Pils is also fermented in the classic square type of vessel and kräusened during lagering; other products go into an ugly forest of unitanks.

Dinkelacker produces a range of bottom-fermenting beers that adopt a middle stance between those of its local rivals Stuttgarter Hofbräu and Schwaben Bräu. In general, Hofbräu's are the sweetest, Dinkel's medium, Schwaben's the driest, but these are fine distinctions since all three breweries produce typically soft southwestern beers. In addition to its pale beers, Dinkelacker has a dark single bock, **Cluss Bock Dunkel★★**, from its affiliate Cluss brewery in nearby Heilbronn – very malty in aroma and palate, but rather weak in finish. At its Stuttgart headquarters Dinkelacker also produces a number of specialities inherited when the local Sanwald brewery was absorbed. These include a rather thin **Stamm Alt★** and two wheat beers, each made to the same specifications: the sparkling **Weizen Krone★★** and the **Sanwald Hefe Weiss★★**.

Schwaben Bräu

The smallest of Stuttgart's three breweries, in the pleasant suburban township of Vaihingen. It has a large, traditional copper brewhouse and splendidly cavernous lagering cellars. The relative dryness of its beers is best exemplified by its **Meister Pils★★→★★★**. The parent company, Rob Leicht, also owns the Kloster brewery at Pfullingen-Reutlingen. Its **Kloster Pilsner★→★★**, is available not only in the local market but travels as far as the USA. It has a lightly hoppy aroma and finish, a quite full, soft, texture, and a hint of sharpness in the finish. Another subsidiary, Bräuchle, in Metzingen, produces a pale **Bock★★** for the whole group. The company plans a small museum of brewing, perhaps as a gesture to beer as a parent product – in the local market, it is almost as well known for its soft drinks.

Stuttgarter Hofbräu

The Hofbräu rivals, and may surpass, Dinkelacker in local sales. Its brewery is not far beyond that of Dinkelacker, on the edge of Stuttgart. It's a curiously rural fold of the city, and

Hofbräu's turn-of-the-century buildings have flourishes that could be Scottish baronial. Inside, however, the brewery is uncompromisingly modern. The name Hofbräu derives from a former royal brewery, but the present company is publicly held, with most of the stock in the hands of one person. The notion that drinkers of German wines have a soft, sweetish palate is emphatically accepted by Hofbräu, and the brewery also takes pride in its beers' not being pasteurized. Its premium product is called **Herren Pils**$\star\to\star\star$.

BAVARIA: MUNICH AND THE SOUTH

Beer-lovers in other countries may be jealous of Germany in general but the focus of envy must be the state of Bavaria. No entire nation, nor even Germany's other states put together, can rival Bavaria's tally of breweries, which still exceeds 800. Between them, they produce about 5,000 beers. Only nine or ten of Bavaria's breweries are, by any standard, large (each producing more than half a million hectolitres a year). More than 500 are very small – 10,000hl or less and of those, about half are tiny, producing less than 2,000hl.

Almost every village has a brewery and some have two or three. The very small breweries almost have their own inn, and often their beer is available nowhere else. There are breweries in monasteries – and convents – and in castles. The castles and baroque-rococo churches are a reminder that Bavaria was a nation of extrovert pride in the 17th and 18th centuries and when in 1919 it joined the German Republic, one of the conditions was that its Pure Beer Law be retained.

Bavaria is the home of more beer styles than any other part of Germany. Its everyday beers are not especially potent, but its specialities include the strongest beer in Germany. It grows good malting barely and virtually all of Germany's hops (and exports them all over the world), it has water in the Alps and the icy caves where the usefulness of cold maturation – lagering – first came to be understood.

The mountain and forest isolation of village Bavaria has helped its culture to survive, not only in costume, everyday dress, worship, music and dance, but also in its sense of being a beer land. Isolation was favoured by the founders of monasteries, too, in the days when they were the sanctuaries of all knowledge, including the art of brewing. If there was communication in these matters, it was across the mountains and within the forests. From the Dark Ages, the cradle of modern brewing has been slung from St Gallen in Switzerland to Munich, to Vienna, to Pilsen in Bohemia. That cradle is filled to bursting point with hearty, thirsty, Bavaria, crying *ein prosit!* at every opportunity.

While the Federal Republic as a whole drinks 140-odd litres of beer per head each year, this figure is greatly exceeded in Bavaria where the figure is closer to 240. No other state has such a defined calendar of drinking dates and styles. It may not matter much which beer you drink in the madness of the pre-Lenten *Fasching* (an answer in southern cities like Munich and northern ones like Cologne to the *Mardi Gras* of Nice and New Orleans, or the *Carnival* of Rio). However, in March and April, the appropriate beer is *Doppelbock*; in May, single *Bock*; in June, July and August Export-type beers at village festivals and *Weissbier* or *Weizenbier* in the beer gardens; at the end of September, and for the weeks that follow, *Märzenbier* for the *Oktoberfest*; by November, it is time to think of *Weihnachts* (Christmas) beer, which may be a variation on the festival speciality, or could be a *Weizenbock*.

Even the beer's accompaniments have a timetable. With the mid-morning beer, the appropriate snack is *Weisswurst*, a pair of succulent veal sausage coddled in a tureen of warm water. The veal is tempered with small proportions of beef and coarse bacon, and there is a seasoning of parsley (occasionally chives) and sometimes onion or lemon. *Weisswurst* is so important that purists argue over its proper contents. For lunch, the beer might be accompanied by *Leberkäse*, which is neither liver nor cheese but a beef and pork loaf, served hot. For an early evening snack, the ubiquitous large radish of the region, which has a black skin and white flesh. The flesh is sculpted into a spiral and assaulted with salt. If the salt on the radish doesn't make you thirsty, the granules on the big, fresh, soft pretzels will do the trick.

To the foreigner, not least the beer-lover, the state of Bavaria may be synonymous with its capital city. Munich. Within Bavaria, while its claims are universally recognized, Munich and its hinterland have competition from other cities and regions where yet more breweries are to be found.

Munich's claims are that it has some of the biggest and most famous breweries, and that it has nurtured more styles of beer than any other city. Within its hinterland, stretching through the regions known as Upper and Lower Bavaria, into the Alps and to the Austrian frontier, are hundreds of breweries. The city itself is ringed by small breweries making excellent beers. The Maisach and Schloss Mariabrunn breweries are just two examples. To the southwest, it is only 32km (20 miles) to the lakes and the beginning of the mountains, with more local breweries to serve the terraces and beer gardens.

South of Herrsching, on the lake called Ammersee, is the monastic brewery of Andechs, whose immensely malty beers were the extremely distant inspiration for the American Andeker brand. The brothers also have their own bitter liqueurs and fruit brandies, and there is a well-patronized *Stube* and terrace. Farther into the Alps, near the ski resort of Garmisch-Partenkirchen, another famous monastery brewery, Ettal, producing well-made and typically Bavarian beers but better known for its fruit brandy. Northeast of Munich near Landshut is the Klosterbrauerei Furth and also the celebrated convent brewery of Mallersdorf, just off the road to Regensburg. Another convent brewery, St Josef's, is at Ursberg, west of Augsburg, near Krumbach, on the road to Ulm.

A monastery brewery founded in 1040 at Weihenstephan, near Freising, less than 32km (20 miles) northeast of Munich, was to have great historical significance. Although the evidence for continuous production is hazy, the brewery survived long enough to be secularized by Napoleon and continues today under the ownership of the State of Bavaria. The Bayerische Staatsbrauerei Weihenstephan thus claims to be the oldest brewery in the world. It may be a cobwebbed claim, but there is none better. Although there are vestiges of the monastery from the 12th century, and today's buildings are set in a restored cloister from the 17th century, the brewery is modern. It also offers some training facilities to the adjoining brewing institute.

There are only a handful of Faculties of Brewing in the world, and Weihenstephan – part of the Technical University of Munich – is the most famous. In recent years it has had difficulties, arising originally from its efforts to deal with brewers who do not work in *Reinheitsgebot* countries, but its name remains a by-word in the industry. The Weihenstephan brewery produces a full range of beers but is perhaps best known for its Kristal Export Weizenbier (very fruity, with hints of blackcurrant, and extremely dry in the finish) and its Hefeweissbier (light for the style and refreshing).

Wheat-beer brewing is especially associated with the area to the east of Munich. About 32km (20 miles) out of the city is the Erding wheat-beer brewery, perhaps the best-known of the specialist and certainly the fastest-growing. Farther east, in Mühldorf, the Jägerhof house brewery of Wolfgang Unerti produces a wonderfully turbid wheat beer.

To the south of Munich another tiny brewery specializes in wheat beers: Gmeineder, at Deisenhofen near Oberhaching. Much farther south, at Murnau, off the road to Garmisch, another notable example of the turbid style of wheat beer is made by the Karg brewery.

Where to drink

Each of the principal Munich breweries has several of its own special outlets in the form of gardens, beer halls and restaurants. The best or most famous are detailed with their entries below. Paulaner has announced plans for a brewpub in Kapuzinerplatz. Kaltenberg has an offshoot called Dasklesne Brauhaus, specializing in wheat beer, in the Luitpoldpark. The Hofbräuhaus of Traunstein has a brewpub making wheat beer in the railway station at Groshesselohe, a suburb of Munich. To the west of Munich and closer to Augsburg, the *Schloss* brewery at Odelzhausen specializes in a double bock called Operator (nothing sinister about the name – it is dedicated to the Munich opera). As is often the case, the *Schloss* (nine bedrooms, ☎08134-6606) is more like a country house, but it has a restaurant. To the north of Munich, the brewery guest-house Goldener Hahn (☎08461-419) is at Beilngries, about half way to Nürnberg. Farther north, at Lengenfeld-Velburg, the Winkler brewery guesthouse (☎09182-326) is widely known for its Kupfer Spezial beer. This much-loved brew is a dark copper colour, with gravity of 14 Plato, bottom-fermented in open vessels and matured for between ten and 16 weeks. A remarkable feature of this family concern is that it grows and malts its own barley. Its beer is hopped with both Bavarian and Bohemian varieties. There are also brewery guest-houses to the northeast of Munich at Adlersberg (Prösslbrau; ☎09404-1822); Böbrach (Brauereigasthof Eck; ☎09923-685); Zwiesel (Deutscher Rhein; ☎09922-1651); and Zenting (Kamm; ☎09907-315).

Altenmünster

The name Altenmünster has become well-known among beer-buffs in the USA thanks to the export of one of its beers in large, 2-litre flagons. These flagons, with a sprung, porcelain "swing top" and pewter handle, are much in demand. In the American market, the brew is identified simply as **Altenmünster★★**, sometimes with the after-thought "Brauer Bier", but no indication of style. In fact, in its full golden colour and big palate, it is a good example of the German style known as

Export. It has a firm body, with a leaning toward maltiness that is typically Bavarian.

Altenmünster is a village near Augsburg, but exports of this beer have been so successful that some are now handled from a sister brewery in Weissenbrunn, northern Bavaria. Both breweries belong to a group embracing several other companies. These include Sailer (it rhymes with "miler"), producing a range of soft, easily drinkable but unexceptional beers in Marktoberdorf, south of Augsburg; Kulmbacher Schweizerhof and Ranchenfels Steinbiere (see separate entries).

Augustiner

The favourite brews among serious beer-drinkers in Munich are those from Augustiner. The beers are generally the maltiest among those produced by the city's major brewers and in that sense are closest to the palate traditionally associated with Munich. This is especially true of Augustiner's pale beers. The everyday **Augustiner Hell**★★★★ qualifies as the classic pale beer of Munich, with its malty aroma and palate, soft entrance and firm, smooth finish. The brewery's interpretation of the German Export type has the brand name **Edelstoff**★★★ in Germany and, confusingly, is described as "Augustiner Munich Light" in the American market. "Light" refers, of course, to its colour and not to its body. This is hardly the lightest of German beers and even the slenderest of those is big by American standards. In recent years Augustiner has been emphasizing its pale beers, perhaps to the detriment of its dark styles. The basic dark beer is called **Dunkel Vollbier**★★★. There is also a **Dunkel Export**★★→★★★, which has occasionally appeared in Germanic areas of the USA. The company has a number of other styles; its **Maximator Doppelbock**★★★ is marketed in the USA under the unexciting description "Munich Dark".

The maltiness of Augustiner's beers has sources close to home. No fewer than three of Munich's brewers have their own maltings and Augustiner is one. Its malt is produced in cellars that stretch like the tunnels of a mine underneath the brewery, which itself belongs to industrial archaeology. Constructed in 1885 and a magnificent example of the proud brewery edifices of the time, it is now a protected building. In the brewhouse only one in three vessels is made from copper; the other two are of stainless steel. The dark beers have the benefit of a triple decoction; the pale a double. Only aroma hops are used, in five varieties, from both Bavaria and Bohemia. Fermentation is in unusual vessels, open but with a lid that can be brought down, without pressure, to collect carbon dioxide. Fermentation is at very cold temperatures and lagering is in traditional vessels, with kräusening. The brewery uses wooden casks to supply beer gardens and some inns in the Munich area. The casks are pitched at the brewery, adding another traditional aroma to that of the malty air.

Augustiner has as its near neighbours Hacker-Pschorr, Spaten and Löwenbräu; all four are in the traditional "brewery quarter" behind Munich's central railway station. Across the river are Paulaner and the Hofbräuhaus brewery. In the heart of the brewery quarter, on Arnulf Strasse, is the Augustiner Keller, relatively small and much loved by the people of Munich. In the centre of the city on Neuhauser Strasse, Augustiner has its elegant, somewhat eccentric, 1890s restaurant and brewery tap, with a small, Italianate garden. This building was originally constructed in 1829 to house the brewery after secularization. As its name suggests, Augustiner was originally a monastic brewery, and its first site was close to Munich's landmark cathedral, the Frauenkirche. The brewery dates at least from the 15th century, though there is some uncertainty about the claimed foundation date of 1328. It is without doubt an institution in Munich, favoured by yet a third famous outlet, the beer garden at the Hirschgarten, a public park near Nymphenburg Castle. This popular picnic spot is said to accommodate as many as 8,000 drinkers, while Löwenbrau's beer garden in Munich's huge central park holds a mere 6,000. How carefully this has been counted is open to dispute.

Ayinger

In Munich, the best-known country brewer is Ayinger. The position it enjoys in the city is evident: its beers are served in the restaurant and cabaret called the Platzl, on the square of the same name, directly opposite the Hofbräuhaus. The restaurant is owned by Ayinger and a special Platzl brew is produced – a miniature barrel of the beer is customarily set in the centre of the table, to accompany the evening's burlesque. After dinner, there might also be a clear fruit brandy, made from apples and pears and served in pot vessels shaped like tobacco pipes.

The Platzl beer is pleasant enough but a half-hour journey out of Munich to the village of Aying will provide just that freshness to make it taste delicious. In Aying (and in the USA) this brew is known as Jahrhundert. The name dates from the brewery's centenary in 1978. **Jahrhundert**★★ is a German Export-type beer. It has some herbal hoppiness in the nose and a big, malty palate that dries in a crisp finish.

Ayinger has a full range of styles, among which several are noteworthy. **Altbairisch Dunkel**★★→★★★ is a splendid example of the Bavarian dark style, with a warm, sweetly fruity aroma and coffee-ish finish. **Fest-Märzen**★→★★ is a little pale for the style but has a lovely malt bouquet, carrying through in the soft palate. **Maibock**★→★★, too, is a classically malty Bavarian beer, with spicy, apricot notes. Most characterful of all is the double bock, labelled in Germany as Fortunator and in the USA as Celebrator. By whichever name, **Fortunator/ Celebrator**★★★ is an outstanding example of double bock style and a beautifully balanced beer, its richness mellowing out in a long, dryish finish. When strong brews are served at the end of winter, Germans talk about taking the "springtime beer cure". Ayinger goes further: it dubs its home village a "beer spa".

Where the Munich basin, with its crops of malting barley, gives way to the foothills of the Alps the village of Aying provides for gentle exploration. Ayinger, with its own elderly maltings and modern brewhouse, stands on one side of the road, facing its guest-house on the other. A small beer garden, little more than a terrace, and an early baroque church complete the village square. In the square, the typical Bavarian maypole is set into a wooden tun that was once a maturation vessel in the brewery. The brewmaster at Ayinger also looks after the local museum.

Ayinger also owns Höll wheat-beer brewery in Traunstein, further up the road. This imposing brewery was built in the late 19th century and has not changed markedly since. It leans sleepily into a hillside in the valley of the river Traun. Four wheat beers are produced at Traunstein. **Export Weiss-bier**★→★★ is filtered and has a full, relatively sweet, fruitiness (ripe plums, perhaps?). The unfiltered **Hefe-Weissbier**★→★★ is much more tart. The **Ur-Weizen**★★→★★★ has a fuller, amber-red colour and bursts with fruitiness. It is also unfiltered and has the classic apples-and-cloves spiciness of a traditional wheat beer. A **Weizenbock**★★★, 17 Plato, pale and filtered, is available in the local market at Christmas.

Forschungs

A secret well kept by the beer-lovers of Munich is the existence of a house-brewery in the market-gardening suburb of Perlach. The place does have the qualities of a mirage. For one thing, it operates only in summer (and even then closes on Mondays). For another, it looks like a cross between a seaside ice-cream parlour and the control tower at a small and dubious airport. It also happens to make the highest-gravity brew in Munich. Its speciality is a 19 Plato beer called **St Jacobus Blonder Bock**★★★. This potent product is soft and sweet but very clean with a big, malty finish. The supporting potion is curiously called **Pilsissimus**★★→★★★. It has both hops and malt in its big aroma and contrives to be both dry and soft in palate. The Forschungs brewery and its small, pebbled beer garden are at Unterhachinger Strasse 76, Perlach (☎089-6701169).

Hacker-Pschorr

There is a resonance about the names of Munich's principal breweries. Not so long ago, Hacker and Pschorr were two of them. They merged, and much more recently have been taken over by Paulaner. Despite that, the brewery continues to operate, with its own range of beers. They are on the dry side and perhaps not as smooth as some Munich brews. However, by the standards of some other regions and countries, they still have a fair degree of character. Hacker-Pschorr has never been identified with any single speciality, though it has recently been concentrating on its **Pils**★. Its *Oktoberfest* **Märzen**★→★★ and **Animator**★★ double bock are both pleasant. The company's beers can be tested at Zum Pschorr-Bräu, in Neuhauser Strasse, and in summer on a terrace in the Marienplatz.

Hofbräuhaus

Perhaps the label "HB" is felt in Germany to speak for itself, but elsewhere in the world the allusion is not instantly clear. It stands for "Hofbräu" ("court brew"), and is the label of brews produced for the world's most famous beer hall. The Hofbräuhaus in Munich was originally the beer hall and garden of the Bavarian Royal Court Brewery. Lesser Hofbräus remain elsewhere in Germany, having passed from minor royalty into commercial hands, but the most important one still belongs to Bavaria, albeit to the state government. The garden is pleasant, though the rambling beer hall smells of stale cigarettes and the detritus of tourism. The beers are excellent, the conventional brews being malt-accented with a spritzy finish. Although the everyday beer is a fresh-tasting, malty **Export**★★→★★★, the Hofbräuhaus (founded in 1589) is credited with having, in its early days, introduced *Bock* beer to Munich. Its immensely tasty, malty **Maibock**★★★★ (18 Plato) has a very deep amber-red colour. Its winter double bock, **Delicator**★★★→★★★★ has the same gravity but a yet darker colour. When the first cask of the springtime beer is tapped at the Hofbräuhaus on May Day, the Prime Minister of Bavaria usually takes part in the ceremony. Maibock tastes especially good accompanied by a couple of *Weisswurst*. Since its earliest days the Hofbräuhaus has also had a tradition of wheat beers. Its **Edel Weizen★★→★★★** has long been enjoyed, but **Dunkel-Weizen★★→★★★** is not to be ignored: a complex beer with dense head, lavish lacework, a sweet start, toasty maltiness, and a lemony tartness in the finish.

Kaltenberg

Although by no means the only brewery owned by an aristocrat, Kaltenberg is perhaps the best known, not least because it is in a classic Bavarian castle. The castle dates from the 13th century, but the present structure was built in the 17th century based on designs by the architect who created Neuschwanstein for "Mad" King Ludwig II of Bavaria. The third King Ludwig was the last and his great-grandson, Prince Luitpold, runs the Kaltenberg brewery. In export markets Kaltenberg is known for a well-made **Diat-Pils★★**, but in its local market it is noted for a malty, dark beer, with a coffee-ish finish, **König Ludwig Dunkel★★→★★★**, which has a gravity of 13.3 Plato.

Kaltenberg Castle is near Geltendorf, less than 50km (30 miles) west of Munich. It has a beer garden and restaurant, and in June holds a beer festival and costumed jousting between "medieval" knights (for information, ☎08193-209). At these festivals, a **Dunkel Ritter Bock★★★** 23 Plato is made available ("Ritter" means "rider" or "knight").

Löwenbräu

Internationally, the best-known name among the Munich breweries is Löwenbräu. About a quarter of its output is exported and it licenses its name to be used on products in other countries, including the USA and Japan. Despite international sales it is not the biggest brewer in Munich, though it comes a good second to Paulaner, which exports far less. In local preference, Löwenbräu's beers are somewhere in the middle of the league table. In general, the beers are malt-accented but well-balanced, with a late hint of hoppiness in the finish. Löwenbräu is not especially associated with any one style, but promotes its **Pils★★**, which is unusually hoppy by Munich standards. The brewery owns the biggest beer hall, the 5,000-seat Mathäser, in Bayern Strasse, near the central railway station. The Mathäser has the look of a railway station itself, with its cafeteria entrance, but its 15 or so inner halls are worth exploring. The cellar restaurant features wheat beer. Löwenbräu also has one of the biggest beer gardens in the huge central park called the English Garden. Löwenbräu's encircles the park's famous pagoda, the "Chinese Tower".

Paulaner

The biggest brewery in Munich is especially associated with its classic **Salvator★★★★** double bock. This extra-strong, very dark beer, with deep amber highlights, has a gravity of 18.5 Plato and is made with three malts. Only Hallertau hops are used, though of both bittering and aroma varieties. The beer has a very rich start, drying out in a long finish. Its alcohol content is around 6 percent by weight, 7.5 by volume. The brewery has its origins in the early 17th century with a community of monks of

St Paul, who became well known throughout the city for the strong beer they brewed, called Salvator (Saviour) to sustain themselves during Lent. Being a very strong beer, it came to be known as a "double" bock and gave rise to that style. Most other double bock beers echo the Saviour's brew by bearing names ending in *-ator*. Double bock beers are drunk to warm the soul as winter gives way to spring and the beer gardens think about reopening. The first new barrel of Salvator is ceremonially tapped by the Mayor of Munich or Prime Minister of Bavaria at the brewery's 3,500-seat beer hall and garden on Nockherberg three to four weeks before Easter.

The brewery was secularized in the early 19th century and has since had several owners, but it still stands on the same site, though it has grown to straddle the hill. From the modern office block, a tunnel through the hillside leads to the maltings and the brewhouse, which is still in traditional copper. The brewery uses classic fermenters and traditional lagering cellars, maturing its everyday beers (which are kräusened) for five or six weeks and its stronger specialities for three to eight months. Paulaner has one of Germany's first refrigeration machines, made for the brewery by Carl von Linde, and an early water turbine powered by a stream that runs down the hill. Paulaner's beers are firm-bodied and dry for Munich, often with an assertive finish. The dark **Alt-Münchner Dunkel**★★→★★★ has a fine colour, a smooth, full body and a maltiness in that dry finish. The export-style **Urtyp 1634**★★ has, again, a full, smooth body but a slightly tannic finish. The pale **Original Münchner Hell**★★→★★★ is similar but milder. The brewery produces a full range of styles – with about ten principal beers – including a dry, rounded **Altbayerische Weissbier**★★→★★★ that has helped popularize wheat beers in the USA.

Schneider

The specialist wheat-beer brewery of George Schneider and Son has been a feature of the Munich scene for more than a century, and has a restaurant on Tal Strasse. However, after World War II the company moved production out of the city, northeast to Kelheim, near Regensburg. Since Munich and the area to the east have such a long and thriving tradition of wheat beers, **Schneider-Weisse**★★★→★★★★ might be regarded as the classic example of the style. For flavour, though, it is exceeded by the brewery's *Weizenbock*, **Aventinus**★★★★ which, with its huge head and insistent sparkle, adds its own flourish to beer drinking in Munich. Both have a beautiful balance of wheat character and maltiness.

Spaten

This is one of the world's most important brewing companies because of its influence on the beers most nations drink today. All lager beers, whether dark, amber or pale, owe much to the work of the Spaten brewery in the 19th century. The influence of this company should be far more widely recognized internationally, but perhaps its reputation has been subsumed, with those of its neighbours, into that of Munich itself.

Although it still takes great pride in earlier styles such as wheat beers (notably the dry, spicy, full-bodied and fluffy **Franziskaner Hefe-Weissbier**★★→★★★ and its cleaner, sparkling **Club-Weisse**★★), Spaten's greatest contributions were in the development of bottom-fermenting beers: in the perfecting of the Bavarian dark style, as typified by its own **Dunkel Export★★★→★★★★**; in the popularization of the amber type, as represented by its world classic **Ur-Märzen★★★★**; and in the perfecting of the Munich pale variety, as exemplified by its **Münchner Hell★★★**. From an historical viewpoint, all these beers are classics, and they are still produced in a manner that blends tradition with modern technology. Spaten has its own maltings, uses traditional kettles and lauter tuns (copper in the old brewhouse, stainless steel in a new one), closed classic fermenters and horizontal lagering tanks.

An especially interesting feature of Spaten's methods is that three different yeasts are used in the production of bottom-fermenting beers. The pale beers of conventional gravities (including a very dry **Spaten Pils★★→★★★**) have one yeast; the **Franziskus Heller Bock★★** another; the darker brews a third. Most breweries would use only one strain for all those types, but Spaten feels that yeasts should be chosen according to their suitability to ferment the different worts and their contribution to background palate.

The company traces its origins to a brewery of 1397, and its name (meaning "spade") is a jocular corruption of Spaeth, an early owner. The royal court brewmaster Gabriel Sedlmayr took over the company in 1807 and his son, Gabriel the Younger, became the father of modern lager-brewing. Studies carried out by Gabriel in the 1830s introduced Bavaria to more scientific methods, notably the use of the saccharometer in the control of fermentation. Sedlmayr gathered disciples who spread the reputation of Bavarian bottom-fermenting techniques, and Sedlmayr's friend and rival Antom Dreher went on to introduce the amber style of lager in Vienna in 1840/41. A year later, the Pilsen brewery produced the first pale lager. In 1873, Sedlmayr worked with von Linde on his first refrigerator, at the instigation of Dreher (Paulaner's Linde machine came later) and in 1876 he introduced the world's first steamheated brewhouse (companies that followed liked to call themselves "steam breweries"). The present company was constituted originally from Gabriel's business and his brother Joseph's Franziskaner brewery.

Spaten is still predominantly owned by the Sedlmayr family. It is proud of its family ownership and of its traditions, and still delivers beer in Munich by horse and dray. Regrettably, the building from which they emerge looks less like a brewery than a fair-sized airport.

NORTHERN BAVARIA: FRANCONIA

For the beer-drinker, Munich and southern Bavaria might seem like the pearly gates, but heaven is further north. Up there Bavaria has a region that is almost a state within a state: Franconia (Franken), with Nürnberg as its largest city and Bamberg (with no fewer than ten) and Amberg (a mere nine) as its most heavily-breweried towns.

There are more small breweries in Franconia than anywhere in the world. It remains a centre of production for dark Bavarian lagers. It has more unfiltered beers than anywhere else and a greater number of eccentric specialities.

From south to north, the region stretches from Regensburg to Bayreuth, Kulmbach and Coburg, on the frontier with East

Germany. Due east the Bohemian Forest forms the frontier with Czechoslovakia, with Česke Budějovice (Budweis) and Pilsen nearby. To the west the small-brewery country of the Steigerwald reaches to Würzburg and wine territory.

Bamberg is the centre for a highly unusual speciality, namely the smoky *Rauchbier*. Kulmbach is the traditional centre for dark beers and produces some especially strong *Doppelbock* brews. Coburg has its unique, revivalist *Steinbiere*, brewed with hot rocks. Bayreuth has a proprietary speciality: the Maisel brewery's *Dampfbier*, and Schierling has its own *Roggen* (rye) beer.

Even in towns not specifically associated with a single style, many breweries have their own minor specialities. Sometimes these are dark beers. Often they are unfiltered. While an unfiltered *Kräusenbier* is cause for comment elsewhere in the country, such brews are not uncommon in Franconia. As its name suggests, this type of beer is kräusened. Then, before the kräusen has worked out, the maturation vessel is tapped, revealing intentionally cloudy beer.

Another type of unfiltered beer is not kräusened. This is *Kellerbier*, which is allowed to settle in the maturation tanks before being tapped. As might be expected it has a notably low carbonation. Traditionally, this type of beer has been heavily hopped to guard against infection. An outstanding example is made by St Georgenbräu, of Buttenheim, just south of Bamberg. Another excellent *Kellerbier* comes from Maisel of Bamberg (there are four Maisel breweries in Bavaria, each quite separate but linked by family).

Bamberg is a town of only 70,000 people but it is a remarkable centre of brewing. On the hill that overlooks the town is the 17th-century Romanesque church of St Michael, part of a former monastery which had a brewery (the monks' brewhouse has now been converted into a Franconian Beer Museum ☎0951-53016). The town itself is a living museum, not only for its German Renaissance buildings but also for its selection of breweries. There is plenty of half-timbering and gilding about the breweries and their guest-houses, too, but their principal contribution is in terms not of architecture but of social and economic history. Two even have their own maltings so that they can do the kilning necessary to produce *Rauchbier* (which is made by kilning the malt over beech logs). There are also two free-standing maltings.

By no means do all of Bamberg's ten breweries regularly feature *Rauchbier* and, though the town is the centre for production, companies elsewhere have been known to produce a beer in this style. In Bamberg, the Heller brewery has Aecht Schlenkerla Rauchbier as its principal product; the family Merz's Hausbrauerei Spezial produces nothing else; Kaiserdom Rauchbier is produced in Eltmann for Burgerbrau-Bamberg; Maisel's Rauchbier is made by another Eltmann brewery. An unfiltered, but bright, *Rauchbier* is made by Fischer Greuth, in Herscheid, south of Bamberg.

Among other Bamberg breweries, Fässla offers as its specialities a *Kellerbier* and a *Märzen* and splendid dark pre-Christmas Bock called Bambergator; Keesman emphasizes its malty but dry Herren Pils; the secular Klosterbräu has a dark beer; Löwenbräu has a range of products; Mahrs has a relatively well carbonated *Kellerbier* and a delicious, rich dark brew called Wunderburger Liesl. The pale beers of Bamberg all have a dry maltiness.

To the west is the Steigerwald, with woodland walks and scores of small breweries, many with their own taverns. About 24km (15 miles) north of Bamberg, at Pferdsfeld, the Kunigunda Leicht brewery lists its production at 250 hecto-litres a year, which probably makes it the smallest in Germany. To the east, in the countryside known as the Frankische Schweiz are more small breweries.

Some towns and villages have communal breweries where members of the public can brew their own beer. Falkenburg, Neuhaus-on-Pegnitz and Sesslach are examples. This facility is generally exercised by barley farms or tavern keepers. In the days before commercial production, a communal brewer who had a new batch ready would display a garland or a six-pointed star outside his house. The latter is a symbol of the brewer, deriving from alchemy rather than from any religious signifi-cance. In some places this practice is still followed, although it is also used by small commercial brewers. Ecclesiastical brewing was significant in the past in Franconia, but only one monastery brewery remains, the Klosterbrauerei Kreuzberg at Bischofsheim, north of Würzburg.

Where to drink

In Bamberg, the obvious places to stay are the guest-houses of Brauerei Spezial (Obere König Strasse 10, ☎0951-24304), which is in the shopping area; or Brauerei Greifenklau (Laurenziplatz 20, ☎0951-53219) which has a spectacular valley view. The mandatory stop for a drink is the Schlenkerla tavern, in Dominikaner Strasse, but other brewery taps are also worth a visit; the low-ceilinged tavern of the Mahrs brewery, in Wundeburg, is a delightful "local". The Steigerwald can be explored from the Klosterbräu Hotel in Ebelsbach (☎09522-235), which specializes in a dark Märzen beer.

To the north, between Bamberg and Coburg, the Goldener Stern at Ebersdorf (24 bedrooms, ☎09562-106163) has a splendid Zwickelbier. Northwest of Coburg, at Gauerstadt, near Rodach, the Wacker brewery (20 bedrooms, ☎09564-225) has a pale draught beer. Northeast of Coburg, the Grosch brewery (17 bedrooms, ☎09563-547) in Rodental, on the way to Neustadt, has an excellent dark beer. In the old brewing town of Lichtenfels, the Wichert Gasthof has a Kellerbier but no bedrooms. The Frankische Schweiz can be explored from the Drei Kronen brewery inn at Memmelsdorf (☎0951-43001), where an unfiltered lager and a dark Märzen is served.

Another Drei Kronen ("Three Crowns") in nearby Strass-geich produces a lovely, firm-bodied Kronenbräu Lager with a gravity of 12.7 Plato and a "1308" Pilsener of 12.4 (unusual, in that everday lagers usually have lower gravities than their companion Pilseners). The "1308" is named for the founda-tion date of this tiny (3,000hl) brewery, which so captured the imagination of an executive from a large international company that its name was bought for use on somewhat lesser beers in Canada and South Africa. This Drei Kronen has no rooms. Neither does the Schinner brewery restaurant in Richard Wagner Strasse, Bayreuth, but it does serve an excellent Braunbier. In Nürnberg, the Altstadt brewery is an essential visit, with beef on sale by the bottle and available on tap nearby. Regensburg has a number of beer-restaurants. In Arnulfsplatz, the Kneitinger brewery produces beer mainly for its own restaurant. The Spitalgarten, in Katharinenplatz, dates from the 14th century and serves local beer.

Altstadthof

The name indicates "Old Town Courtyard", which is the corner of Nürnberg where this delightful *Hausbrauerei* is to be found. The brewery, a bakery and one or two wholefood shops share a restored courtyard off Berg Strasse. In the Old Town, in a building dating from the 16th century and with brewing rights from that time, the *Hausbrauerei* first charged its traditional copper kettle in 1984, taking care to use organically grown barley malt and hop blossoms. Fermentation is in open, wooden tuns like those in drawings of medieval breweries and lagering is in wooden hogsheads of the type often kept as museum pieces in large breweries. The year-round product is an unfiltered dark beer with a gravity of 12–12.5 Plato. **Hausbrauerei Altstadthof★★★** beer has a deep, tawny colour, almost opaque; yeasty fruitiness and malty sweetness in the aroma; a yeasty dryness overlaying the rich, smooth, malty palate; dark malt tones in the finish, with some local, Hersbrucker hop coming through. Seasonal *Bock* and *Märzen* versions have also been produced. A tiny antique bottling machine fills the beer into swing-top litres, which are then sold at the brewery in crude wooden six-packs. The beer is also available on draught at two Altstadthof cafes (one, opening at lunchtime, is called the Dampfnudel and specializes in sweet steamed puddings; the other, opening in the evening, is the Schmelztiegl). The brewery has only two full-time employees.

The *Hausbrauerei* was established, initially out of enthusiasm for beery history, by the owners of the Lamms brewery in Neumarkt, south of Nürnberg. Lammsbrau provides not only the yeast but also the water for Altstadt. The *Hausbrauerei* does not have an adequate supply of its own water, nor space for treatment facilities.

EKU

The EKU brewery in Kulmbach boasts the highest ratified gravity of any bottom-fermenting beer in the world, with its **Kulminator 28★★★→★★★★**. As its name suggests, this beer has a guaranteed gravity of 28 degrees – though analysis has revealed levels as high as 30.54. The brewery claims to mature the beer for nine months with a short period of freezing to settle protein. Since this is not done specifically for the purpose of raising alcohol content, Kulminator 28 is not labelled as an *Eisbock*. As the name Kulmin*ator* implies, it is a *Doppelbock* by style, though it is labelled merely as *Urtyp* ("original") and *Hell* ("pale"). In fact it is not especially pale – the great density of malt provides an amber cast – but it is not a dark beer. It has an intensely malty nose and palate, with a strongly alcoholic character. Its alcohol content has been analyzed at 10.92 by weight, 13.5 by volume – though this, too, can vary slightly.

The world heavyweight title is contested between Kulminator 28 and the Swiss Hürlimann brewery's Samichlaus (a Christmas beer). Samichlaus has a lower gravity (27.6), a longer period of maturation (a year) and a higher alcohol content (11.2 by weight; 13.7–14 by volume). While this contest is too hard to resist, such muscle has limited application. These are beers of excellent quality but they would best be dispensed from small barrels suspended from the necks of mountain-rescue dogs. Whether they revive or stun the recipient depends upon the constitution of the drinker. Certainly, in their fermentation, the yeast is stunned by the alcohol it produces. That explains why these beers take so long, and are so difficult to make. Nor do they contain any of the sugars (or, sometimes, enzymes) that are used in the relatively lightweight strong beers (or "malt liquors") of the USA.

EKU also has a dark double bock, simply called **Kulminator★→★★★** (with a gravity of 18.5); a pale, single **Edelbock★★**; a conventional dark export-style beer called **Rubin**; a rather full-bodied **Pils★→★★**; and a pleasant **Weizen★**.

The first two initials of EKU stand for Erste ("First") Kulmbach. The "U" derives from the union of two earlier breweries that created the company in 1872.

Hofmark

The traditionalist Hofmark brewery is interesting for a number of reasons: its location, east of Regensburg at Cham on the Bavarian side of the Bohemian Forest, means that its soft water emerges from the same quartz-granite bed as that of Pilsen; it was founded in 1590 and has been in one family for more than 200 years; and it still uses some traditional techniques, not least the method of fining with beechwood chips. It is also unusual in that its premium beer Das feine Hofmark is prepared in two variations: mild and bitter (designations that sound more English than German). Both are firm, smooth, beautifully balanced beers of some complexity. Das feine Hofmark **Würzig Mild★★** has a malt accent; **Würzig Herb★★→★★★** (meaning "dry" or "bitter") has a lovely hop character in both nose and finish. This brewery was a pioneer in the use of swing-top bottles.

Kaiserdom

A full range of beers is marketed under the Kaiserdom label by the Bürgerbräu brewery of Bamberg. Most tend toward the dry maltiness of the region but are unexceptional. However **Kaiserdom Rauchbier★★★** has the distinction of being the only smoked beer exported to the USA.

Kulmbacher Mönchshof

The dark-beer tradition of Kulmbach is best maintained by the "Monks'" brewery. Its **Kloster Schwarz-Bier★★★★** rates as a classic, with a gravity of 12.5, a full smooth body and a dark-malt palate unrivalled among major labels. The connoisseur of Bavarian dark beers might, of course, prefer the earthier character to be found in some of the many *Hausbrauerei* examples. Mönchshof goes back to the beginnings of monastic brewing in Kulmbach in 1349. It was secularized in 1791, becoming a family brewery, and is now part-owned by Kulmbacher Reichelbräu. Even at the peak of Kulmbach's international repute as a brewing centre, at the turn of the century, Mönchshof was one of the smaller houses. Today, it remains an active exporter, especially to the USA. Its range includes a very full-bodied dark double bock called **Urstoff★★→★★★**; a very flavourful single **Klosterbock Dunkel★★★**; a malty **Märzen★★**; a malty export called **Maingold★★**; and what is for Bavaria an unusually dry **Mönchshof-Pilsener★★**.

Kulmbacher Reichelbräu

If Germany can have *Eiswein*, then it can have icy beer, too. The tradition of *Eisbock* is especially kept alive by Kulmbacher Reichelbräu. *Eisbock* is a strong beer in which alcohol content is enhanced by freezing and then removing the ice.

Because alcohol has a lower freezing point than water this concentrates the brew. The resultant **Eisbock Bayrisch G'frorns★★★→★★★★** ("Bavarian Frozen") has a gravity of 24 and an alcohol content of around 8 percent by weight, 10 by volume. It is a most interesting beer, dense and potent. Reichelbräu, which is named after its founder, has the biggest local sales and offers a full range of styles.

Kulmbacher Schweizerhof

Kulmbacher Schweizerhof was founded in 1834, but since 1980 has been part of the same group as Rauchenfels, Altenmünster and Sailer. It has a range of styles but its principal beer, identified simply as **Kulmbacher Schweizerhof-Bräu★→★★** ("feinherb aus Kulmbach") is a rather malty Pilsener with a firm, dry palate.

Maisel

Among the four Bavarian brewing companies called Maisel, this one in Bayreuth is by far the biggest. It has also become well known for its speciality brews, notably its highly individualistic **Maisel's Dampfbier★★★**. This is a top-fermenting beer, very fruity, with vanilla-like tones. It has a gravity of 12.2 Plato, is made with a triple decoction mash from four barley malts, hopped with Hallertaus and fermented with its own yeast in open vessels. It emerges slightly redder and paler than a Düsseldorfer Altbier, and about 4 percent alcohol by weight, 5 by volume. It is not pasteurized, even for export to the USA. "Dampfbier" is a registered name, not intended to indicate a recognized style and Maisel earnestly disavows any intention to sound like Anchor Steam (which is different both in production process and palate). In the late 1970s, the brewery decided that, "all beers were beginning to taste the same. We wanted something distinctive. We experimented, and this was the brew we liked." The decision may also have had something to do with the move out of a magnificently castellated and steam-powered brewery of 1887 into a remorselessly modern plant next door. There is an element of nostalgia to a "steam beer" (which is how Dampfbier would, inescapably, translate). For the two Maisel brothers who own the brewery, nostalgia is not a cheap emotion. The entire old brewery has been mothballed, in working order, and is now open for tours, at 10 o'clock each morning, or by appointment.

Meanwhile, Maisel continues in its spotless new brewery to produce an interesting range of products, including three wheat beers. **Weizen Kristall-Klar★★★** is, as its name suggests, a crystal-clear beer, very pale, with a champagne-like sparkle and a tannic, apple fruitiness. **Hefe-Weiss★★** is fermented out with a mixture of yeasts, kräusened and given a dosage at bottling. It has a deep bronze colour, an apple-like palate and a big, fluffy body. **Weizenbock★★→★★★**, at 17.5 Plato, has a deep tawny colour, a big body, and a sharpness that recedes into smooth vanilla and licorice tones at the finish.

Rauchenfels Steinbiere

One of the world's oddest speciality beers, Rauchenfels Steinbiere, is also among the most drinkable. This is a 1980s revival of a brewing method used before the development of metal kettles. When brewing vessels were made from wood they could not be heated directly, and one method of boiling the brew was to mull it with hot stones. This is said to have been done in Alpine areas where stone could be found that would accept great heat, and sudden cooling, without shattering.

The inventive and entrepreneurial German brewer Gerd Borges, on the lookout for new specialities, acquired a quarry with suitable graywacke stones, developed a way of handling the hot stones in a brewery and revived the technique. A clay hearth and a beechwood fire heat the stones, which are held in a steel basket, to a temperature of 1,200°C. The stones are then immersed in a pre-heated brew. The kettle bubbles, hisses, and exhales steam as though it were a volcano. Within a few seconds, the malt sugars in the brew have caramelized on to the stones.

In this modern version, the heating function of the stones is less significant than the caramelization of the malt sugars. "Stone Beer" is top-fermenting, but the caramelized malt comes back into play when the cooled stones are placed in the maturation vessels with the brew. At this point, a violent secondary fermentation starts, settling down over a three-week period. **Rauchenfels Steinbiere★★★ → ★★★★** has a very smoky palate, less dry than smooth, with a long, rounded finish. The Steinbiere contains a substantial proportion of wheat malt, but not as much as its companion brew, **Rauchenfels Steinweizen★★★**. This beer, with 60 percent wheat, has more sharpness and acidity. It is the more popular of the two beers in Germany. The beers are made at Neustadt, near Coburg, in an old-established brewery acquired for the purpose.

Schäffbräu

After a bruising collision with the *Reinheitsgebot*, the Schäffbräu brewery now probably produces the purest beer in Germany. Whatever its other claims to fame, it is notable for its "Fire Festival" double bock. **Schäff-Feuerfest★★★** has a gravity of 25 Plato, and the brewery claims that it is matured for 12–18 months before emerging with an alcohol content of more than 8 percent by weight; 10 by volume. It is a dark, fruity beer, with a low carbonation. Although the brewery recommends Feuerfest as an aperitif, both its name and its prune-brandy palate seem more suited to accompany *crêpes Suzette*. So does its bottle, with wax seal and limited-edition number. The brewery is south of Nürnberg, in the Altmühltal Natural Park at Treuchtlingen.

Schierlinger Roggen

"The first rye beer for 500 years", says the advertizing, discounting the Finnish speciality *Sahti*. The local brewery in Schierling is a subsidiary of the aristocratic Thurn and Taxis, of Regensburg. *Roggen* simply means rye. **Schierlinger Roggen★★★** is a newish, top-fermenting, speciality. It has a tawny, dark, colour; the dense head and fruity aroma of a wheat beer; a dry, grainy palate; and a dash of spicy, slightly bitter, rye character in the finish. A welcome innovation.

Schlenkerla Rauchbier

The most famous Bamberg *Rauchbier* is Schlenkerla, pro-duced for the tavern of that name by the Heller brewery. Like Scotch whisky, *Rauchbier* gains its smoky palate at the malting stage. Again as with Scotch, the method stems from the available means of kilning the malt. What the Scots had at hand was peat; the Franconians had beechwood. As more modern methods of kilning evolved, a degree of tradition survived in both Scotland and Franconia, especially in the wooded countryside that surrounds the town of Bamberg.

Ricks of beechwood logs still wait to burn in the tiny maltings (though it has both Saladin and drum systems) of the Heller brewery, which dates from 1678. The traditional brewhouse, in copper trimmed with brass, sparkles. In another room, a whirlpool makes a strange contrast before the open fermenters.

Ninety-five percent of the brewery's production is *Rauchbier*, usually at a *Märzen* gravity of just over 13.5 percent. It is made entirely from smoked malt, mashed by double decoction, hopped only once (the magic cone can hardly fight the smoke), bottom-fermented, matured for six or seven weeks without kräusening and not pasteurized. The resultant beer has a smoky aroma and a dryness the moment it hits the tongue, and a full, smoky flavour that lingers in a long finish.

Some people have to drink as many as five litre glasses before they begin to enjoy *Rauchbier*. It is, not only among beers but also among all alcoholic drinks, a classic. **Aecht Schlenkerla Rauchbier Märzen★★★★** is the definitive example, and in October, November and December there is a 19 Plato version called **Ur-Bock★★★**.

The brewery also has a *Helles*, but even that has a hint of smokiness.

Spezial

The oldest *Rauchbier* producer is believed to be Bamberg's Brauerei Spezial, which dates from 1536. It is an unassuming *Hausbrauerei* in a main shopping street. The Christian Merz family have their own tiny maltings and produce only smoked beers. Their everyday product, if it can be called that, is a *Rauchbier* simply called **Lager★★★**, at 12 Plato. It has a gently insistent smokiness and a treacle-toffee finish. A **Märzen★★★→★★★★** version of around 13.5 is even smokier in texture, bursting with flavour in the finish. There is also a November **Bock★★★**.

Tucher

One of the two large breweries that dominate the Nürnberg market is Tucher, the other being Patrizier. On their home ground, both have upset beer-lovers by swallowing smaller breweries, but Tucher's exports have brought a welcome taste of Germany to parts of the New World.

The brewery has a full range, including a dryish **Pilsener★→★★**, a tasty malty dark beer called **Alt Franken Export Dunkel★★**; a smooth double *bock* called **Bajuvator★★**; and a couple of wheat beers, **Weizen★** and **Hefe-Weizen★**. Sad to say, the splendidly bitter **Doppelhopfen** has not been available in recent years.

Würzburger Hofbräu

Würzburg in wine country and tried, in 1434, to banish its brewers forever. A couple of hundred years later it had acquired a Hofbräuhaus, which still produces pleasant beers, malt-accented but well-balanced. Its **Pils ★→★★**, has a malty nose, a firm body and a hoppy finish. **Burkardus★** (in some export markets **"Bavarian Dark"**) is tawny and translucent with a dry, malty palate. **Oktoberfest★** is on the dark side and quite dry. There is also a **Maibock★**, a **Sympator★** double bock and the fresh, plummy, Julius Echter **Hefe-Weissbier★★**.

BERLIN

"The champagne of beers" is a soubriquet too generously disposed. It is appropriate only to wheat brews, notably *Berliner Weisse*. Napoleon's troops during their Prussian campaign coined the description "the champagne of the north". Long after Napoleon was vanquished, the same "champagne" was a fitting toast in Imperial Berlin.

"Berlin white beer" has a very pale colour, an insistent sparkle, a fragrant fruitiness in the nose, a sharp, dry palate and a *frisson* of quenching, sour acidity in the finish. It is served in large bowl-shaped glasses, like beer-sized champagne saucers. To soften its acidity, it is often laced with a dash (a *Schuss*) of raspberry syrup, as though it were a *kir royale*. The green essence of the herb woodruff is also sometimes used for this purpose.

The term "white" has been used over the centuries throughout northern Europe to describe pale, sometimes cloudy, wheat beers. In the north of Germany it became the practice for such beers to contain a relatively low proportion of wheat and be characterized by a lactic fermentation. No doubt the lactic fermentation was originally accidental, but it is now a feature of the style. There are vestiges of this type of brewing elsewhere in the north, notably in Bremen, but it is mainly associated with Berlin. Because it is intended as a light, refreshing drink, *Berliner Weisse* is produced to a low alcohol content and with a very gentle hop rate. A typical gravity is around 7.5–8 Plato, with an alcohol content of just under 2.5 percent by weight; around 3 by volume. The beer may well have only four or five units of bitterness.

Between a quarter and a half of the mash comprises wheat, which is malted. The rest is barley malt. A top-fermenting yeast is used, in a symbiosis with a lactic culture. In the production of the Schultheiss brewery's *Berliner Weisse*, there is also a blending with a wort that is three to six months old. The brew then has between three and six months' maturation at warm temperatures, is re-innoculated, and has four weeks' bottle-conditioning at the brewery. Devotees of the style will keep the beer for a further one to two years in a cool, dark place (but not a refrigerator) to bring out the delicacy and complexity of its fruitiness and fragrance.

Schultheiss Berliner Weisse★★★★ is a beautifully complex example. The generic **Berliner Weisse★★★→★★★★** brewed in East Berlin by V.E.B. Getrankekombinat has similar characteristics, with a notably pale colour and lots of refreshing, lactic, acidity. **Berliner Kindl Weisse★★★**, made by the biggest producer, scores points for assertiveness, but is lacking in complexity and length.

Where to drink

Berliner Weisse is widely available, and is especially popular at the city's various lakes in summer. The Berlin Museum (Linden Strasse 14) has a Weissbierstube, with an interesting collection of glasses, the *Kindl* version of the beer, and traditional snacks. "Haus der 100 Biere", at Mommsen Strasse 45, Charlottenburg, is worth a visit. Opposite the Charlottenburg Palace, the Luisen-Brau brewpub produces a soft, sweetish, unfiltered Vienna-style lager. There is a newer brewpub, called Rixdorfer, at Glasower Strasse 27, in Neu Koln. Others have foundered.

SCANDINAVIA

The northernmost nations of Europe evoke images of icy *fjords* bristling with longboats full of Norsemen inflaming themselves with mead or some early form of beer. Nordic legend certainly lays great stress on brewed beverages, but the modern reputation of Scandinavia in this respect derives from elegant, civilized Copenhagen.

Outside Germany, the Danes did more than anyone to popularize lager brewing, and they did so with great resourcefulness. In 1845, pots of bottom-fermenting yeast were brought from Munich to Copenhagen by the founder of the Carlsberg brewery. In a journey of at least 965km (600 miles), by stagecoach, he is said to have kept the yeast cool under his stovepipe hat and by dousing it with cold water at every stop. In 1883, the Carlsberg laboratory crossed another frontier by isolating for the first time a single-cell yeast culture. Pure bottom-fermenting yeasts were subsequently identified as *carlsbergensis*.

Denmark continues to remember its earlier, top-fermenting wheat beers by producing a barley malt derivative, of low alcohol content, called *hvidtøl*. But it is, of course, best known for pale lagers, brewed in an unusually wide variety of strengths, and typically with a malty mildness of palate.

Not only in tradition but also in consumption of beer per head, Denmark is an important brewing nation. It has, though, only about 20 breweries. Among those, Carlsberg also owns Tuborg, Wiibroe and Neptun, and has a stake in Ceres and others.

Norway has 15 breweries (owned by nine companies), producing by law all-malt beers, principally clean, crisp Pilseners. Probably the best-known brewery is Ringnes, producing good examples of the style, while the beers of its associate Frydenlunds have more hop character. In the same group are two provincial breweries, Arendals and Lundetangens. Most towns have their own breweries, marketing only locally. One of them – Mack, in Tromsø – is the world's most northerly brewery. In Tromsø, which is north of the Arctic Circle, beer is served with a snack of seagulls' eggs.

A typical Norwegian brewery might produce a Pilsener of 10.5–11 Plato (1042–44), with around 3.6 percent alcohol by weight; 4.5 by volume. Other products may include a summer beer of around 10.5, attenuated to a similar alcohol content and hopped for flowery aroma rather than bitterness; a "Bavarian-style" dark lager of 11–12 (1044–48), less well attenuated, to achieve again a similar alcohol content; a

German-style "Export" of 13, 1052, 4.5, 5.6; a Christmas beer of 15, 1060, 4.8, 6; and a dark *Bock* of 17, 1068, 4.9, 6-plus. There might also be a special product marking an anniversary or other celebration, usually at around 11.5, 1046, 3.6, 4.5.

In Norway and Sweden, beers are heavily taxed, and their strength and availability is beset with restrictions. Sweden's laws on beer strength mean that supermarkets sell only low-alcohol or light beers. The former, designated as Class I, have a maximum of 1.8 percent alcohol by weight (2.25 by volume). The latter, Class II, have 2.8 (3.5), from a gravity of at least 10.5 Plato (1042) and often considerably higher. Although such a specification is not unusual elsewhere in the world, Swedes complain that restrictions make it difficult for them to find a beer of a more typically international "medium" strength (which they describe as *Mellanøl*, at 3.6, 4.5). Given this difficulty, serious beer-lovers in Sweden often find themselves in restaurants or state liquor stores where strong beers (Class III, 4.5, 5.6) are available. Thus laws that are intended to favour low-strength beers have the opposite effect.

Sweden has 14 breweries, four of which are owned by Pripps. Despite the rigid alcohol brackets, most brewers have a wide variety of products. The same product may be brewed in two or three strengths, each clearly labelled as to its class.

The most unusual Swedish beers are two from a company called Till, which has three breweries in the far north. One, with the Viking name **Röde** (Red) **Orm**, is described as a mead. It is primed with honey, and spiced, though it is brewed from barley malt, and hopped. It has hints of honey in the aroma and finish. Despite its fierce name, it is a low-alcohol beer (Class I). The other, in Class II, is called **Spetsat**. It is a dark beer seasoned with juniper, angelica and sweet gale (*Myrica gale*, also known as bog myrtle). It has some juniper in the nose and a sweetish, faintly resinous, palate. All three ingredients were widely used in brewing in Europe before the ascendancy of the hop, and may still be found – along with alder twigs – in traditional home-brews in Nordic countries.

Finland has nine breweries, owned by three companies. The Fins do not tax beer so heavily, since they see it as a temperate alternative to hard liquor. Their alcohol limits on beer are also generally a little higher. Finland's Class I beers may have a maximum alcohol content of 2.25 by weight; 2.8 by volume. Class II (3; 3.75) is generally ignored by brewers. Class III has 3.7; 4.5. Class IV has 4.5; 5.6. Most Finnish beers are mainstream lagers, but there is the odd Märzen or Christmas beer, and one excellent Porter (see Koff). A commercial "home-brew" called *Sahti*, sometimes made with rye and juniper, is produced in several forms to the northwest of Helsinki. A sweetish lager called Lapin Kulta is made in Finnish Lapland. Scandinavia now has two brewpubs: Bryggeriet Gpollo, next to the Tivoli Park, in Copenhagen; and Bogstadveien, Oslo.

Aass

Embarrassingly named (at least to English-speakers) brewery in Drammen, near Oslo. The name means "summit", so perhaps the owning family originally came from the mountains. A small brewery by international standards and only middle-sized in Norway, but an exporter. Range includes the well-matured **Aass Export★★**, firm and smooth, with Saaz hops in the nose; **Aass Bayer Øl★★**, a good example of the Bavarian style; **Aass Jule Øl★★★**, a Christmas beer with a tawny colour and a lovely, nutty finish; and **Aass Bokk★★→★★★**, splendidly creamy.

Albani

Medium-sized independent producing a typical range of Danish beers, with some good strong seasonal specialities as well as the popular **Giraf★★** pale lager (15.4 Plato; 1063; 5.4 percent alcohol by weight; 6.8 by volume) and an all-malt **Porter★★→★★★** (20; 1083; 6.2; 7.8).

Carlsberg

International name, producing or licensing its beers in at least a dozen countries, some of which have as many as four or five different strengths and styles of Carlsberg. The company also makes at least half a dozen special export beers, and within its own country has yet more. The basic **Lager Beer★→★★** (known in some markets as Hof, after the Danish Royal Court), has the soft, smooth, malty dryness that is typical of Carlsberg and its home country. The same character can be found in the much stronger **Elephant★★** (in some markets, Carlsberg '68), which has 16 Plato; 1064; 5.7; 7.1. There is, predictably, a chewier character to the yet stronger **Carlsberg Special Strong Lager★★★** (6.8; 8.5), representing something of a style in itself. At Easter, Danes have the pleasure of **Carlsberg Påske Bryg 1847★★★** (17.4; 1069; 6.2; 7.8), which has a lovely, deep-amber colour, a restrained sweetness in the nose and a malty dryness in the finish. A beautifully balanced and delicious beer. A similar brew, of slightly lower gravity, is produced for Christmas. **Gamle Carlsberg Special Dark Lager★★** is a true Munich-style beer, of conventional gravity. **Gammel Porter** (or **Imperial Stout)★★★** has a gravity of 18.8; 1075, producing 6.1; 7.5. It is bottom-fermenting, but has a splendidly stouty "burnt toffee" palate. Carlsberg's premises include the world's most beautiful brewhouse, like a cathedral of beer. The original owners turned the company into a foundation to support the arts and sciences, and it remains such.

Ceres

While it own **Ceres Pilsner★→★★** has a classically clean maltiness, this medium-sized Danish company also has hoppier beers from its associate Thor brewery. The group produces a very wide range of tasty beers in typically Danish styles. A beer colourfully dubbed **Red Eric★★** has a gravity of just under 13; 1058; and an alcohol content of 4.5; 5.6. It is a firm, dry lager, pale in colour despite its name. A pink version was dropped after a Community ruling on food colourings.

Faxe

Unpasteurized beers, sterile-filtered, from an aggressive company. The principal local product is **Faxe Fad**★→★★ (meaning "draught-style"), at 3.6; 4.5. An export version called **The Great Dane**★→★★ has 4.5; 5.6. In some markets there is a **Fest Bock**★→★★, at 6; 7.5. Typically Danish beers, perhaps less distinctive than they were a few years ago.

Koff

A genuinely top-fermenting **Porter/Imperial Stout**★★★ →★★★★, dry, very roasty and satisfying, is an especially noteworthy product from this Finnish brewery. Full name Sinebrychoff.

Neptun

A green beer is the speciality product of this house. The beer is called Rooster in the American market, Bacchus in Japan, and **Pinsebryg**★★ (Whitsun brew) in Denmark. The colour was devised to celebrate the beginning of spring, but it merely distracts attention from a pleasantly soft, dryish palate, big body, and alcohol content of 6; 7.5. Another brewery provides the wort; Neptun ferments and matures.

Polar Beer

Iceland (with only 200,000 people) has just one brewery, and severe laws mean that its local products, a "Pilsner" and (surprisingly) a "*Märzen*-type", have only 6.2; 1025; 1.78; 2.25. However, the brewery does export a well-made **Polar Beer**★→★★ of 13; 1052; 4.2; 5.3.

Pripps

Sweden's biggest brewing company. Its **Nordik Wölf**★→★★, is very well attenuated (9; 1036; 3.8; 4.75). In Sweden, it rates as a Class III beer, and it has more alcohol and flavour, especially hop character, than most competing "light beers" in the US market. In the Swedish market, the brewery is very proud of its **Royal**★★, a Pilsener-style beer with a lot of Hallertau hop in the nose, a soft palate and a spritzy but long finish. The most distinctive of all the Pripps products is Sweden's only top-fermenting brew, **Carnegie Porter**★★★→★★★★, which in its reintroduced Class III version has a big, dry, "burnt" palate. Each year, there is one vintage-dated bottling of this product, conditioned for a minimum of 12 months at the brewery.

Spendrup's

Sweden's most aggressive independent. Its all-malt premium **Spendrup's**★★ and its super-premium **Old Gold**★★ have a lot of hop character, in both aroma and palate.

Tuborg

International name, producing a full range of Danish styles. Tuborg's beers are perhaps a little lighter in body and hoppier than those of its partner Carlsberg.

THE NETHERLANDS

The home not only of Heineken and Amstel but also Grolsch, once a country brewer but now internationally chic. While these companies originate from the north and east, the beer culture of The Netherlands was traditionally in the south, in the Dutch provinces of Brabant and Limburg, and they still have the greatest numbers of old-established small breweries. (The names Brabant and Limburg also occur in neighbouring parts of Belgium and Germany.)

In recent years, micros and brewpubs have sprung up all over the country. Under a windmill in Amsterdam, the 't IJ micro-brewery produces dryish, assertive brews. These have included an abbey-style Double called **Natte**★★ (meaning "wet"), at 6 percent alcohol by volume; a pale Triple, **Zatte**★★ → ★★★ ("drunk"), at about 8; a "Super Double" **Struis**★★★, said to exceed 10 percent ("Struis" means ostrich, but also implies big and strong); and a slightly less potent, dry-hopped "Super Triple", **Columbus**. A more recent product is a hugely hoppy **Plzen**★★ → ★★★.

Farther north, the Dutch province of Friesland has a range of ales with an intentional tartness from a cowshed brewery near Sneek. **Buorren**★★ → ★★★ (6), broadly in the style of a Double, is the flagship product of the Friese brewery. In the Frisian provincial capital, Leeuwarden, a home-brewer has commercially marketed fruit beers under the name Middelzee.

Near the northern city of Gronigen, a dry, malty ale is produced by a micro-brewpub called Peizer Hopbel, jointly established by Grolsch and the Gulpener brewery. This is in the village of Peize.

In the eastern town of Almelo, the old town hall and courthouse has been turned into a brewpub, initially making a hoppy, fruity, unfiltered ale (Almelosche Pub, Het Oude Verkeershuis, 80 Grotestraat).

In the eastern province of Gelderland, a micro making fruity, spicy ales began in a schoolhouse in Herwijnen, then moved to Heuekenlem. Also in Gelderland, at Wageningen, a micro called Onder de Linden began by making a strong ale.

Near Nijmegen a farmhouse and maltings and brewery dating from at least the 1700s has been revived under the name De Raaf, "The Raven" (Rijksweg 232, Heumen, ☎080-581177). Its products include a Belgian-style "white" beer, **Gelderse Witte**★★★ tart and spicy; a very complex and tasty bronze ale, **No 12**★★ → ★★★ and a well-rounded, abbey-style **Dubbel**★★ and **Tripel**★★.

In Limburg, a micro in Roermond makes the outstandingly hoppy **Christoffel**★★★, a very assertive

Pilsener. The province of Zeeland has two micros: in Middelburg, De Hop Bloem specializes in a Triple; in Goes, De Gans makes a very dry Bitter and a roasty, chocolatey, top-fermenting Bock. In the middle of the country, the town of Utrecht has a brewpub, at a chic restaurant called the Stadskasteel; and Amersfoort has De Drie Ringen, producing a fruity, sweet ale.

Until recently, a typical Dutch brewery would produce a low-alcohol Old Brown (around 9 Plato; 1036; 2-3 percent by weight; 2.5-3.5 by volume); a Pilsener (in The Netherlands, this term indicates the classic gravity of 11-12 1044-48; with an alcohol content of around 4.5); a "Dortmunder-style" (some, as might be expected, at around 13.5; 1054; 4.7; 5.9, but others considerably stronger); and a seasonal *Bo(c)k* (15.7-16.5; 1063-66; 5-5.5; 6.25-7). Now, new styles are being introduced, often with a Belgian accent. There are 20-odd breweries.

Where to drink

The Dutch pioneered speciality beer bars. The best in Amsterdam are Het Laatste Oordeel (17 Raadhuisstraat), which also organizes lectures and tastings for groups of visitors: ☎020-254634; and In De Wildeman (3 Kolksteeg at Nieuwe Zijds Kolk), off the shopping street Nieuwendijk), a former gin-tasting room. Not far from Dam S9, The Nederlands Bier Proeflokaal (Jonge Roelen Steeg 4) specializes in Dutch beers. De Zotte (Raamstraat 29, near Leidsplein) offers Belgian brews. There are also a number of speciality beer shops in Amsterdam. The best is De Bierkoning (Paleisstraat 33, near Dam S9). Another good example is D'Oude Gekroonde Bier en Wijn Winkel (21 Huidenstraat, running between Herengracht and Keizersgracht, a couple of blocks north of Leidsestraat).

Most of the main cities of The Netherlands have at least one speciality beer bar and some of the best are members of the Alliance of Beer-Tappers. A list of member-cafes throughout the country can be obtained from Het Laatste Oordeel of In De Wildeman. Many of these bars do not open until mid-afternoon.

Each year at the end of October and beginning of November, the Dutch beer-lovers' organization PINT runs a festival of Bock beers at the Artis Zoo in Amsterdam. There is a national beer museum, with a bar called De Boom, in the cheese town of Alkmaart (Houttil 1).

Alfa

Small Limburg brewery making exclusively all-malt beers, smooth and well-balanced, with Hallertau and Saaz hopping. Noted for its sweetish **Super-Dort★★★**, the strongest example of the style (16-16.5; 1064-66; 5.5; 7)

Arcen

Revivalist brewery that was a forerunner of the boutiques in The Netherlands, making a wide range of interesting, all-malt, top-fermenting specialities. These include **Arcener Grand Prestige★★★**, at 10 percent one of the strongest beers in The Netherlands. It is very dark brown, with a rich aroma and palate, full of dry, smooth fruitiness and with a strong, warming finish. An excellent winter brew that could be styled as a strong old ale, bottle-conditioned, but is described on the back label as a barley wine. Other specialities include **Arcener Stout**★★★ (6.5), dryish, with some smokey notes; **Altforster Altbier**★★→★★★ (5), dry and on the thin side; and **Arcener Tarwe**★★→★★★ (5), a Bavarian-style wheat beer of the lightest and most delicate type.

Bavaria

Light, malty-tasting beers under the **Bavaria**★ and **Swinkels** names. This brewery, in Lieshout, Brabant, produces a wide range of supermarket and other "own-brand" labels.

Brand's

Oldest brewery in The Netherlands - founded in 1871, and in recent years acquired by Heineken. Its basic **Pils**★★ has a delicate hop character in its aroma and palate and is very clean indeed. It has attracted attention in the US (where it is labelled as Royal Brand) by being marketed in a porcelain-style bottle. The super-premium **Brand Up**★★→★★★ is nonetheless more interesting. The suffix is meant to indicate "Urtyp Pilsener" and this all-malt beer (12.5; 1050; 4.5) has much more hop character, especially in the palate. It has 36-37 units of bitterness. A soft, malty, clean, amber-coloured Bock called **Imperator**★★→★★★ (6.5 by volume) has now been joined by a Double Bock (too early to rate). The speciality **Sylvester**★★★ is brewed in late August or early September for release in November. It should be sold out after January, but some bars retain stocks through the year. This is now an all top-fermenting beer, of 18-18.5 Plato (1072-4; 6.4; 8), having a deep bronze colour, a wonderfully complex and sophisticated fruitiness in the aroma and palate with a nice dryness in the finish. An *eau-de-vie* among beers.

Breda

This Brabant town gives its name to a company making the once-famous **Three Horse(shoes)**★ beers (generally fresh-tasting, with some hoppiness), and now linked with Rotterdam's **Oranjeboom**★ (whose products tend to be firmer in body, as part of Allied Breweries (with the bland **Skol**★ labels). A confusion of similar-tasting beers, with export markets also having the low-cost **Royal Dutch Post Horn**.

Budels

Small Brabant brewery with several interesting new products: **Budels Alt**★★→★★★ is in the German style but from the relatively high gravity of 13.5 (1054; 4.4; 5.5). **Parel**★★→★★★ is a top-fermenting pale beer of 14 (1056; 4.8; 6). **Capucijn**★★→★★★ (16; 1064; 5.2; 6.5) is a most unusual beer, with hints of smoked applewood. All of these beers are notably smooth, and are not pasteurized.

Dommels

Brabant brewery owned by Artois, of Belgium. **Dominator Dommelsch Speciaal**★★, a strong (4.8; 6), very pale lager, dry and lightly fruity, is a new product.

Grolsch

The pot-stoppered bottle was set to be phased out in the 1950s, but consumers objected. It helped **Grolsch**★★ become a cult beer, first in The Netherlands, more recently in export markets. Judged (as it now must be) among the bigger-selling Dutch Pilseners, Grolsch has a hint of new-mown hay in the nose; a soft, fluffy body; and a dryish palate. It is unpasteurized. Other products include **Grolsch Amber**✭✭, in broadly the style of an Altbier.

Gulpen

Small Limburg brewery already known for one speciality, and now gaining attention for a second. The original speciality, **X-pert**✭✭→✭✭✭, is a super-premium Pilsener with a notably full colour, a gravity of 12 (1048; 4.5), and a lot of Tettnang hop in both aroma and palate. It is krausened, and well-matured. The newer product, **Mestreechs Aajt**✭✭✭→✭✭✭✭, is a revival of a regional speciality, with a nod in a southerly direction. It is a sour-and-sweet summer beer, claret in colour, and with some gentian notes. It is brewed from a refreshingly low gravity of 8.5 (1034; 3.2; 4), and a blend in which a proportion has wild yeast and lactic fermentation and ageing for at least a year in unlined barrels.

It is ironic that Gulpen should intentionally produce a sour beer. In the days before refrigeration, if beer in a brewery went sour, it would be sold off as malt vinegar. Gulpen's vinegar was so popular among the locals that the company continues to produce it (by less empirical methods), and also makes mustard.

Heineken

International trade (in beer even before tea, spices and diamonds) has always been a way of life in The Netherlands, a tiny but densely populated nation pushing into the sea. Heineken was the first brewery in the world to export to the United States at the repeal of Prohibition, and the company now controls the production of more beer in the international market than any rival. Its principal product, **Heineken Lager Beer**✭→✭✭, is in the Pilsener style, and in its production the company stresses the use of summer barley and a total process time of not less than six weeks. The beer has a characteristically refreshing hint of fruitiness, only a light hop character, and a spritzy finish. In the Dutch market, the company produces a full range of local styles. It also has specialities like the tasty, though bottom-fermenting, **Van Vollenhoven Stout**✭✭→✭✭✭ (16.2; 1065; 4.8; 6).

Seasonal *Bock* beers have been marketed locally under the Heineken, Hooijberg and Sleutel names, in what seems to be an ascending order of dryness.

A full range of beers is marketed internationally under the Amstel brand. These are generally lighter, and sharper, in palate (see also Canada). A third international brand is Murphy (see Ireland). The company also has substantial stakes in the local brewing industries of France, Italy and several smaller countries.

De Kroom

Very small Brabant brewery. A new speciality called **Egelantier**✭✭ is a bronze, bottom-fermenting beer of conventional gravity but full body. The Dortmunder-style **Briljant**✭✭ (12; 1048; 5.2; 6.3) seems to have developed more of its own character in recent years. It has a malty nose, firm but surprisingly light body, and dry palate.

De Leeuw

Small Limburg brewery. It is to be hoped that the soft, all-malt **Jubileeuw**★★ (originally produced for the brewery's centenary) has a permanent place in the range. This is a pale, bottom-fermenting beer of conventional gravity. **Super Leeuw**★★ (13.5; 1054; 4.7; 5.9) is a well-liked Dortmunder. These beers are unpasteurised.

Lindeboom

Small Limburg brewery noted for its gently dry **Pilsener**★★ and a pleasant **Bock**★★. Has now added a bronze, malty beer in broadly the Vienna style called **Gouverneur**★★→★★★.

De Ridder

Small Limburg brewery noted for its creamy, fruity, Dortmunder-style **Maltezer**★★. The products of this brewery do not seem to have changed in character since it was acquired by Heineken.

Schaapskooi Trappist

The only abbey brewery in The Netherlands is called Schaapskooi ("Sheep's Pen"), and has, since the 1880s, operated within the monastery of Koningshoeven, near Tilburg. Its **Dubbel**★★→★★★ (1064) has a deep, ruby, colour; a yeasty fruitiness in the nose; and a depth and complexity of pruny, sherryish flavours. Its **Tripel**★★★ (1070-plus) is paler and drier, with notes of Goldings hops and perhaps coriander. The double appears under the La Trappe, Koningshoeven and Tilburg names, but is much the same beer in each case. The Tripel is at its spiciest in the La Trappe version; maltier under the Koningshoeven label; and hoppier and paler in its Tilburg form.

BELGIUM

The secret is out. Beer-drinkers have begun to realize that Belgium has the most diverse, individualistic brews in the world. Its cidery, winey, spontaneously fermenting *lambic* family predate the pitching of yeast by brewers and its cherry *kriek*, strawberry *framboise* and spiced "white" brews predate the acceptance of the hop as the universal seasoning in beer. Other countries have monastery breweries but it is only in Belgium that the brothers have evolved their own collective style. Whether produced in the country's five monastery breweries or in secular plant, "abbey"-style beers are always strong, top-fermenting and bottle-matured. They often have a heavy sediment and a fruity palate, sometimes evincing hints of chocolate. Within these characteristics, however, there are substantial differences between the brews, and a couple of subcategories, but that is the way of Belgian beer. Some Belgian specialities are hard to categorize, although most are top-fermenting and many are bottle-matured. No country has a more diverse range even within the bottle-matured group – the Belgians are keen on this means of conditioning and sometimes refer to it as their *méthode champenoise*.

In a Belgian cafe, the list of beers will identify at least one member of the *lambic* family (occasionally a sweet *faro*, often a sparkling *gueuze*); perhaps a honeyish "white" beer (*witbier* or *bière blanche*) from the village or a brown (*bruin*) from the town of Oudenaarde; a local *spécial*; and a strong, bottle-conditioned monastery (*abdij* or *abbaye*) brew. There may also be a Belgian *ale*, as well as local interpretations of English, Scottish and sometimes German styles. This is in an ordinary cafe; there will be a far greater categorization in a cafe that makes a feature of speciality beers, listing them by the hundred. After decades of decline when they were regarded as "old-fashioned", speciality beers began to enjoy a revival in the late 1970s. They are a joy to the visiting beer-lover, although it is necessary to know what to order. A request simply for "a beer" is likely to be met by a mass-market Pilsener.

With the revival of interest in speciality beers within Belgium, more of them have also entered export markets. They present a bewildering choice. As always, the selection of beers reflects both history and geography. The influence of the brewing customs of the surrounding nations has been accepted with shrewd selectivity by the Belgians, yet they have also contrived to be conservative and inward-looking to the point that their principal regions maintain their own traditions. The country is divided not only into its Dutch-speaking north (Flanders) and French-speaking south (Wallonia) but also has a German-speaking corner in the east and a bilingual knot around the city of Brussels. Some styles of beer are perceived as belonging not to a region but to a province, river valley, town or village.

The Belgians like to talk about beer as their reply to Burgundy. They suggest that beer is to them what wine is to France. Cheese might be an even better comparison. The beers of Belgium, like the cheeses of France, are often idiosyncratic, cranky, artisanal. Some drinkers could never learn to enjoy one of the cloudy, sour specialities of the Senne Valley any more than they could acquire a taste for a smelly cheese. In both cases, the loss would be theirs. This is drink at its most sensuous. In its native gastronomy, Belgium is a land of beer, seafood and – after dinner – the world's finest chocolate. It is a land of German portions and French culinary skills. Beer may be served, with some ceremony at a family meal, and might well have been used in the cooking. Other countries have the odd dish prepared with beer, but Belgium has hundreds. The Belgians even eat hop shoots, as a delicacy, in the brief season of their availability, served like asparagus.

Beer is also a central theme in Belgium's history and culture. St Arnold of Oudenaarde is remembered for having successfully beseeched God, in the 11th century, to provide more beer after an abbey brewery collapsed. He is the patron saint of Belgian brewers, some of whom display his statue by their kettles. (French-speakers can, if they prefer, remember another beery miracle, that of St Arnold at Metz.) The 13th-century Duke Jan the First of Brabant, Louvain and Antwerp has passed into legend as the King of Beer: "Jan Primus" has been corrupted into "Gambrinus", by which name he is remembered not only in Belgium but also in Germany, Czechoslovakia and far beyond. Jan Primus is said to have been an honorary member of the Brewers' Guild, although their present gilded premises on Brussels' Grand' Place were not built until 1701. Today, the "Brewers' House" is the only building on the Grand' Place still to be used as the headquarters of a trade guild. Today's Confederation has about a hundred members, and that represents roughly the number of breweries in Belgium. The figure has been declining for some years, although recently a number of new micro-breweries have opened. Many Belgian breweries are family owned, which can lead to problems when there is no clear succession. But however much the number of breweries fluctuates, the tally of beers increases, with new specialities constantly being launched. At any one time, there are probably more than 800 Belgium beers on the market.

FLANDERS

Flemish painters like Bruegel and the aptly named Brouwer depicted the people of their home stage as enthusiastic beer-drinkers. It has been like that for a thousand years. As Emperor of Europe, Charlemagne took an interest in brewing, and perhaps he brought the news from Aix to Ghent. The nationalistic Flemings might, however, secretly resent their famous artists' depiction of beery excess. They take pride in being hard-working, and the Early and Late Flemish schools of painting were made possible by the prosperity of Flanders at different times as an exporter of beer as well as textiles, and as a commercial centre. Flanders emerged as a principal component of the new Belgium in 1830, and has in recent years reasserted itself through the trading prosperity of the river Scheldt – with beer exports once again on the upswing.

As a region, Flanders stretches from the Dutch side of the Scheldt to a slice of northern France. Politically, it comprises the Belgian provinces of West and East Flanders, Antwerp and Limburg.

West Flanders, with its 15th-century canalside capital Bruges, has traditionally been known for its sour, burgundy-coloured style of beer – the classic example is Rodenbach. The province is well served by small breweries and has two of the strongest beers in Belgium, from the revivalist Dolle Brouwers and the monastery brewery of Westvleteren. East Flanders, with the proud city of Ghent as its capital, is noted for slightly less sour brown ales, produced in or near the town of Oudenaarde, which has a cluster of small breweries to the east.

The province and city of Antwerp is noted for the beautifully made De Koninck beer (a copper ale). The province also has the monastery of Westmalle, which created the Triple style of abbey beer, and in the south, the strong, golden ale called Duvel, the potent, dark Gouden Carolus and the well-liked Maes Pils.

Limburg has a less gilded capital, the pretty little town of Hasselt, which is known for the production of *genever* gin. It is a thinly breweried province but has the distinctive Sezoens beer from the Martens brewery; and Cristal Alken, an especially well-respected Pilsener beer.

Where to drink

Beer cafes with huge selections have opened and closed in Antwerp. The most reliable, although service varies from the obliging to the dour, is the small cafe Kulminator (32–34 Vleminckxveld) with 350–400 beers. Patersvaetje (1 Blauwmoezelstraat) has about 80 beers.

There are good selections in many other places, although Belgian cafes in general do not always offer much to eat. Where they do, Flanders is at its best with seafood. Vagant (25 Reyndersstraat) has some interesting beers and gins, and offers herring in season (in the same street, De Groote Witte Arend marries beer with fine art and recitals of chamber music). De Arme Duivel (in the street of the same name) has *kriek* on draught, and mussels in season; 't Waagstuk (20 Stadswag) has 60 beers and offers fish dishes; Fouquets (17 De Keyserlei) has beers, oysters in season and desserts. After Antwerp, the largest city in Flanders is Ghent, which has a popular and well-run specialist beer cafe called De Hopduvel ("The Hop Devil", at 10 Rokerelsstraat). The Hopduvel also features the growing number of Belgian cheeses.

Bruges, too, has an excellent beer cafe, a pubby place called 't Brugs Beertje (5 Kemelstraat). Farther afield, the gin town of Hasselt has 't Hemelrijk, on the street of the same name.

Cristal Alken

The hoppiest of the principal Belgian Pilseners is **Cristal Alken**★★→★★★. This well-made Pilsener with a notably pale colour, fresh, hoppy nose; very clean, crisp palate and a smooth dryness in the finish. It is hopped principally with blossoms, including Saaz for aroma, fermented at relatively cold temperatures, lagered for a respectable period and not pasteurized. Cristal is a much-loved beer and its character has been maintained despite a change in the ownership of the brewery. Alken and its former rivals Maes are now part-owned by Kronenbourg of France.

De Dolle Brouwers

"The Mad Brewers", they call themselves. It is a typically Flemish, sardonic shrug on behalf of a group of enthusiasts who rescued from closure a village brewery near Diksmuide, not far from Ostend. As a weekend project, they renovated the brewery, which dates from the the mid 19th century and is a classic of its type. (Tours welcome; ☎051-502781.) They specialize in strong, top-fermenting beers, bottle-matured. The house speciality is **Oerbier**★★★, very dark and smooth, with a sweetness that is offset by licorice tones (original gravity 1100; alcohol content 6 percent by weight; 7.5 by volume). There are also several seasonal products: the brassy-coloured, honey-primed **Boskeun★★★**, an Easter beer of about 8 percent by volume; the pale, dry-hopped **Arabier★★★**, for summer, with a similar alcohol content; and **Stille Nacht★★★**, a claret-coloured Christmas brew, with hints of apple in its aroma and palate, and an alcohol content of around 9 percent. The Ostend area also has a micro-brewery called 't Steedje, producing an ale and a "Triple".

De Koninck

A classic. This perilously drinkable, copper-coloured, top-fermenting beer fits in stylistically somewhere between an English ale (a fruity "best bitter") and a smooth Düsseldorf *Altbier*. For all its complexity of character, it pursues an unassuming occupation as the local beer of Antwerp, from the city's only brewery. The company stayed with top-fermentation when other big-city breweries were switching to Pilseners. Its sole product is **De Koninck★★★**, an all-malt beer of 12 Plato, brewed by direct flame in a cast-iron kettle. It is cold-conditioned and emerges with an alcohol content of a little over 4 percent by weight and 5 by volume. De Koninck has an excellent malt character, a yeasty fruitiness and a great deal of Saaz hoppiness, especially in its big finish. Its full palate is best experienced in the draught form, which is unpasteurized. Opposite the brewery, at the Pilgrim Cafe (8 Boomgardstraat), drinkers sometimes add a sprinkle of yeast to the beer. In the heart of Antwerp, the beer is available at the city's oldest cafe, Quinten Matsijs (17 Moriaanstraat) and at Den Engel (3 Grote Markt).

Duvel

This means "Devil" and is the name of the world's most beguiling beer. With its pale, golden sparkle, **Duvel★★★★** looks superficially like a Pilsener. Its palate is soft and seductive. Beneath its frothy head, behind its dense lacework, this all-malt, top-fermenting beer has the power (6.7 percent alcohol by weight; 8.2 by volume) to lead anyone into temptation. The pale colour is achieved with the help of the brewery's own maltings; Styrian and Saaz hops are used; a very distinctive yeast imparts a subtle fruitiness (reminiscent of Poire Williams); the cleanness and smoothness is enhanced by both cold and warm maturation; and, in the classic, sedimented, version, the *mousse* develops from bottle-conditioning. Duvel is customarily chilled as though it were an *alcool blanc*. It is produced by the Moortgat brewery in the village of Breendonk near Mechelen/Malines. Other Moortgat products include tasty, abbey-style beers under the **Maredsous★★** label, for the monastery of that name. Duvel is sometimes compared with the various monastic Triple beers, but this is self-evident heresy. Duvel is lighter in body, less sweet, more delicate. It is the original, and therefore classic, example of what has become a distinct style. Broadly in this style are **Deugniet★★**, **Hapkin★★→★★★**, **Lucifer★**, and perhaps the darker **Sloeber★★**.

Gouden Carolus

This is the classic strong, dark ale of Belgium. Its name derives from a gold coin from the realm of the Holy Roman Emperor

Charles V, who grew up in the Flemish City of Mechelen (better known by its French name, Malines) where this beer is brewed. **Gouden Carolus*** → ★★★★**, has a dense, dark colour, a gentle, soothing character, a hint of fruitiness in the finish and, from a gravity of 19 Plato, an alcohol content of 6 percent by weight; 7.5 by volume. A lovely after-dinner beer; or, better still, a nightcap.

Kwak Pauwel

The odd name derives from an antique Flemish speciality. This revival, a strong (9 percent by volume), garnet-coloured, top-fermenting brew, is notable for its licorice aroma and palate. Licorice is actually added; the character does not derive from the malt, as it does in some dark brews. **Kwak Pauwel*** is a hearty, warming brew. When it first appeared in Belgium, it won attention by being served in a "yard of ale" glass, of the type allegedly handed up to coachmen in times past when they stopped for a restorative drink.

Liefmans

Liefmans is the classic brown-ale brewery in Oudenaarde where such products are a speciality. In recent years, it has twice had new proprietors, and is currently owned by the commercially minded company Riva, of Beutergem. It is to be hoped that standards are maintained. The brewery's basic brown ale, known simply as **Liefmans★★ → ★★★**, is made from at least four styles of malt and a similar number of hop varieties. It spends an extraordinarily long time in the brew kettle – a whole night – and is cooled in open vessels. It is pitched with a pure-culture, top-fermenting yeast that has a slightly lactic character, imparting the gentle sourness typical in such beers. It has six weeks' warm-conditioning in tanks and is then blended with a smaller proportion of a similar beer that has had eight to ten months' conditioning. It has an original gravity of around 12 Plato (1048) and an alcohol content of 3.7 percent by weight; 4.6 by volume.

The longer-conditioned "vintage" brew is bottled "straight" as **Liefmans Goudenband★★★★** (Golden Band) and is surely the world's finest brown ale. After tank-conditioning, it has 3–12 months' bottle-maturation (without dosage) in the brewery's *caves*. It is called a *provisie* beer, indicating that it can be laid down. If it is kept in a cool (but not refrigerated) dark place, it will continue to improve, perhaps reaching its peak after two years. For a brown ale, it is unusually spritzy and very dry, with a finish reminiscent of Montilla. It has an original gravity of about 13 Plato (1052), and an alcohol content of 4.4; 5.5. The brown ales are also used as the basis for the unusual **Liefmans Kriek★★★**, which has a notably smooth body, a sour-and-sweet palate and a port-wine finish. It has an original gravity of 18.25 Plato (1073), 5.76 by weight; 7.2 by volume. Liefmans craft-brewing approach is emphasized by the use of a tissue-wrapped bottles. These appear in a variety of sizes including, for very good customers, hand-filled Nebuchadnezzars containing enough beer to fill 20 normal bottles.

The town of Oudenaarde also has brown ales from its Cnudde and Clarysse breweries, the latter under the Felix label, and in a less sour style from Roman. Similar beers are made nearby by the wonderfully artisanal brewery of Crombe in Zottegem and Van Den Bossche in St Lievens-Esse, and there are many more distant imitators.

Maes

A flowery "Riesling" bouquet imparts distinctiveness to **Maes Pils**★★. This is a light, soft, dry Pilsener-style beer. The brewery is in the village of Waarloos, north of Mechelen. The company also produces two top-fermenting beers for the abbey of Grimbergen, a Flemish village near Brussels. **Grimbergen Double**★★ is a dark, fruity beer, with a chocolatey palate; it has a gravity of 15.8 Plato and an alcohol content of 5.2 percent by weight; 6.5 by volume. **Grimbergen Tripel**★→★★ is paler, fruity, but with a more winey character; it has a gravity of 19.6 Plato and an alcohol content of 7.2 by weight; 9 by volume. (See also Curée de L'Ermitage.)

Rodenbach

The unimaginative are apt to consider Rodenbach's beers undrinkable, yet they are the classics of the "sour" style of West Flanders. They gain their sourness, and their burgundy colour, in a number of ways. The sourness derives in part from the top-fermenting yeast, a blend of three strains that has been in the house for 150 years, and from cultures resident in wooden maturation tuns. The colour, too, originates partly from the use of reddish Vienna-style malts but also probably from the caramels and tannins extracted from the oak of the tuns. These vessels, made from Slavonian oak, from Poland, are uncoated. They make a remarkable sight, each tun standing vertically from floor to ceiling. The smallest contains 15,000 litres of maturing beer; the largest 60,000 litres. There are 300 in all, filling several halls, as though this were a winery or a brandy distillery. When the maturing beer has attained its typical palate, it is stabilized by flash pasteurization so does not mature in the bottle and is not intended for laying down.

The basic **Rodenbach**★★★→★★★★ is a blend of "young" beer (matured five to six weeks) and "vintage" brews (matured 18 months to two years). The longer-matured beer is also bottled "straight" as **Rodenbach Grand Cru**★★★★. The basic Rodenbach has an original gravity of 11.5–11.75 Plato, emerging with 3.7 percent alcohol by weight; 4.6 volume. The Grand Cru has an original gravity of 15, but an alcohol content of only around 4.1; 5.2. The gravity is heightened by the use of non-fermented sugars and the alcohol content is diminished because some of the fermentation is lactic. There is both a sharpness and a restorative quality about these beers: perfect after a game of tennis. The Grand Cru has a slightly bigger palate and a smoother texture. Even then, some Belgians add a touch of grenadine, as though making a red *kir*. The Rodenbach brewery is in Roeslare, the centre of an agricultural area.

Several breweries in West Flanders produce similar beers to Rodenbach's but none with such a distinctive character. Examples include Paulus from Van Eecke; Bacchus from Van Honsenbrouck; Petrus from Bavik; and Vichtenaar from Verhaege. This brewery also has a sweeter beer in this style, called Bourgogne des Flandres. In East Flanders, the Bios Brewery has a drier entrant with the similar, Flemish-language, name **Vlaamse Bourgogne**.

St Louis

The widely marketed St Louis beers of the *lambic* family, including a novel strawberry brew, come from the Van Honsenbrouck company in Ingelmunster. In buccaneering fashion, this brewery tackles a wide variety of "speciality" styles and carries this off suprisingly well on occasion. St Louis **Gueuze Lambic★** may be a trifle on the sweet side but the **Kriek Lambic★→★★** is well balanced, if a little bland. The **Framboise★★** is full and fruity. In addition to its sweetish **Bacchus★→★★** (see previous entry), the brewery has an interesting top-fermenting speciality called **Brigand★★**. This is an amber, strong brew, with a secondary fermentation in its corked bottle. It has a gravity of 20 Plato, emerging with 7.2 percent alcohol by weight; 9 by volume. While it superficially resembles a *saison* in its immense liveliness and fruitiness, it has a more rounded texture and its palate is less citric, more reminiscent of soft fruit.

St Sixtus

See Westvleteren, Trappist Monastery of St Sixtus.

Sezoens

While seasonal *saison* beers from summer are a recognized style in the French-speaking part of Belgium, they are less evident in Flemish tradition. **Sezoens★★★** has the same connotation, but is the registered trademark of a distinctive and delightful product from the Martens brewery, in the Limburg village of Bocholt. It has a delightful label, too, showing a well-clad personification of winter handing the beer to a sunny "Mr Summer".

Sezoens is a pale, golden top-fermenting brew of 13.5 Plato, with 4 percent alcohol by weight; 5 by volume. It has a fresh, hoppy aroma (Saaz is used), a firm, clean, notably dry palate, and plenty of hop character throughout, especially in the finish, where the hearty dryness is that of the Northern Brewer variety. At the moment, this product is not bottle-conditioned though it might be in the future. In all of these respects, Sezoens is quite different from the amber, stronger, yeastily fruit *saison* brews of French-speaking Belgium. Martens also produces a rather German-tasting **Pils★★**.

Devotees who track these beers down to their far-flung home village should arrange in advance to visit Martens' museum (Brouwerij Martens Museum, Dorpstraat 32, Bocholt, Belgium B3598; ☎011-461705), which is open by appointment only. In Brussels, Sezoens is the speciality of the cafe De Ultieme Hallucinatie (316 Koningsstraat), which is in an Art Nouveau house near the Botanical Gardens.

Stropken

The first Stropken was assertively spicy, with a hint of anis, but this subsequently yielded to a more refined Grand Cru version. **Stropken Grand Cru★★→★★★** is a well-made, top-fermenting beer, with an original gravity of 17.5 Plato and an alcohol content of around 5.5 percent by weight; 6.75 by volume. The name Stropken is an ironic Flemish reference to the halters that the rebellious Lords of Ghent were obliged to wear by Emperor Charles in the 16th century. Stropken, originally produced as the house brew at the Hopduvel specialist beer cafe in Ghent, is now produced under contract by the Slaghmuylder brewery also in East Flanders. Slaghmuylder produces well-made abbey-style brews.

Westmalle, Trappist Monastery

The classic example of the pale, Triple style of Belgian Trappist brew is produced by the monastery of Westmalle, a village northeast of Antwerp. The monastery, established in 1821, has brewed since its early days, though it was slow in making its beer available commercially, and remains one of the most withdrawn of the Trappist monasteries. Visits are not encouraged, though the brewery can sometimes be seen by appointment. The smart, traditional copper brewhouse is in a strikingly 1930s building. It produces three beers. The "Single", confusingly known as **Extra**, is available only to the brothers; a shame, since this pale, top-fermenting brew is a product of some delicacy. The **Double**★★ is dark brown, malty, but quite dry. It has an original gravity of around 16 Plato and an alcohol content of about 5.5 by weight; just under 7 by volume. The **Triple**★★★★ offers an unusual combination of features, being a strong, top-fermenting beer of pale, almost Pilsener, colour. Its mash is entirely of Pilsener malts from Czechoslovakia and France but, in the classic procedure, candy sugar is added in the kettle. There are three hopping stages, using Fuggles, a number of German varieties and Saaz. The brew is fermented with a hybrid house yeast, then has a secondary fermentation of one to three months in tanks, and is given a priming of sugar and a further dosage of yeast before being bottled. It is warm-conditioned in the bottle before being released from a gravity of around 20 Plato, it emerges with an alcohol content of around 6.4 percent by weight; 8 by volume. With its faintly citric fruitiness, its rounded body and its alcoholic "kick", the Triple expresses a very full character within six months of leaving the monastery, though bottles from 1927 are still in good condition. Westmalle is jealous of the individuality of its product, but several secular breweries produce beers in a similar style, using the designation Triple (in Flemish, Tripel). Good examples include Vieille Villers Triple from Van Assche; Witkap from Slaghmuylder and the slightly fuller-coloured Affligem from De Smedt.

Westvleteren, Trappist Monastery of St Sixtus

One of Belgium's strongest beers comes from by far the smallest of the country's five monastery breweries. This is the monastery of St Sixtus, at the hamlet of Westvleteren, in a rustic corner of Flanders, near the French border and between the coast and the town best known by its French name Ypres (Ieper in Flemish). Although it overlooks a hop garden, the monastery produces beers in which malty sweetness is the predominant characteristic, with spicy and fruity tones also notable. As well as being tiny, the brewhouse is antique. Its own output is limited – artisanal Trappist beers, bottled without labels and identified by the crown cork – though further supplies are produced by arrangement in a nearby commercial brewery. From the monastery's own output there is no Single, and the basic beer, with a green crown-cork, is called **Double**★★. Then comes the **Special**★★ (red crown-cork), drier, with hints of vanilla and licorice, a gravity of around 15 Plato and an alcohol content of about 4.8 percent by weight; 6 by volume. The **Extra**★★ (blue) has more fruity, acidic tones and some alcohol character (20 Plato; 6.4; 8). Finally, the strongest beer in the monastery (and the country) is the **Abbot**★★★★ (yellow), very full-bodied, creamy, soft and sweet. This is sometimes known as a 12-degree beer, its gravity in the Belgian scale. That works out at about 30 Plato (1120) and the beer has around 8.48 percent alcohol by weight; 10.6 by volume.

These beers can be bought by the case at the monastery and sampled next door in the Cafe De Vrede, but they are less easy to find elsewhere. Their crown-corks identify the beer as Westmalle, while the commercially produced version has a label and is designated St Sixtus. The commercially produced counterpart to Abbot, with a yet yeastier character (very lively, and with an acidic finish) is exported to the USA simply as **St Sixtus★★★**. This is remarkable in that the producing brewery, St Bernard, is itself very small. St Bernard is in Watou, near Poperinge. Its local rival Van Eecke produces a similar range of tasty yeasty, abbey-style brews, and a hoppy speciality called **Poperings Hommelbier★★ → ★★★**.

BRUSSELS AND BRABANT

Within the extraordinarily colourful tapestry of Belgian brewing, the most vivid shades are to be found in the country's central province, Brabant, and especially around the capital city, Brussels. If the Germanic north of Europe and the Romantic south intertwine in Belgium, it is in the province of Brabant and the city of Brussels that the knot is tied. As the nearest thing Europe has to a federal capital, Brussels has some lofty French kitchens, but it also takes pride in the heartier *carbonades* of what it terms *"cuisine de biere"*, in which several restaurants specialize. On its Gallic avenues, it has some splendid Art Nouveau cafes, but the Grand' Place and the older neighbourhoods are Flemish in flavour and so is the beer.

To the east, the Flemish village of Hoegaarden is the home of the Belgian style of "white" beer. Louvain (in Flemish, Leuven) is the home of Stella Artois and the biggest brewing city in Belgium. The greatest splash of colour by far is, however, Brussels. Although it has one conventional brewery, Brussels is the local market for the *lambic* family, the most unusual beers in the world, with palate characteristics that range from a hint of pine kernels to a forkful of Brie cheese. *Lambic* is produced in the city itself and, in great variety by a cluster of specialist brewers and blenders in the Senne Valley.

The Senne is a small river that runs diagonally, often underground, from northeast to southwest through Brussels. There used to be *lambic* breweries on both sides of the city and even today *lambic* is served as a local speciality on the eastern edge of the city at Jezus-Eik. South of Brussels it is served at Hoeillaart-Overijse, where Belgium's (dessert) grapes are grown. However, it is on the western edge of Brussels that production is concentrated today spreading out into the nearby scatter of farming villages collectively known as Payottenland. Traditional *lambic*-makers brew only in the winter, and the number in production at any one time varies. So does the extent to which traditional methods are still used.

There are a couple of *lambic* breweries within the western boundary of Brussels itself and a further eight or nine active ones in Payottenland. There are also four or five companies that contract or buy brews which they then ferment, mature or blend in their own cellars. A further two or three breweries beyond the traditional area also produce beers of loosely this type (notably St Louis and Jacobins, both from West Flanders). With 20-odd houses producing *lambic* beers to varying degrees of authenticity, and seven or eight derivative styles, some available in more than one age, there are usually about 100 products of this type on the market, though many are obtainable only on a very limited scale and in specialist cafes.

The *lambic* family are not everybody's glass of beer, but no one with a keen interest in alcoholic drink would find them anything less than fascinating. In their "wildness" and unpredictability, these are exciting brews. At their best, they are the meeting point between beer and wine. At their worst, they offer a taste of history, as though one of those stoneware jars of beer had been lifted from the canvas of a Bruegel or Brouwer.

The basic *lambic* is a spontaneously fermenting wheat beer, made from a turbid mash of 30–40 percent wheat and the rest barley. The barley is only lightly malted; the wheat not at all. The boil can last three to six hours and the brew is hopped very heavily but with blossoms that have been aged to reduce their bitterness. The hops are used for their traditional purpose as a preservative; their bitterness is not wanted in a fruity wheat beer. In the classic method, the brew is taken upstairs to the gable of the roof, where vents are left open so that the wild yeasts of the Senne Valley may enter. The brew lies uncovered in an open vessel, and consummation takes place. The brew is allowed to be aroused in this way for only one night, ideally an autumn evening, and only the wild yeasts of the Senne Valley are said to provide the proper impregnation.

After its night upstairs the brew is barrelled in hogsheads, where primary and secondary fermentations take place, further stimulated by microflora resident in the wood. For this reason, *lambic* brewers are reluctant to disturb the dust that collects among the hogsheads, which are racked in galleries with no temperature control.

Brewers outside the traditional *lambic* area who wish to make a beer of this type have been known to acquire a barrel of a Senne Valley vintage to use as a starter. In the classic method the brewer never pitches any yeast. No doubt it was originally just a question of supply, but some barrels used in the maturation of *lambic* originally contained claret, port or sherry – the last reminiscent of whisky-making in Scotland. Like the whisky-maker, the *lambic*-brewer wants his barrels to respond to the natural changes in temperature.

The primary fermentation takes only five or six days, the secondary six months. If a brew of less than six months is made available for sale, it is customarily identified as young (*jong*) or "fox" (*vos*) *lambic*. The classic maturation period, however, is "one or two summers" and occasionally three.

Terminology is imprecise, not least because of the two languages in use (and Flemish manifests itself in several dialects). *Lambic* may appear as *lambiek* and both the beer and yeast are said to derive their name from the village of Lembeek, in Payottenland. In its basic form *lambic* is hard to find, but it is served on draught in some cafes in the producing area. The young version can be intensely dry, sour, cloudy and still, like an English "scrumpy" or rustic cider. The older version will have mellowed, settled, and perhaps be *pétillant*.

A blended version of young *lambic* sweetened with dark candy sugar is known as *faro*. If this is then diluted with water, it becomes *mars*. Sometimes cafes provide sugar and a muddler. If the sugared version is bottled, it is effectively chaptalized and develops a complex of sweetness in the start and fruity sharpness in the finish. If young and old versions of the basic beer are blended in the cask to start yet a further fermentation, the result, sparkling and medium-dry, is known as *gueuze-lambic*. This term is also sometimes used to describe a version that is blended and conditioned in the bottle, though such a product is properly known simply as *gueuze* and is the most widely available member of the family. The bottle-conditioning may take three to nine months, though the beer will continue to improve for one or two years after leaving the brewery and will certainly last for five. Until recent years, small lambic brewers did not use labels. They simply put a dab of whitewash on each bottle to show which way up it had been stored. Now, labels are required by law, but some of the old whitewashed bottles are still in the cellars of cafes. They are likely to contain vintage beers, made at a time when all aspects of production were more traditional.

The version of lambic in which cherries have been macerated in the cask is known as *kriek*. If raspberries are used, it is called *framboise*. In recent years. Some very un-traditional fruits have also been used. The cherry version is a very traditional summer drink in the Brussels area, and the original method is to make it with whole fruit, which ferment down to the pits. Another technique is to macerate whole fruit in juice and add the mixture to the brew. The original beer is brewed from a conventional gravity of 12–13 Plato (1048–52), though the density and alcohol content varies according to dilution, blending and maceration. A basic *lambic* has only about 3.6 percent alcohol by weight; 4.4 by volume. A *gueuze* might have 4.4; 5.5. A *kriek* can go up to 4.8; 6.

Even with all of these variations at their disposal some cafes choose to offer their own blend, perhaps to offset the sourness of a young *lambic* with fruitiness of a mature one. Such a blend may be offered as the *panache* of the house. These beers are sometimes accompanied by a hunk of brown bread with cheese, onions and radishes. A spready *fromage blanc*, made from skimmed milk, is favoured. Or a salty *Brusselsekaas* might be appropriate. The beers are served at a cool cellar temperature of around 10°C (50°F). In the USA they have proved themselves to be elegant aperitifs, over ice, as though they were vermouth.

As if such colour were not enough, there are also a number of ale breweries in Brabant, especially northwest of Brussels.

Where to drink

In Brussels: Beer-lovers who also enjoy Art Nouveau will appreciate the cafe De Ultime Hallucinate (Koningsstraat 316). Something a little later, reminiscent of the bar in a railway station, is offered by the wonderful 1920s Mort Subite (serving the *lambic* beers of the same name) at Rue de Montagne-aux-Herbes Potagères, not far from Grand' Place.

Another *lambic* cafe, even closer to Grand' Place, is Bécasse, in an alley off Rue Tabora. Easily drinkable and sweetish *lambic* beers are brewed for the house by De Neve and served with snacks in a cosy "Dutch kitchen" atmosphere. On Grand' Place, La Chaloupe d'Or has a wide selection of beers. Another cafe in the "Dutch kitchen" style, also in the centre of the city, is 't Spinnekopke at Place de Jardin aux Fleurs, with a good range of well-kept beers. Not far away, Place Sainte Catherine has several atmospheric cafes selling *lambic* beers.

Around the edge of the city-centre are several specialist cafes with very large selections. These include Le Miroir, Place Reine Astrid 24, in Jette; Moeder Lambic, at Savoiestraat 68, St Gillis and (for draught beers) at Boendaalse Steenweg 441, near the university; and Le Jugement Dernier, Chaussée de Hacht, Schaarbeek.

In Louvain/Leuven, the town-centre brewpub Domus, in Tiensestraat, has a wide selection of beers. Its own, copper-coloured *Domusbier* is yeasty, fruity, hoppy and dry. There is also a beautifully balanced honey-flavoured beer, called *Dubbel Domus*. Nearby, Gambrinus is a delightful Art Nouveau cafe, and the old market square is lined with student taverns and terraces.

In Payottenland, every village has at least one cafe serving *lambic* beer. In the aptly-named village of Beersel, with its 13th-century castle, the cafe Drie Fonteinen blends its own *quenze-lambic*. In Schepdaal, De Rare Vos has traditional dishes and a huge selection of *lambic* beers.

Artois

A major European brewing company that is the biggest in Belgium. The name derives from a family, not the region of northern France. **Stella Artois★★** is a Pilsener-style beer with a hint of new-mown hay in the nose.

In recent years, Stella has gained in hop character, with a notable Saaz accent. Artois, based in Leuven, also produces a "Danish"-style premium lager called **Loburg★**. Products of its subsidiaries include **Vieux Temps★** and **Ginder★**, both Belgian-style ales, and the **Leffe★★** abbey-style ales. Stella and its erstwhile rival Jupiler now form a joint company called Interbrew.

Belle-Vue

In so far as the phrase "mass-market" can be applied to *lambic* beers, it describes the relatively bland and sweet **Belle-Vue★** products from the sizeable Vandenstock brewery in Brussels. The same company owns the excellent De Neve *lambic* brewery in Payottenland at Schepdaal. In its unfiltered form, **De Neve Lambic★★→★★★** has an almondy, aperitif dryness. Also in Payottenland, the sister Brabrux brewery makes medium-sweet *lambics*.

Boon

A well-respected brewer and blender of *lambic* beers, Frank Boon (pronounced "Bone") has contributed much to the revival of interest in *lambic* styles since he started to blend his own products some years ago at the former De Vit brewery in, appropriately, Lembeek. Boon's *lambic* beers are aromatic, very lively, fruity and dry. He makes a speciality of offering a variety of ages and even of *caves*. His speciality blends are labelled **Mariage Parfait★★★→★★★★**. Other blenders include Moriau and Hanssens.

Cantillon

Tiny, working "museum brewery" producing *lambic* beers in Brussels. Well worth a visit at 56 Rue Gheude, Anderlecht (☎5214928). Its beers are smooth, with a sustained head, dry and with a sharply fruity finish. Its vintage-dated **Lambic Grand Cru★★→★★★** and **Framboise Rosé de Gambrinus★★★★** are classics.

De Troch

Very small *lambic* brewery in Wambeek in Payottenland. Despite its small scale it exports to France where its beer is well-regarded. **De Troch★★★** beers are generally on the dark side, quite full in body, and rather carbonic. There is also a blender called De Troch in Schepdaal.

Eylenbosch

The extreme dryness and woodines formerly found in the Eylenbosch *lambic* beers seems to have retreated since the brewery was rented to new management. The beers are still dry but balanced with hints of sweetness against a smoother background. Distinctiveness has been traded perhaps for a broader acceptability. An Eylenbosch speciality has been the **Festival Supergueuze★★★**, which has more than three years' maturation before being bottled, according to the brewery, which is at Schepdaal, in Payottenland.

Girardin

A good, traditional *lambic* brewery in Payottenland at St Ulrik's Kapelle. Girardin produces big-bodied, fruity and rather bitter beers. Its **Lambic Girardin★★★** is a well-regarded example of the basic style.

Haacht

Beyond its everyday beers (usually on the malty side), this brewery, in Boortmeerbeek, has made some effort to promote a **Gildenbier★★★**. This is an unusual, Belgian style of top-fermenting dark brown beer that is notable for its rich sweetness. It may have limited application – as a restorative, perhaps – but is a part of tradition. This example has a hint of iron in the nose and licorice tones in the finish. The style was originally local to Diest, not far away on the northeast border of Brabant.

Hoegaarden "White"

Hoegaarden is a village in the far east of Brabant that is famous for cloudy "white" wheat beers. There were once 30 breweries in the area producing beers in this style. The last closed in the mid 1950s and a decade later a revivalist brewer re-started production on a small scale. This unlikely venture has proved to be both a critical and commercial success. The brewery is called De Kluis and the beer **Hoegaarden★★★★**. It has a very old-fashioned specification: in percentages, 45 wheat, 5 oats and 50 barley. The wheat and oats are raw, and only the barley is malted. This strange brew is also old-fashioned in that it is spiced, with coriander and curaçao, both of which were more commonly used before the universal adoption of the hop as a seasoning. A top-fermenting yeast is used and there is a further dosage in the bottle, with a priming of sugar. The nature of the grist and the use of a slowly flocculating yeast in the bottle help ensure the characteristic "white" cloudiness. The beer has a conventional gravity of 12 Plato, and emerges with an alcohol content of 3.84 percent by weight; 4.8 by volume. As it ages, it gains a refractive quality known as "double shine", and its fruity sourness gives way to a honeyish sweetness.

A similar beer, aromatic and pale but stronger (18.4 Plato. 7; 8.7) and made exclusively from barley malt, is called **Hoegaarden Grand Cru★★★**. As its name suggests, a beer of nobility and complexity.

Meanwhile, the Hoegaarden brewery's taste for experimentation is unquenchable. Another of its products is called Forbidden Fruit. **Verboden Vrucht**✴✴→✴✴✴ (Le Fruit Defendu) is a claret-coloured, all-malt, strong ale of 19.5 Plato (7.2; 9), which combines a spicing of coriander with a hefty helping of Challenger and Styrian aroma hops. The spicy, sweet fruitiness is very evident in the aroma, and the earthy hoppiness in the palate. A very sexy strong ale, as its label implies. There are several further colourful specialities. In funding its growth, the brewery sought partners, and is now owned by Interbrew. Connoisseurs will be monitoring the quality of its white beer, which is still widely regarded as the best in the market, despite competition from a growing number of imitators. Among them, Brugs Tarwebier and Dantergemse Witte are the most convincing.

Lindemans

This classic Brabant farmhouse brewery in *lambic* country at Vlezenbeek seems an unlikely location from which to attack world markets. Nonetheless, its craftsman-made **Faro**✴✴, **Gueuze**✴✴, **Kriek**✴✴→✴✴✴ and **Framboise**✴✴✴ are variously well-known in The Netherlands, France and the USA. In their whitewashed brewery the Lindemans family have seen *lambic* beer, once written-off as a "farmers' drink", capture the imagination of wine-lovers. In so doing, their products have lost a little of their sharpness and become very much sweeter, but they remain accessible examples of their style.

Mort Subite

The name may mean "Sudden Death", but it derives simply from a dice game played at the famous Mort Subite cafe in Brussels. Despite the Bruxellois joke "from beer to bier", the Mort Subite brews are not especially lethal. On the contrary, they have a conventionally modest alcohol content. They are brewed by the De Keersmaeckers in Payottenland.

The family have been brewers since the 18th century and still have some cellars dating from then, though their 1950s brewhouse is modern by *lambic* standards. Their beers, including a **Faro**✴✴, a **Gueuze**✴✴ and a **Kriek**✴✴, have in the past varied from being sharp to being on the bland side. Recently there have been some rather sweet, "beery" bottlings.

Palm

Typically Belgian ales are produced by this medium-sized family brewery in the hamlet of Steenhuffel, to the northwest of Brussels. In Belgium, a top-fermenting beer of no regional style is often identified simply as a "special" to distinguish it from a Pilsener. Hence **Spéciale Palm**✴✴, now exported to the USA under the more precise name Palm Ale. It has an original gravity of around 11.25 Plato and its yeast is a combination of three strains. Palm Ale has a bright, amber colour; a light-to-medium body; a fruity, bitter-orange aroma and a tart finish. Other products include the dry-hopped, bottle-conditioned **Aerts 1900**✴✴✴, an outstanding example of the style.

Timmermans

Widely available *lambic* beers made at Itterbeek in Payottenland. Timmermans' **Lambic**✴✴→✴✴✴, **Gueuze**✴✴→✴✴✴ and **Kriek**✴✴→✴✴✴ are all fruity and acidic but easily drinkable.

Vanderlinden

Excellent *lambic* beers, produced at Halle in Payottenland. Vanderlinden's **Vieux Foudre Gueuze**★★→★★★ has a full colour, a dense, soft, rocky head and a palate that is smooth and dry, with a "sour apple" tartness. **View Foudre Kriek**★★→★★★ is lively, with lots of aroma, starting with hints of sweetness and finishing with a dry bitterness. The brewery also has a fruity **Framboise**★★→★★★. Its house speciality **Duivel**★★★ is an odd combination of a *lambic* with a conventional top-fermenting beer.

Vandervelden

Arguably the most authentic tasting of the *lambics* from the country breweries are the **Oud Beersel**★★★→★★★★ products of this house. Very dry, with a hint of pine kernels. The brewery is in Beersel.

FRENCH-SPEAKING
BELGIUM

Perhaps it is the softness of the language: summer beers called *saisons*, winter-warmers like Cuvée de l'Ermitage and Chimay Grand Reserve, aperitifs like Abbaye d'Orval. Or maybe the rolling, wooded countryside, occasionally hiding a brewery in its folds. The French-speaking south seems a restful, contemplative place in which to drink. Just as there are fewer people in the south, so the breweries and beer styles are thinner on the ground, but they are rich in character.

When, as sometimes happens, a beer menu in Belgium lists "Wallonian specialities" (in whichever language), it is referring to *saisons* and monastery beers from four provinces. Among these, the province of Hainaut (with interesting industrial archaeology around the cities of Mons and Charleroi) has the most breweries, including the celebrated one at the abbey of Chimay. The province of Namur, named after its pleasant and historically interesting capital city, has the Rochefort monastery brewery. The province of Liège also named after its principal city, has the Jupiler brewery, producing the biggest-selling Pilsener in Belgium. This province also has the German-speaking pocket in which the Eupener Brauerei produces an excellent Pilsener and a stronger, amber Kapuciener Klosterbrau.

Where to drink

Almost every town in Belgium has at least one specialist beer cafe, and there are many in the French-speaking provinces. Good examples include: in Mons, Le Bureau, on Grand Rue, and La Podo, in Marché aux Herbes; between Brussels and Charleroi, at Nivelles, Le Pado; near Namur, at Jambes, Escapade, and – a little further away – Le Relais de la Meuse, at Lustin; between Namur and Liège, at Huy, Tavern Big Ben; in Liège, Le Cirque d'Hiver and Le Pot au Lait; south of Liège, in the direction of the Ardennes, Le Vaudrée, at Angleur.

Bush Beer

This distinctive and extra-strong brew takes its name from that of the family Dubuisson (*buisson* means "bush") by whom it is made, in the village of Pipaix in the province of Hainaut. The family re-named the beer Scaldis, for the American market, to avoid conflict with the US brewers Busch. Scaldis was the Latin name for the river Scheldt. Under either name, **Bush Beer/ Scaldis★★★** might be more accurately described as an ale. It has a copper colour, a gravity of 9.5 Belgian degrees (24 Plato; 1095) and an alcohol content of at least 7.34 percent by weight; 9.4 by volume. Some samplings have shown alcohol contents as high as 11.7 by volume. Produced with a top-fermenting yeast matured for three months and filtered not pasteurized, it emerges with a chewy, malty, perhaps nutty, palate and with a hoppy dryness in the finish.

Chimay Trappist Monastery

The best-known and biggest monastery brewery in Belgium. Its long-serving brewmaster, Father Théodore, is a greatly respected figure in the industry, and Chimay's products have been a model for many others. They are, in the monastic tradition, top-fermenting strong ales, conditioned in the bottle. Within this tradition, the Chimay beers have a house character that is fruity, both in the intense aroma and the palate. Beyond that, each has its own features. Each is distinguished by its own colour of crown cork (*capsule*). The basic beer, **Chimay Red★★★**, has a gravity of 6.2 Belgian degrees, 15.5 Plato, 1063, with 5.5 percent alcohol by weight; 7 by volume. It has a full, copper colour, a notably soft palate and a hint of blackcurrant. The quite different **Chimay White★★★** has a gravity of 7 Belgian; 17.35 Plato (1071) and an alcohol content of 6.3; 8. It has a firm, dry body, slender for its gravity, with plenty of hop character in the finish and a quenching hint of acidity. This noble beer is very highly regarded by the brewery, but it does not have the most typically Chimay character. A return to type is represented by the **Chimay Blue★★★★**, which has a gravity of 8; 19.62 (1081) and an alcohol content of 7.1; 9. This has, again, that characteristically Chimay depth of aromatic fruitiness – a Zinfandel, or even a port, among beers. Chimay Blue is vintage-dated on the crown cork. If it is kept in a dark, cool place (ideally 19°C/65°F, but definitely not refrigerated), it will become markedly smoother after a year and sometimes continues to improve for two or three, drying slightly as it progresses. After five years, it could lose a little character, but some samples have flourished for a quarter of a century. A version of Chimay Blue in a corked 75 cl bottle is called **Grande Reserve**. The larger bottle size and different method of sealing seem to mature the beer in a softer manner. With different surface areas and air space, a slightly larger yeast presence and the very slight porosity of cork this is not fanciful.

The full name of the abbey is Notre Dame de Scourmont, after the hill on which it stands near the hamlet of Forges, close to the small town of Chimay in the province of Hainaut. The monastery was founded in 1850, during the post-Napoleonic restoration of abbey life. The monks began to brew not long afterward, in 1861–62. They were the first monks in Belgium to sell their brew commercially, introduced the designation "Trappist Beer" and in the period after World War II perfected the style. The monastery was damaged in the war and has been extensively restored, but in traditional style. It has a classic copper brewhouse and very modern fermentation halls.

The monastery also makes a cheese, called Chimay, of the Port Salut type. A restaurant not far from the monastery sells both beer and cheese.

Cuvée de l'Ermitage

Hermitages were the first homes of monks in the western world and there were many in the forests of Hainaut in the early Middle Ages, but no one is certain which of two sites gave their name to this brew. It is certainly worthy of being enjoyed in a reflective moment, though not necessarily to the ascetic taste. **Cuvée de l'Ermitage***** is a very dark and strong all-malt brew of 18.7 Plato, with an alcohol content of 6 percent by weight; 7.5 by volume. It is produced from three malts and heavily hopped with an interesting combination of Kent Goldings and Hallertaus (both for bitterness) and Northern Brewer and Saaz (both for aroma). It has a distinctively creamy bouquet, a smooth start, with hints of sweetness, then a surprising dryness in the finish – almost the sappiness of an Armagnac. Cuvee is the local speciality of the old Union brewery at Jumet, on the edge of Charleroi. The brewery produces a range of top-fermenting beers of its parent, Maes.

Jupiler

The biggest-selling Pilsener beer in Belgium takes its name from Jupille, near Liège, where it is produced by a brewery that for many years rejoiced in the odd name Piedboeuf. In recent years, the company itself has become known as Jupiler. Although it has lost some of its hoppiness, **Jupiler*** remains dry and soft and is a pleasant enough mass-market beer.

Orval Trappist Monastery

There is a purity of conception about both the brewery and the monastery of Orval. The brewery provides its own distinctive interpretation of the monastic style and offers just one beer: **Orval*****. This brew gains its unusual orangey colour from the use of three malts produced to its own specification, plus white candy sugar in the kettle; its aromatic, aperitif bitterness derives from the use of Hallertau and (more especially) Kent Goldings, not only in the kettle but also in dry-hopping; its characterful acidity comes from its own single-cell yeast in its primary and secondary fermentations and a blend of four or five bottom cultures in a slow bottle-conditioning. As to which of these procedures is most important in imparting the *gout d'Orval*, there may be some debate. The triple fermentation process is certainly important, but the dry-hopping is perhaps the critical factor. The beer has an original gravity of 13.5–14 Plato (1055 +) and emerges with an alcohol content of more than 4.5 percent by weight, around 6 by volume. Its secondary fermentation lasts for five to seven weeks, at a relatively warm temperature of around 15°C (60°F). Its bottle-conditioning, regarded by the brewery as a third fermentation, lasts for two months, again at warm temperatures. The beer should be kept in a dark place, ideally at a natural cellar temperature. If it was bought in a shop, give the beer a few days to recover its equilibrium and pour gently. It should improve for about a year and, although its character may then diminish, it could keep for five years.

This is a short period in the life of an abbey that was founded in 1070 by Benedictines from Calabria, rebuilt in the 12th century by early Cistercians from Champagne and sacked in several conflicts along the way, in the 17th century leaving most of the ruins that stand today. From the 18th century, there are records of brewing having taken place in the restored abbey, which was then sacked in the French Revolution. The present monastery, with its dramatic, dream-like purity of line, subsumes Romanesque-Burgundian influences in a design of the late 1920s and 1930s. The monastery makes its beer, crusty brown bread and two cheeses, of the Port Salut and (in a somewhat distance interpretation) Cheddar types, and sells them to tourists in its gift shop.

Meanwhile, in its corner of the province of Luxembourg, not far from the small town of Florenville, the "valley of gold" dreams. Legend says that Countess Mathilda of Tuscany lost a gold ring in the lake in the valley. When a fish recovered the ring for her, Mathilda was so grateful that she gave the land to God for the foundation of the monastery. The fish with the golden ring is now the emblem of Orval and its beer.

No other beer can be said to match the character of Orval but there are secular products in a broadly similar style. An example from this part of Belgium is the beer of the micro-brewery at Montignies sur Roc. From Flanders, there is Augustijn, produced by the Van Steenbergen brewery.

Rochefort Trappist Monastery

A low profile is perhaps appropriate to a Trappist monastery and it cannot be said that Rochefort, in the province of Namur, has any clear image. The first impression created by its beers is that they are classic examples of the Trappist style and certainly very well made. If they have a house characteristic, it is a subtle chocolate tone. **Rochefort★★★** has beers at 6, 8 and 10 Belgian degrees.

Saison Dupont

With its big bouquet, dry, peppery fruitiness and great complexity, **Saison Dupont★★★★** is the classic of this style. Beers in the *saison* style usually have a big, rocky head; good lacework; a full, amber colour; a firm but somtimes quite thin body and a delicate balance between sour acidity and sweet fruitiness; with a soft, clean finish. They are usually bottle-conditioned and often dry-hopped.

Other examples include *saisons* Pipaix, Roland and Voisin. These artisanal *saisons* come in corked wine bottles and are something of a speciality in the western part of Hainaut.

There are beers that are not described as *saisons* but are similar in style. These include the Allard and Groetembril range from Hainaut and La Chouffe from a new micro-brewery in the province of Liège.

Saison Régal

This is the most widely available *saison* beer, from the Du Bocq brewery of Purnode in the province of Namur and Marbaix in Hainault. **Saison Régal★★** is neither the strongest nor the most efflorescent example of the style, but it is a useful introduction. It has a gravity of around 13 Plato (1052) and around 4.5 percent alcohol by weight; 5.6 by volume. It is produced with a mash of more than 90 percent malt, pale and crystal, has a Kent Goldings accent in the hopping (with also Hallertau and Saaz) and spends a month stabilizing in closed tanks. The beer has a full, amber colour, a surprisingly light but firm body, and a teasing balance between aromatic hoppiness and fruitiness. The brewery also produces a characterful strong ale, **Gauloise★★ → ★★★**. (This has nothing to do with the well-known brand of cigarette.) The beer celebrates those most brave of Gauls, the early Belgians. Gauloise is available 6 and 8 degrees Belgian gravity, producing slightly higher figures for alcohol by volume. Du Bocq produces a great many other products, in some instances marketing the same beer under more than one name. It is a colourful old brewery, but this practice of "label-brewing" does not win friends in Belgium.

Saison Silly

"Saison" is emphasized in English-speaking markets to prevent this name from sounding too silly. In fact, Silly is the name of the village in Hainaut where the beer is made. In Belgium, **Saison Silly**★★ → ★★★ has a gravity 13.75 Plato, a firm body, a hint of intentional, quenching sourness in the palate and a sweeter, soft finish. The *saison* sold in the US is **Speciale Enghien**★★★, which has a higher gravity, at around 20 Plato, with a softer, rounder palate, quenchingly acidic but notably clean in its long finish. A companion of 15 Plato is called **Doublette Enghien**★★ → ★★★.

THE GRAND DUCHY OF LUXEMBOURG

Although it shares its name with a province of Belgium, and has economic ties with that country, the Grand Duchy of Luxembourg is a sovereign state. In the matter of beer, the Grand Duchy leans in the opposite direction, towards Germany. It even claims that its Purity Law is similar to that of Germany, though it does, in fact, permit adjuncts. The typical product range of a Luxembourgeoise brewery includes a relatively mild Pilsener; a slightly more potent brew, perhaps in the Export style; and a bottom-fermenting strong beer, sometimes seasonal.

Luxembourg has five brewing companies, each with just one plant. The biggest, just, is Diekirch, which has a fairly big-bodied, clean-tasting, all-malt **Pils**★★, with a good hop aroma. There have also been occasional sightings of a stronger (4.9 by weight; 6.1 by volume) pale, bottom-fermenting beer called **Premium**★★ from Diekirch.

The second largest brewery (Artois, of Belgium, has a small stake) is Mousel et Clausen, with the Royal-Altmünster brand. Then Brasserie Nationale, of Bascharage, with the Bofferding and Funck-Bricher labels. The small Simon brewerly, of Wiltz, produces some excellent beers. So does the tiniest of them all, Battin, of Esch, with its Gambrinus label.

FRANCE

As well as making the world's most complex wines, France has a beer tradition stretching from the beginnings of brewing. Most evident in the north: the Flemish corner specializes in top-fermented beers; Alsace and Lorraine in bottom-fermented brews. A newer development is the spread of tiny, British-style ale breweries like Les Brasseurs, in Lille (opposite the main metro station) and La Micro Brassene (Rue de Richeheu 106, Paris) and the odd micro, like bobtail (at St-Séverin, in the Périgord).

Just south of Valenciennes, Duyck produces **Jen-lain★★★→★★★★**, a classic *Bière de Garde*, with a deep, amber colour, fruity nose and hints of licorice, in its long finish. In the tradition of this style, it is a top-fermenting brew, all-malt, 16 Plato (1064; 5.2; 6.5), not pasteurized, although, it is filtered (ideally, it should not be – the original idea of a *Bière de Garde* was that it could be laid down).

The area between Valenciennes, Lille and Boulogne is the heartland of this style. A good example is the bottle-conditioned **La Choulette★★★**, counter-pointing a citric fruitiness with a hoppy dryness. The same beer is the basis for a *Framboise*. Another excellent *Bière de Garde* is **Trois Monts★★★**, from a brewery that also makes a malty **Bière de Mars**.**★★★** Seasonal "March beers" are a new fashion. So are wheat beers, like the herbal **L'Angelus★★★**. Outside France, the easiest *Bière de Garde* to find are the relatively hoppy **St Léonard★★→★★★** and the malty **Lutèce★★★**.

The Lille area also has the world's strongest pale (truly golden) lager, **La Bière de Démon★★★** (21.7; 9.6; 12). For its weight, this beer is surprisingly dry, but with honeyish tones. It is brewed by Enfants de Gayant, who also own the Boxer brewery in Switzerland, George Killian's **"Irish Red"★★→★★★** is brewed by Pelforth of Lille (16.8; 1067; 5.3; 6.6) in a malty, full-bodied interpretation that also characterizes the brewery's darker **Brune★★**. Both are top-fermenting. Pelforth and Union de Brasseries (whose brands include **"33"** and **Mützig**) are part-owned by Heineken.

A yet more unusual speciality, **Adelscott★★★** (16.2; 1065; 5.2; 6.5) is produced with whisky malt, which in this case imparts a very light smokiness. It is brewed by Fischer/Pêcheur, a major independent based in Alsace. Fischer also makes a ginseng-flavoured lager called *La Bière Amoureuse*. Meteor and Schutzenberger are smaller independents in Alsace, and Amos in Lorraine. Kronenburg, also in Alsace, is France's biggest brewery.

THE BRITISH ISLES

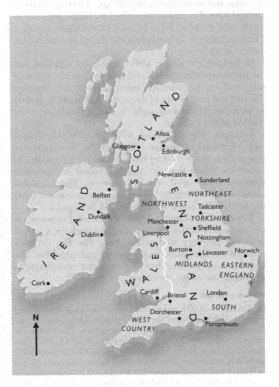

England, Wales and Scotland are the only nations in which the principal brewing tradition is to produce ales. Ireland is the only nation in which the principal tradition is to produce stouts.

These island nations were at the peak of imperial arrogance when the rest of the world started to abandon such top-fermenting brews in favour of bottom-fermenting lagers, in the mid and late 19th century. Imperial power may be a mixed blessing, but there is something to be said for national pride.

Even to the British, their ales present a taste which has first to be acquired. The writer Graham Greene, whose own family have a renowned brewery, recalls in his book *A Sort of Life* that he "hated" his first pint but that when he tried a second, he "enjoyed the taste with a pleasure that has never failed me since". The delights afforded by the classic draught ales of Britain might be compared to the pleasures offered by the red wines of

Bordeaux. Both have subtlety of colour; a fresh fruitiness; dashes of sweetness and counter-strokes of dryness; and sometimes a hint of oak. The dry stouts of Ireland have the qualities ascribed by Hugh Johnson in his *World Atlas of Wine* to true Amontillado sherries: "Dry and almost stringingly powerful of flavour, with a dark, fat, rich tang".

In Britain, the seeker after "real" ales will look out for the designation "cask-conditioned" at the point of sale, and for hand-pulled pumps, the most common (though not only) form of dispense. A British ale served as cask-conditioned draught is like a Bordeaux wine bottled at the château.

Britain's "Big Six" (Bass, Allied, Whitbread, Grandmet (Watney), Courage, Scottish & Newcastle, in descending order of size) have between them about 30 breweries. More than 50 old-established independent companies have well over 60 breweries. There are also about 70 newer micro-breweries, all established since the late 1970s, and a further 60-odd brewpubs.

The number of micro-breweries varies, but some are by now a part of the mainstream, and perhaps a couple of dozen are very well established. The Big Six own some of the brewpubs, but most are independent. The Big Six may become five if Grandmet completes its intended sale of its breweries.

Where to drink

Of Britain's 70,000 pubs, half serve the cask-conditioned product. Among those, the 5,000 chosen each year for the *Good Beer Guide* are the ale-lovers' favourites. This invaluable guide is published by the Campaign for Real Ale (34 Alma Road, St Albans, Herts AL1 3BW ☎0727-67201), and available from WH Smith and other bookstore chains. Not every visitor to Britain has time to visit all 5,000 although it is praiseworthy to try. The *Good Beer Guide* also indicates which pubs offers accommodation. Most visitors land in London, where there are some good "real ale" pubs, but where out-of-town brews can be expensive and badly kept (to be fair, most don't travel well).

A much more satisfying experience will be obtained if the drinker does the travelling, whether for a long weekend or for a browse of two or three weeks around the British Isles. Below, the ale territories are viewed anti-clockwise from London. Since Britain has not only a great many pubs but also a huge range of ales, only those of special interest or reputation (and not all of those) can be detailed, and scores are accordingly high. The ★ and ★→★★ ales generally did not make the list.

LONDON AND THE SOUTH

Perhaps because the classic hop-growing county of Kent is in the southeast, many of the ales brewed in this part of the country are bitter and aromatic. London has two classic independent breweries, Young's and Fuller's, and both produce splendidly hoppy beers. In Central London, Young's

is well served at the Lamb (94 Lamb's Conduit St, Blooms-
bury); Fuller's at the Star Tavern (6 Belgrave Mews West,
Belgravia). The breweries are both on the west side of town, in
Wandsworth and Chiswick respectively, whence their pubs
generally fan outward toward pretty London "villages" like
Richmond. Lamb's Conduit St also has the Sun, famous for its
wide range of out-of-town ales. The Beer Shop (8 Pitfield St,
near Old St Underground station) has a wide selection of
bottled products, and has its own, excellent, contract-brewed
London Porter★★★ and an award-winning old ale called **Dark
Star★★★**. London has many brewpubs. None stands out for its
beers, but the Firkin chain is famous for having popularized
the idea. A good example is the Frog and Firkin (41 Tavistock
Crescent, near Portobello Road market). The Orange (37
Pimlico Rd) is recommended for its **Porter★★** and the farther-
flung Greyhound (151 Greyhound Lane, Streatham Common)
for its **Pedigree Mild★★**.

Where to drink: long weekends

West to Oxford. Along the Thames Valley, where every
brewery offers good, country ales. Go via Henley (Brakspear's
ales at many pubs; try the Three Tuns, 5 Market Place);
Abingdon (for Morland's hoppy ales at the riverside Old
Anchor); to Oxford (Morrell's fruity **Varsity**, and an interest-
ing Sweet Stout, at lots of pubs; try the Old Tom, 101 St
Aldates). Venture farther north to Banbury for Hook
Norton's dry, hoppy ales, or return via the B474 to visit the
Royal Standard of England (for Marston's Owd Roger at Forty
Green, near Beaconsfield). South to Brighton. Via Horsham
(King and Barnes; the Stout House) or Lewes (lovely, buttery-
malty brews, including a mild, a sweet stout and barley wine,
from Harvey's/Beard's; try the Brewer's Arms). Near Brighton, at Hove, Firkin founder David Bruce has the new
Belcher's brewpub (100 Goldstone Villas). East to Canterbury. Via East Kent hop country. Stop in Faversham for a pint
of the local Shepherd Neame (the Anchor, Abbey St). Ale from
the Goacher micro-brewery can be sampled at the George,
Shalmsford St, a hamlet near Chartham, just W of Canterbury.
Return via Tunbridge Wells, to sample Larkin's ales, micro-
brewed by hop-farmers (Sussex Arms, Neville St).

Brakspear

Among a remarkably good crop of breweries in the Thames
Valley, Brakspear, at Henley, is outstanding. Its "ordinary"
Bitter★★★★ (1035), hoppy from its nose to its lingering finish, is
the classic example of this English style.

Fuller

Persistent award-winner. Beautifully balanced ales, with fresh
hoppiness being countered by honeyish fruitiness as gravities
ascend. Delightfully flowery **Chiswick Bitter★★★** (1035+);
complex "special", **London Pride★★→★★★** (1041+); muscu-
lar, stylish **Extra Special Bitter★★★★** (1055+). The bottled
Golden Pride★★★ (1084–92) has the colour, smoothness and
warming finish of a cognac.

Gales

The corked and bottle-conditioned **Prize Old Ale★★★→★★★★**
(1092–98) has such a dry fruitiness, and alcoholic warmth, as to
be reminiscent of a Calvados. This dry fruitiness characterizes

the range, which also includes two characterful bitters and pale and dark milds. The brewery is about 96km (60 miles) from London, on the edge of Portsmouth.

King and Barnes

Nutty, dexterously balanced ales, notable for their very long finish, from a country brewery (in Horsham, Sussex) that has very modern equipment. **Sussex Bitter★★→★★★** (1032–36) and the heftier **Festive★★→★★★** (1050) are good examples. They also have a good example of a Southern-style **Brown Ale★★★**.

Shepherd Neame

The Queen Court vineyard, growing a prize-winning Müller-Thurgau, is owned by this brewery. Since the location of both, the country town of Faversham, is in the "Grande Champagne" of the English hop, it seems a shame that Shep's no longer grow their own East Kent Goldings. After a period of flirtation with other hops, the brewery is, however, now re-emphasizing this wonderfully aromatic local variety. The hop bitterness comes through most strongly in the "ordinary" **Masterbrew Bitter★★★** (1036). **Shepherd Neame Stock Ale★★★** (1037) is dark and dry, with a lot of character for its gravity. **Masterbrew Best** (1044) is dry, "best" bitter with a nice balance of hop and malt.

Watney

Once-famous brewery, subsumed into the drinks and fast-food conglomerate of Grandmet. Future uncertain.

Whitbread

National bottled products include the definitive sweet or "milk" stout (both brewed and primed with lactose), **Mackeson★★★** (1038–42 in Britain; higher in the Americas). Surprisingly, this brew is not filtered, just fined. The brewing world's answer to Bailey's Irish Cream perhaps? Whitbread also has **Gold Label★★★** (1098; 8 percent alcohol by weight; 10 by volume), a classic pale barley wine, which spends three hours in the brew-kettle, has its own yeast and in the bottled (but not canned) form is unpasteurized. Strong and warming, but mellow. Whitbread has angered ale-lovers by closing breweries like Fremlin's and Higgon's, and taking over Boddington's.

Young

Fiercely independent London brewery serving real ale in all of its pubs. Its "ordinary" **Bitter★★→★★★** (1036), soft and complex, is still a classic, despite being less assertively dry than it once was. Its **Special★★★→★★★★** (1046) is beautifully balanced, with a malty finish. Its bottled **Ramrod★★** (1046) has a smooth bitterness and an interesting balance of maltiness and strength. **Young's Export Special London Ale★★★→★★★★**, (1062–3) has, when it is fresh, a massive bouquet of floral East Kent Goldings. **Old Nick★★★→★★★★** (1084) is a classic dark barley wine, warming, with some liqueurish fruitiness (a hint of banana?) in the finish.

EASTERN ENGLAND

From London, a round-trip east for two or three days will reveal some intensely traditional ales and interestingly rural (of often flat) countryside. The first stop would be one of the villages near Chelmsford, where Ridley's brewery sells its very hoppy, dry beers, often from wooden casks.

Beyond Ipswich, the road heads for the pretty little harbour town of Southwold, the home of Adnams brewery.

Further north in Norwich, the Rosary Tavern, in Rosary Road, is renowned for its selection. From Norwich, the road runs through The Fens to Wisbech, where Elgood's fruity **Bitter**★→★★ is brewed. Cambridge has a brewpub, the Ancient Druids, in Napier St. There is a good selection at the Cambridge Blue (85 Gwyair St, off Mill Rd).

The return journey presents a tough problem: to the east lies Bury St Edmunds, with the classic Greene King brewery; to the west is Bedford, home of Charles Wells. Whichever the way home, pass through Hertford, home of McMullen's, noted for its **Original A.K.**★★★. This classic example of a pale mild has a lovely balance of malt; fruit and restrained hop. At 1031–35, it shows just how much flavour a low gravity beer can have.

Adnams

Noted wine merchants as well as brewers. It seemed like a Scotch whisky allusion, too, when British beer-writer Roger Protz observed that he found a salty, tangy, "seaweedy" character in Adnams' tawny ales. Some say this trait has vanished, but there is still an elusive house character. The **Mild**★★ (1034), **Bitter**★★→★★★ (1036) and **Extra**★★★ (1044) are all distinctive and very complex. Adnams also has some outstanding bottled beers, most notably **Broadside**★★★ (1064–72), a complex and smooth strong pale ale. The barley wine **Tally-Ho**★★★ (1075) is available on draught at Christmas.

Greene King

Graham Greene, as a celebration of his 80th birthday, mashed a special "edition" of the family brewery's **St Edmund Ale**★★★ (1056–62). This pale strong ale has a surprising crispness in its malty palate. More remarkable from a technical viewpoint is **Strong Suffolk**★★★→★★★★ (1058), the last surviving link between traditional British methods of making barley wines and the wood-aging techniques used in the production of Flemish ales like Rodenbach. Like that celebrated Flemish ale, this English speciality is a blend in which a proportion is aged for between one and two years in unlined oak tuns, with a view to providing an intentionally vinous note. In the English product, this vinous note is against a fruity, rich, smooth background. Greene King's ales are in general on the fruity side – notably so in the much-loved strong Bitter **Abbot Ale**★★★ (1046–52).

Ruddles

Still the famously alliterative Ruddles of Rutland, although the county was subsumed into Leicestershire and the brewery into the Watney/Grandmet group. **Best Bitter**★★→★★★ (1037) has lots of Fuggles character, while the **County**★★★ (1050) speaks more of Goldings. Two excellent ales.

YORKSHIRE AND THE NORTHEAST

Instead of being happy to be England's biggest county, Yorkshire has always felt itself to be a nation in its own right, steadfastly preserving its customs. Even today, its brewing tradition of using double-deck fermentation vessels leaves it with a family of yeasts that are as headstrong as a Yorkshireman. Perhaps that is why the character of its creamy, nutty ales has been better sustained than that of the brews from the counties further north, clustered around the city of Newcastle.

An ale tour might follow the Pennine hills and dales, whose villages are always within easy reach of the big industrial cities. In South Yorkshire, the city of Sheffield has a brewpub, the Frog and Parrot (Division St, ☎0742-21280), which has in recent years brewed a winter (October and November) dark ale, aiming for a world-record gravity of 1125 and a commensurate alcohol content. **Roger and Out★★★→★★★★** is immensely potent yet soft and smooth. Sheffield has two breweries owned by Bass, one producing the tasty **Stone's Best Bitter★→★★**. It also has a Whitbread brewery, producing **Trophy Bitter★**. Yet a third sizable brewery, owned by Vaux, produces the under-rated Ward's ales. In the nose, they seem drily malty, but there is a dense interplay of hop and yeast in a full flavour and texture that is typically Yorkshire.

In West Yorkshire, Wakefield has a boutique called Clark's, with an adjoining pub, the Henry Boon, in Westgate, selling its flowery **Bitter★★** (1038). Huddersfield has some colourful ales at the brewpub Sair (Lane Top, Linthwaite). Halifax has a Watney subsidiary, Webster, making dry ales with a pleasantly oily texture. Keighley, near Bradford, has a classic brewery, Timothy Taylor's. Leeds has another classic, Tetley's. In East Yorkshire, at Snaith, the award-winning Old Mill microbrewery has a herby **Traditional Bitter★★→★★★** (1037) and the appropriately hoppy **Bullion Bitter★★→★★★** (1044). Hull brewery has an excellent dark **Mild★★→★★★**.

In North Yorkshire, the village of Tadcaster became for reasons of its water an important centre. It has the classic Sam Smith's; former family rival (now part of the Courage group) John Smith's, producing a pleasantly drinkable **Bitter★→★★** with some Yorkshire character; and a Bass brewery with several local ales. North Yorkshire has, not far from Ripon, in the village of Masham, the classic Theakston brewery, owned by Scottish & Newcastle. Beyond the Yorkshire border, there are lovely, nutty ales from Cameron's in Hartlepool. Nearby, a Whitbread brewery produces sweetish ales at Castle Eden.

Vaux has its principal brewery at Sunderland. Its **Samson★→★★** is a fruity "best" Bitter. Its range also includes Britain's first **Weizenbier★★★**, lightly tart and quenching, **Double Maxim★★→★★★**, a brown ale in the higher-gravity style (around 1045) regional to the Northeast; not so much brown as amber red, with a full, crystal-malt character, its sweetness steadied with an underlying dryness. Its neighbour and more famous rival **Newcastle Brown Ale★★→★★★** (1045) has a winey note. Another example of this style, **High Level Brown Ale★★** is among the well-liked, slightly buttery, brews from products by Federation, a brewery owned by working men's clubs. This brewery is just across the river Tyne from Newcastle. The city also has two micros: Big Lamp, making very hoppy ales; and Hadrian, whose products are fresh-tasting and beautifully balanced.

Samuel Smith

Classic exponent of the Yorkshire brewing system, fermenting in "stone" (actually, slate), double-deck vessels, which make for a circulation of the yeast. The character developed by the yeast in this system produces brews with a very full texture. "Sam's" products also have their own roundness. They are often thought to be malty, but they also have a great deal of interwoven hop character. While British drinkers seek them out as cask-conditioned draught (always from the wood), export markets have to make do with bottled products. Britain's **Museum Ale**★★★ (1048) has become chic in the US as Samuel Smith's Pale Ale.

So, at the same gravity, have Britain's **Strong Brown**★★★, known in the US as Nut Brown (it is, indeed, nutty-tasting) and the delightfully named **Nourishing Strong Stout**★★★ (again, 1048), confusingly offered to Americans as Porter (it is arguably dry enough, but surely too full-bodied for that designation?). If the British have a serious complaint it is that they cannot buy the silky **Oatmeal Stout**★★★★ (1048) or a new **Imperial Stout**★★★ → ★★★★ (1072), immensely rich, with a flavour of slightly burnt currants on a cake.

Tetley

Classically creamy Yorkshire ale, **Tetley Bitter**★★★ (1035.5), comes from this independently minded outpost of Allied Breweries. **Tetley Mild**★★★ has a distinctively rummy note.

Theakston

Never mind the spelling, **Old Peculier**★★★ (1058–60) is a strong dark ale with a sweet richness that is positively embracing in the cask-conditioned draught. In bottled form, it is as satisfying as a chaste kiss. If it is chilled, so is the kiss. **Theakston Best Bitter**★★ has a light, yeasty dryness.

Timothy Taylor

A splendidly Yorkshire-sounding brewery, in the land of the Brontës. A quirky but wide, and excellent, range includes a hoppy, heathery "best", **Landlord**★★★ (1042) and the beautifully balanced, dark **Ram Tam**★★ (1043).

SCOTLAND

A cold country that specializes in rich, warming ales. Scotland, and especially Edinburgh, were once known throughout the world of brewing for their strong ales. The quality and diversity of these products was pummelled by brewery takeovers in the 1960s, and the dust has yet to settle, despite the arrival of one or two boutiques.

Among the British giants, Bass has two Scottish breweries, mainly concerned with the better-than-average Tennent's lagers. They also have one or two cask ales, and a famously tasty, malty dark strong brew called **Fowler's Wee Heavy**★★★ (1067–73), produced under contract by Belhaven. Allied produces Skol in the brewing town of Alloa, and has a cask ale called **Archibald Arrol's 70/-**★★★ (1037), with a typically Scottish maltiness in the entrance and surprising hoppiness in the finish. The **80/-**★★ is less equivocal.

Micros have come and often, regrettably, gone. Harvies-toun, at Dollar near Stirling, makes fullish, fruity ales. The West Highland brewpub's wonderfully named **Severe Strong Ale** (not tasted) in the working railway station at Taynuilt, near Oban. The celebrated **Borve House Extra Strong**★★★ (1085)

is now made at Ruthven, Aberdeenshire. The Orkney Brewery has among its products a cidery, sherryish, beer made from the grain bere, a precursor to barley.

Belhaven

With monastic beginnings and a site in the harbour village of Dunbar (between Edinburgh and the border), Belhaven has always had romance. It has also had classic Scottish ales of unrivalled complexity. The brewery has done its best to maintain consistent quality during constant changes of control. In Scotland, its brews have held up well. In England, they are often badly served. Belhaven's **70/- Heavy★★→★★★** (1035–6) has been known over the years for its remarkable balance and depth of character; the **80/- Export★★★** as a classic draught "Scotch Ale".

Broughton

A member of the Younger brewing family founded this micro, producing very well-made Scottish ales at Broughton, near Biggar (between Glasgow and the border). The principal product is **Greenmantle Ale★★** (1038), with an interesting balance of malt and hop. **Broughton Special★★** (1038) is a dry-hopped version. **Merlin's Ale★★** (1044) is golden and dry. **Old Jock★★→★★★** (1070) is dark, malty and very tasty.

Caledonian

With its open kettles, fired by direct flame, and even the odd copper fermenter, Caledonian holds the deepest traditions of Edinburgh as a brewing centre. Its much-appreciated range of tasty ales have gained in malty freshness, hop aroma, and complexity since the brewery's return to independence. **Merman★★★→★★★★** is an outstanding dark ale. The brewery's speciality, the strong **Caledonian Ale★★★→★★★★** (1077–1080), marketed in the US as *MacAndrew's*, has an unusually pale colour for the style and a wonderfully clean maltiness, dried by the alcoholic power of the finish. A Lowland Single Malt of the beer world.

Maclay

The lesser known of Scotland's two old independents, probably because its ales can be hard to find outside its home town of Alloa. Rarity value aside, there is a school of drinkers that favours Maclay's as the best ales in Scotland. Some are, perhaps, on the hoppy side, but the **60/-Light★★★→★★★★** (1030) is an undisputed Scottish classic.

McEwan/Younger

In Scotland, the ale known as **80/-** or **IPA★★** (1042) is enjoyed for its fullness of flavour. In England, the richer and darker **Younger's No 3★★** (1043) has a small cult following. In Belgium and the US, another dark brew, **McEwan's Scotch Ale★★★** (1088), packs a more obvious punch.

Traquair

A manor house (perhaps even a castle?) in which Bonnie Prince Charlie once took refuge. Like any other large residence, it had its own brewery, enterprisingly put back into operation by the Laird in 1965. The castle can be visited (☎0896-830323). At its best, **Traquair House Ale★★★★** (1073–1080) is the classic example of a dark Scottish ale, rich and full but with its sweetness balanced by earthy, oaky dryness. Uniquely among British breweries, Traquair ferments all of its ales in uncoated wooden vessels. The Laird died in 1990, and it is to be hoped that both the beer and its unique character survive.

THE NORTHWEST

South of the Scottish border, the Lake District, Cumbria and Lancashire are dotted with breweries all the way to Manchester, which has a cluster of its own. Manchester and the nearby towns produce some excellent mild ales (although this is not always realized elsewhere in Britain). They also tend toward very dry, fruity bitters. The wonderfully eccentric West Coast Brewery, at the King's Arms (Helmshaw Walk, Chorlton-on-Medlock, Manchester) is well worth a visit.

Between Manchester and Liverpool, the town of Warrington is an important brewing centre. The number of breweries in the region as a whole makes for a lively variety, though that has been eroded by takeovers in recent years. Matthew Brown, which produces pleasant but unexceptional ales in Blackburn, is now owned by Scottish & Newcastle. Allied's Tetley subsidiary has a brewery in Warrington which also brews under the name Walker. Also in Warrington, Greenhall Whitley (making unexceptional ales) additionally owns Shipstone (in the East Midlands). A third Warrington brewery, the independent Burtonwood, produces creamy, pleasant ales.

Boddington
Known for an unusually pale **Bitter★★** (1035) that remains dry but is no longer as hoppy as it was in its vintage years. Now owned by Whitbread.

Holt
Unpretentious to the point of reticence, but famously popular among beer-lovers in Manchester for its quiet devotion to cask-conditioned ales. A notably low-tech brewery whose products have distinctive notes of black malt, high hop-rates, and the dry fruitiness of the house, hybrid yeast. The **Mild★★★** (1033) is roasty and dry. The **Bitter★★★** (1039) is wonderfully intense.

Hyde
Country-style brewery in the urban heart of Manchester. So low in profile as to be easily overlooked, but should not be. Its dark **Mild★→★★** (1032) has some caramel notes; the pale **Best Mild★★** (1034) has a clean maltiness, with some hop notes; the **Bitter★★→★★★** (1036-7) has a seductively creamy texture, a clean fruitiness and a long, hoppy finish.

Jennings
Rural independent in isolation in Cockermouth, Cumbria. Noted for its hoppy, fresh-fruity **Bitter★★→★★★** (1034-5).

Lees
Clean, dry ales from a well-respected brewery among the cotton towns on the edge of Manchester. Especially noteworthy is its vintage-dated **Harvest Ale★★★→★★★★** (1100; 10.5 percent alcohol by volume), made each year from the new season's malt (Maris Otter, Yorkshire) and hops (Goldings, East Kent). This pale strong ale has a warm, fruity aroma; a smooth, malty palate; and a lot of hop in the finish.

Robinson

Sizable independent in Greater Manchester. Products include a bronze-coloured **Best Mild**★★→★★★ (1032) that is a very good example of the style; a pale, dryish **Bitter**★★ (1035); and the strong, dark fruity **Old Tom**★★★ (1074–82), with lots of warming alcohol in the finish. Robinson also owns Hartley, of Ulverston, Cumbria. Hartley is known for a beautifully balanced "best" Bitter, **XB**★★→★★★ (1040).

Thwaite

Especially noted for its intense, complex, dark **Best Mild**★★★ (1034), among a range of nutty-tasting ales. Thwaite's is in the old brewing town of Blackburn.

BURTON
AND THE MIDLANDS

The most famous brewing centre in Britain is Burton, a small and rather scruffy town between the West Midlands city of Birmingham and the East Midlands cities of Derby and Nottingham. Burton originally became a brewing centre because of the qualities of its water, and its renown grew when its brewers were the most active in the popularization of pale ales.

The town's original fermentation system, using linked wooden barrels called Unions, no doubt shaped the local brewing yeasts and made its own contribution to the Burton palate. Burton's ales can have a faintly sulphury, sweet-and-tart fruitiness that is compellingly moreish to the devotee.

Burton has no fewer than five breweries. Two are of considerable historical importance, and both are large, working breweries. They are the original Bass brewery (with an award-winning museum ☎0283-45301) and Allied's Ind Coope Burton brewery (which produces ten cask-conditioned ales). The last brewery to use the Burton Union system is Marston, which produces some of Britain's classic ales. Everard's principal production has moved to Leicester, and its Burton brewery has become the Heritage Museum (☎0283-69226).

A fifth brewery is new: the micro Burton Bridge, which produces ales very much in the town's tradition. **Bridge Bitter**★★→★★★ (1042) has a big, plummy aroma and a fruitiness that carries right through to its soft finish. **Burton Porter**★★★ (1045) is dry and coffeeish.

Away from Burton, palates and styles change. In the West Midlands, both dark and pale milds are traditional, and there is often little to distinguish the latter from the region's characteristically sweet "bitters". The area also has no fewer than three out of the four original brewpubs in Britain (that is to say, the old ones that had continued to operate before the new wave).

Not far from the Welsh border, in the Shropshire village of Bishop's Castle, is the Three Tuns (☎0588-638797), a pub with its own traditional tower brewery. Also in Shropshire, near the town of Telford, at Madeley, is Mrs Lewis's All Nations (☎0952-585747). Yet more urban is Ma Pardoe's Old Swan (☎0384-53075), at Netherton, near Dudley. This brewpub, nothing short of an institution, has had several changes of ownership.

An eight-pub brewery may be small, but it has to be regarded as a free-standing independent. In nearby Brierley

Hill, behind its Vine pub (locally known as the Bull and Bladder), is Batham's, a classic small Midlands brewery. Its **Bitter★★→★★★** (1043) has a subtly balanced Midlands maltiness in palate and body with a light hoppiness in the finish. Its local rival in Dudley is Holden's, not a great deal bigger, with a characteristically malty range.

The East Midlands' other big city, Nottingham, has three breweries, but only one remains independent. That is Hardy & Hanson, which produces sweetish ales. A local rival, Shipstone, which makes drier ales, belongs to Greenall Whitley. The oddly-named Home Brewery, with its well-rounded ales, has been taken over by Scottish & Newcastle. Also in Nottinghamshire, the Mansfield brewery now has a couple of excellent cask-conditioned ales, with something of an across-the-county-line Yorkshire taste.

Banks

A cult following attends the malty, tasty, medium-dark **Mild★★★** (1036) from this brewery, at Wolverhampton, in the West Midlands. A very similar, but nuttier, **Mild★★★** is made by the associate brewery Hanson, at nearby Dudley. Wolverhampton & Dudley breweries is a large independent company.

Bass

The biggest brewing company in Britain, dating from 1777, and now with an international reputation. The classic ale under the Bass name is cask-conditioned, and therefore available only in Britain. **Draught Bass★★★→★★★★** (1044) has lost a dash of its Burton character since the brewery stupidly discarded the Unions, but it remains highly distinctive. The company's classic bottled product is **Worthington's "White Shield" Fine Burton Ale★★★★** (1049–53), with its fresh, fruity aroma; smooth palate; and spritzy, acidic finish. White Shield is sedimented with a *dosage* of yeast. Bass also owns Mitchell & Butler, which has three breweries in the West Midlands. One of these is unique in that it produces only mild. Its product, **Highgate Mild★★★** (1036) is therefore a local classic. It is dark mild, smooth, with a nice balance of maltiness and fruitiness.

Bateman

Classic country brewery in the East Midlands, in the Lincolnshire seaside resort of Skegness. Its "best" bitter, **XXXB★★★** (1048) is rightly celebrated for its huge character and complexity. It is full of hops in the aroma and, more especially, the finish. It has a smooth, malty start, with lots of hop and fruit in the palate.

Ind Coope

Biggest component of Allied Breweries. Its **Burton Ale★★★** (1048) is inclined to be under-estimated. It has a great depth of flavour, syrupy in the start, then aromatic in its fruitiness and big hop character. Allied's Burton brewery also produces the well-respected **Ansell's Mild★★★** (1035.5), medium dry, with notes of fruit, chocolate and coffee.

Marston

"Grand Cru" brewery. Classic products include **Merrie Monk★★★** (1043), a soft, complex, chocolatey, dark ale; **Burton Bitter★★→★★★** (1037), with the fruitiness characteristic of the town; **Pedigree**★★★★ (1043), with a hint of Cox's apple in the nose, a nutty maltiness and a flowery, hoppy, elegance in the finish; and **Owd Roger**★★→★★★ (1080), dark, powerful, but creamily drinkable.

WALES

The Welsh seem to have been known for their mead before they brewed ale. They even used honey to spice their ale in Saxon times (an antecedent for the sweet character of ales on the Celtic fringe?). Such thoughts might inspire one of the brewpubs or micros that pop up in various parts of Wales. There is a sweetness, though purely from the malt, in **Sam Powell's Original Bitter**★→★★ (1038), made by a microbrewery in Newton, Powys, Central Wales. The longer-established breweries are all in South Wales, close to the centres of population.

Admirers of the writing of Dylan Thomas might fund themselves in the area of Swansea, near which is Llanelli, famous for Rugby Union and the manufacture of tinplate. Britain's first canned beer was made here by Felinfoel, one of Wales' two classic breweries. Felinfoel makes a nutty **Mild**★★ (1031); a very fruity **Bitter**★→★★ (1033) and the reddish, nutty, dry-but-malty **Double Dragon**★★→★★★ (1040), the latter typifying a good Welsh ale. The brewery has links with its neighbour Buckley, which has undergone changes of ownership. Buckley's products include a lightly fruity, well balanced, **Best Bitter**★→★★ (1036).

As Felinfoel is a Welsh classic, so undoubtedly is Brain's, in Cardiff, the capital. Brain's **S.A.**★★★ (1042) is smooth malty, dryish and delicious – arguably the most Welsh of them all. Bass has Welsh brewers, producing pleasant ales under the Hancock brand. Whitbread and Allied have breweries whose products are of no special interest.

THE WEST COUNTRY

The most westerly brewery in Britain is also one of the oddest. It is the Bird in Hand brewpub, in Paradise Park, at Hayle, Cornwall. The name derives from the fact that Paradise Park is a garden in which rare birds are bred. It supports itself by attracting visitors – and by selling them three hearty ales in its pub. An earlier brewpub, in fact one of the original four, is also a popular stopping place for visitors to Cornwall; the Blue Anchor, in Helston, produces a range of strong ales under the name **Spingo**★★→★★★.

The most westerly of the free-standing breweries is Devenish, at Redruth, Cornwall. With a change of ownership, it is now also using the name Cornish Brewery. Under that name, a range of super-premium **Newquay Steam Beers**★★→★★★ has been launched. These are not steam beers in the American sense but they are, indeed, made by an unusual process: they have two primary fermentations and a cold conditioning. They are also all-malt. The two bitters in the range are similar in style to German *altbier*. Despite the western location of the brewery, the brown ale is in the Northern style. There is also a dry stout. Cornish on one occasion raised from 1086 to 1143 the gravity of its **Domesday**★★★ strong ale. The specially labelled bottling, more sherryish than ever, was listed in the Guinness Book of Records as the strongest beer in the world.

The Newquay ales are notably malty, but western brews in general are of a hoppy-fruity character. The other free-standing brewery in Cornwall takes its name from its home town, St Austell, producing a well-balanced, but hop-accented, ale called **Tinners' Bitter**★★ (1083) after the local mining industry.

The centralized big brewers have found distribution difficult along the craggy coasts and hilly countryside of the thinly populated West, so brewpubs and boutiques bristle through Devon and Somerset, around Bath and Bristol, and into Gloucestershire.

In Totnes, the Blackawton Brewery, founded in 1977, is now Devon's oldest. Among the older-established examples in Somerset, and producing excellent ales, are Golden Hill and Cotleigh (both in Wiveliscombe), and the Miners' Arms (Britain's first new brewpub, except that it was actually a restaurant; now in Westbury-sub-Mendip). In the county of Avon, Butcome and Smiles were both pioneers.

An ale-tour on this route might continue to arc north through Gloucestershire (via the Uley brewer in Dursley), to the Cotswold Hills. There, the prettiest brewery in Britain is to be found; Donnington, at Stow-in-the-Wold, producing malt-accented ales of great subtlety. Still in Cotswold country, but no longer in the West, Hook Norton, at Banbury, has a magnificently traditional tower brewery and some delicious, dry, hoppy ales.

An alternative route (or the southern half of a round-trip) would sample the ales of three old-established firms in Dorset: Palmer of Bridport (with a thatched brewery and lightly hoppy ales), Hall & Woodhouse of Blandford Forum (with the magnificently tasty, hoppy, **Tanglefoot**★★→★★★, 1048), and Eldridge Pope of Dorchester (see entry). There would then be a sampling of ales from Ringwood (see entry) and the old-established Wiltshire breweries of Gibbs Mew in Salisbury (noted for **Bishop's Tipple**★★→★★★, 1062–70, an intense and dry, strong, dark ale), Wadworth of Devizes (see entry), and Arkell of Swindon (don't miss the complex, assertive, **Kingsdown**★★, 1050). Archer, of Swindon, is an excellent micro-brewery. Another micro, Wiltshire Brewery of Tisbury, has been known to produce an alcoholic ginger beer.

Courage

This member of the national Big Six has its principal production of cask-conditioned ales in the West, in Bristol. Its **Directors' Bitter**★★→★★★ (1046) is a British classic: a cask-conditioned "super-premium", with a firm, medium-to-full body, a malty palate with fruity undertones, but most notable for its dry-hopped quality. Courage's vintage-dated **Imperial Russian Stout**★★★★ is the classic example of the style. Its appearances are sporadic, sometimes at 1098 rather than the original 1104, and not always bottle-conditioned, but such pettiness cannot detract from its being the world's most intense brew, in all its tar-like, satisfying robustness. Courage also produces **Bulldog**★★★ (1068), a warm-conditioned, citric, pale ale that is a minor classic. The company is now owned by Elders, of Australia.

Eldrige Pope

The famous, vintage date, **Thomas Hardy's Ale**★★★★, is produced by this old-established company in Dorchester.

Much of Hardy's work was based in and around the town, and he wrote lyrically of the local beer. For a Hardy festival in the 1960s, the brewery produced a celebration ale, and has continued to do so ever since. Thomas Hardy's Ale is produced in numbered, limited editions. It is a bottle-conditioned dark ale of 1125.8; 9.98; 12.48. When young, it is very sweet, but it dries with age, gaining a sherryish character. Remarkably some vintages have actually been aged in sherry wood. The company is also known for a super-premium bitter called **Royal Oak**★★→★★★ (1048), with a notably soft, fresh, fruity character. Although this product is dry-hopped, with Goldings, their character is more evident in **Pope's 1880**★★→★★★ (1041), a premium, bottled ale. **Goldie**★★★ (1085) is a magnificently hoppy pale barley wine.

Ringwood

The godfather of boutique breweries in many parts of the world is Peter Austin, founder of Ringwood. After leaving an established brewery, he set up his own, in the New Forest, and as a consultant has since helped many others to do the same thing. Ringwood's ales all have a firm body, a dry maltiness, and plenty of hop character. Ringwood **Fortyniner**★★ (1049) and **Old Thumper**★★★ (1060) are both widely admired.

Wadworth

Classic country brewery that has quietly won the respect of ale-lovers everywhere. Its **Henry Wadworth IPA**★★ (1034) has a hoppy acidity; its **6X**★★ (1040), often served from the wood, is bigger than its gravity would suggest, with a more obvious fruitiness and some "cognac wood" notes. In the darker **Farmer's Glory**★★→★★★ (1046), the two elements reach a hefty balance: the hoppiness in the start is almost herbal, and there is a rich fruitiness in the finish.

IRELAND

The land of dry stout, the style of beer famously typified by Guinness. While the best-known dry stouts of Ireland are produced by Guinness, of Dublin, there are also fine examples from two other brewers, Murphy and Beamish, both in Cork, the second city of the Republic.

It is commonly held that the Guinness in Ireland is better than that sold elsewhere. This is true of the draught product in so far as the fast turnover encourages the brewery not to pasteurize. **Draught Guinness**★★★ in Ireland therefore has a freshness, and perhaps a softer character, than its counterpart in other countries or in its canned "Draught" form, (infected with nitrogen). In both Ireland and most of Britain, the bottled product is supplied in pubs (but not necessarily in other outlets) in unpasteurized form, under the designation **Guinness Extra Stout**★★★★. It may be far less creamy, but the yeasty liveliness imparted by bottle-conditioning, and the lack of any pasteurization, frees the full, hoppy intensity that characterizes Guinness. In the United States, the stout name has been foolishly used to label an inconsequential lager, *Guiness Gold*.

Despite their fullness of both flavour and body, dry stouts tend to have fairly standard gravities in Ireland: around 1037–40, with an alcohol content in the region of 3.5 by weight 4.3 by volume. The same is true in Britain, but the various American and Continental markets get their stouts at anything from 1048 to 1060-plus. Tropical countries have the version of Guinness known, rather quaintly, as **Foreign Extra Stout**★★★ → ★★★★, at 1073. This highly distinctive, extra-strong stout is first slightly soured in its conditioning, then pasteurized for stability. It thus has a hint of sharpness to balance its immense weight.

Murphy and Beamish are both excellent dry stouts, each with their own distinctive characters. **Murphy's Stout**★★ → ★★★ is firm-bodied, with a roasty character. **Beamish**★★ → ★★★ is very creamy, only medium-dry, with some chocolate notes. The Murphy brewery has recently received considerable investment from its owners, Heineken. Beamish is also owned by a large brewing company, Carling O'Keefe of Canada. (It is coincidental that the original O'Keefe came from Cork.)

Ales are a minor category in Ireland, although the number of brands has increased in recent years. Guinness, together with Allied Breweries of Britain, has a company called Irish Ale Breweries. They have breweries in Dundalk and Kilkenny. Irish ales are generally full in colour (often reddish), full-bodied, sweet, sometimes with hints of butteriness. While this last characteristic would be unacceptable in a lager, it is a distinguishing feature of some ales. Irish Ale Breweries' products are, in ascending order of sweetness: **Macardle's** ★ → ★★ and **Phoenix**★ → ★★; **Perry's**★ → ★★; **Smithwick's** ★★★; and the newer **Twyford's**★★★. There is also a **Smithwick's Barley Wine**★★★. In Britain, the brand-name Smithwick's has become associated with an alcohol-free ale. In some countries, Smithwick's products are marketed under the name Kilkenny.

"Real ale" has not been a success in the Republic, but good examples are produced in the northeast by Hilden in Lisburn, County Antrim. **Hilden Ale**★★★ (1040) is a splendidly hoppy bitter.

Among lagers, **Harp**★ has Irish origins, but no specifically Hibernian character.

SOUTHERN EUROPE

The fastest-growing consumption of beer in Europe is in Italy, where the bright young things of prosperous northern cities like Milan regard wine as a drink for their parents. Brewers in other European countries have poured their most sophisticated beers into the Italian market, and now local companies are responding with their own specialities.

One of the more interesting Italian breweries (with its "moustachioed man" trademark) is Moretti, headquartered in Udine, north of Venice. In winter, the restaurant adjoining its offices serves a yeastily unfiltered version (ordered as *integrale*, meaning "whole") of the basic **Moretti★★** beer, which in its normal form is a clean and lightly spritzy Pilsener. Moretti is also very proud of its export-style **Sans Souci★★** (15 Plato; 1060; 4.5; 5.6), which has a flowery hop aroma and a smooth, malty finish. The brewery also has a higher-gravity (16; 1064; 5; 6.25), all-malt version of a Munchener dark, called **Bruna★★→★★★**. Its most specialized beer, however, is the deep red **La Rossa★★★** (18; 1072; 6; 7.5), that is also all-malt, as evidenced by its rich aroma and palate. Sad to say, Moretti is no longer family owned. A controlling share is now held by Labatt, of Canada, which also owns Prinz Bräu in Italy.

The smallest brewery in Italy is Menabrea. The largest is Peroni, producer of **Nastro Azzuro★→★★★**, and the very similar **Raffo★→★★**, both well-balanced Pilseners in the light Italian style.

A beer in the style of a "red ale", **McFarland★★→★★★** (13.5; 1054; 4.4; 5.5) is made by Dreher (now owned by Heineken). The most exotic speciality, a deeper copperred in colour, is **Splügen Fumée★★★**, made with mediumsmoked Franconian malts, by Poretti (in which Carlsberg has a share).

Elsewhere in Southern Europe, Spain has some pleasantly dry Pilseners and a good few Stronger lagers in broadly the Dortmunder Export and *bock* styles.

On Malta, the top-fermenting specialities of the **Farsons★★★** brewery are all worthy of attention: a genuine **Milk Stout** (1045); a darkish mild ale, **Blue Label** (1039); a very pale, dry ale called **Hop Leaf** (1040); and a darker, fuller-bodied ale, **Brewer's Choice** (1050). Greece has, for reasons no one can remember, a German-style law insisting upon all-malt beers. Yugoslavia, on the other hand, is a hop-growing country, so that ingredient tends to be emphasized by its brewers. Some, like Karlovačko, also have a bottom-fermenting **Porter★★★** (1064).

CANADA

I n several other countries, beers from Canada have enjoyed a fashionability based on images of mountains, forests, wildlife and lakes. To drape all this behind names like Labatt and Molson, mass-market brewing companies based in big cities, is to stretch a point. Nor has the Canadian identity of these companies been sharpened by Labatt's takeover of breweries in other countries, and Molson's merger with erstwhile rival Carling (the joint company is owned 50-50 with Foster's, of Australia). The mainstream brews of Canada are mild, pale lagers and (to some degree in Ontario, and to a greater degree in Quebec) equally light-tasting golden ales, plus the odd sweetish porter. Eastern Canada has been more loyal to the "Colonial" ale tradition than its neighbours across the international border. The Quebecois are said to prefer fuller flavours, and in some products the national brewers have a higher specification for that market.

If the Canadian brews have any common characteristic, it is the typical employment of six-row barley, the tougher husk of which can impart a "rougher" texture than the two-row varieties often used elsewhere. Traditionally, they have been marginally hoppier than their counterparts across the border, but this distinction is now barely perceptible. The difference in strength between US and Canadian beers is often exaggerated by misunderstanding. While most everyday beers in the US have between 3.2 and 3.9 percent alcohol by weight, the standard in Canada is just one small notch higher, at 4 percent by weight. However, 4 by weight is the same as 5 by volume and the latter, larger-sounding, measure is used in Canada.

A further area of misunderstanding: in the US, "Light" means low-calorie; in Canada, it indicates lower alcohol: usually a 3.2 percent by weight (ie 4 percent by volume) beer.

Micros and brewpubs have been opening at a fast rate in Canada, and the best of them have produced some very interesting beers. Unfortunately, there are also many, especially among the brewpubs, that choose to make mainstream beers, often from malt extract. There has been a high closure rate among this latter group. The speed of openings and closures among brewpubs and micros, and the demise or sale of surplus-to-requirement big brewery plants following the Molson-Carling merger, make for a very fast-changing scene.

Where to drink

The Montreal area has several interesting brewpubs. Le Cheval Blanc (809 rue Ontario E, near rue Berry), a long-established, socially mixed, bar turned brewpub which changes its beers seasonally, and has featured some fruity, yeasty specialities. Le Cervoise (4457 St Laurent, near rue Mt Royal) has featured a fruity golden beer and a darker ale, and promises a honey brew. The disco-ish Crocodile Club, on St Laurent, produces a pale ale, among other brews. Local microbrews can be found at a Belgian-accented beer cafe, Futenbulles (Bernard and Parc).

Two hours east of Montreal, the cantons (townships) around Sherbrooke have a couple of brewpubs. At Lennoxville and near Bishop's University, the Golden Lion has a Ringwood-inspired brewery. Its Blonde des Cantons is a good example of a Canadian ale; Lion's Pride has a more English character. A Pilsener and a hoppy winter ale have also been produced. Further south, the stylish Pilsen bar-restaurant and Massawippi Brewery are at North Hatley (see entry under Massawippi).

Toronto has one or two bars with notable selections. C'est What (67 Front St E.) has more than a dozen Ontario micros on tap, presents beer tastings, and has something of a cellar atmosphere to go with its live music ever night. Allen's has half a dozen micros on draught, more than 60 bottled beers, and a very knowledgeable patron and staff; an authentic New York saloon in a Greek part of Toronto (143 Danforth Ave).

There are a great many brewpubs in Toronto and elsewhere in Ontario, many making mainstream beers, others with more interesting products (see entries for Rotterdam/Amsterdam and Growler's). In the town of Waterloo, the Heuther Hotel, which housed a well-known brewery in the late 19th century, has restored that tradition. Its Lion Brewery and small beer museum offers a clean-tasting lager and ales in the Canadian and British styles. Some enthusiasts find in the Ansley's Ale a hint of Draught Bass

In the west, good watering holes are fewer. In Calgary, there is a good selection of beers at Buzzard's (140 10th Ave SW. ☎403-264-6959). Several western cities have branches of the Elephant and Castle pub chain, with Edmonton notably beer-aware (West Edmonton Mall. ☎403-444-3555). Fogg n'Suds (1215 Bidwell St, Vancouver. ☎604-683-2337 plus several branches) specializes in beer, has a very large selection, and sometimes runs tastings. In the Vancouver suburb of Coquitlam, The John B (1000 Austin Ave. ☎604-931-5115) has a good range of local draught beers. See also Spinnakers and Swans.

Bottled beers can often be bought at the brewery. Although the law may be changed, it has until now made it difficult for breweries to sell outside their own provinces. Labatt and Molson-Carling have breweries in most provinces.

Algonquin

Marketing-oriented micro on the site of a famous old brewery (1870-1971) in Formosa, Ontario. Products include **Country Lager**$\star \rightarrow \star\star$, sweetish and flavourful, with a faintly astringent finish; and the pleasant but mild **Special Reserve Ale**$\star\star$, with a fuller colour and a fruity, tart, palate.

Amstel

The Dutch alter ego of Heineken bought a brewery formerly owned by Henninger, of Germany. The brewery, in Hamilton, Ontario, has been used to produce Amstel brands along with the more Canadian-sounding **Grizzly**$\star$, which is sweetish and slightly fruity. **Steeler Beer**$\star$, named after the local industry, is unexceptional.

Belle Gueule

From a Montreal micro called Les Brasseurs GMT, better known by the name of the beer. **Belle Gueule** is a hoppy, yeasty, pale lager. Too early to rate.

Big Rock

In foothills of the Rockies, at Calgary, Alberta. This micro is getting bigger at a remarkable rate. Its well-made brews, unpasteurized but tightly filtered, have included: a perfumy, malty, dry, **XO Lager**★★; the hoppy **Royal Coachman Dry Ale**★★; an aromatic, fruity, smooth, golden **Pale Ale**★★; a straw-coloured **Bitter**★★→★★★, malty in the palate and nicely hoppy in the finish; an amber-red, dry, malty-fruity **Traditional Ale**★★→★★★; the malty-buttery **McNally's Extra**★★★ (7 percent by volume), a classic Irish-style ale; **Springbok Ale**★★ (5 percent by volume), with a bronze colour, a flowery aroma, a light start and a very hoppy, dry, finish; a coffeeish, creamy, **Porter**★★, with a gently roasty finish; and the stronger, richer, **Cold Cock**★★→★★★ (6 percent by volume) winter porter.

Boccalino's Brewpub

Italian-Swiss restaurateur Peter Johner enjoys a beer, and decided to offer a house brew to his customers in downtown Edmonton, Alberta. The fruity, dry **Bocca Blonde**★→★★ and the sweeter **Bocca Ale**★→★★ are produced from extract.

Boreale

From a micro called Les Brasseurs du Nord, in St Jerome, north of Montreal, better known by the name of the beer. **Boreale** is an aromatic, mild, smooth, amber-red ale. Too early to rate.

Brick

Pioneering, sizable micro in the brewing and distilling town of Waterloo. Principal products are the very light, fresh-tasting, **Red Baron**★→★★; and the all-malt **Brick Premium Lager**★★, sweetish, firm-bodied, with some dryness in the finish. Seasonal specials have included a tawny, malty-roasty **Brick Bock**★★→★★★ (6.5 percent by volume), with a warming finish. On the label, the brewery says this product is matured for three months. There is also a winter **Bock** (not tasted). These products change in specification each year.

Burlington Brewing

South of Toronto, in the town of Burlington. This micro's products have included a dry, malty **Lager**★→★★; a hoppy **Dry**★→★★ (5.5); A smooth, lightly malty, dryish, **Brown Ale**★→★★ (5.0), a pleasant brew, but too pale to carry that designation; and a deep amber, aromatically malty springtime **Bock**★→★★ (6.5). More seasonal brews are planned.

Carling

See Molson.

Conners

After a period of expansion, this micro seems now to have settled in Don Valley, near Toronto. **Conners Ale**★★ has a fruity-hoppy character, with a note of Cascades, its refreshing acidity resting on a good malt character. **Conners Bitter**★★ is, despite its name, sweeter and maltier. **Conners Imperial**

Stout★★→★★★ is smooth, slightly viscous, roasty, perhaps even smoky, and very dry. Despite its designation, this is a stout of only conventional strength.

Creemore Springs

Spring water is taken 3km (2 miles) by tanker to the brewery, in the town of Creemore, about 100km (83 miles) northwest of Toronto. Creemore was a railhead for an agricultural region, and now has second homes for Toronto weekenders and skiers. The brewery is in an 1890s hardware store. The only product, **Creemore Springs Premium Lager**★★★, has a dense head; a light, Saaz-accented, hoppiness in the aroma; a firm, malty body; a soft, hoppy, palate; and an elegant, light but lingering, hoppy finish. It is not pasteurized.

Drummond

Regional brewery in Red Deer, Alberta. Products have included **Wolfsbrau Amber Lager**★★, lightly aromatic, firm-bodied, and on the dry side.

Granite

Remote brewpub in Halifax, Nova Scotia (1222 Barrington St). Early products were a Ringwood-style **Best Bitter**★★★, and **Peculier**★★★ (1056-8) modelled on Marston's Owd Roger.

Granville Island

Pioneering, sizable, micro in a trendy-touristy shopping area of Vancouver. Products have included the all-malt **Island Lager**★★, with a good dash of hop character, a smooth body and a dry finish; **Island Märzen**★★★, amber-red, with a dry, malty, start and a long, hoppy, finish; and **Island Bock**★★★ (6.5 percent by volume), with a very deep amber colour, a smooth body and a depth of malty flavour. Granville Island is now part of the Potter group, which also owns the Pacific Western.

Great Lakes

The name occurs in several places in North America. This one is a micro brewing from extract, in Brampton, Ontario. **Great Lakes Lager**★★ is pleasant, soft, sweet, with an aromatically malty palate and a dryish finish. Unicorn Ale has a full, amber-red, colour, and a sweetish palate with some astringency in the finish. Tastings have been very variable (not rated).

Growler's

Glitzy, cafe-style brewpub in Toronto, with some participation from Prince Luitpold of Bavaria. Products include **Unfiltered Lager**★★ (ordered by this description), heavily sedimented and slightly sticky; the regular, filtered **Lager**★★, clean, sweetish and soft; and **Royal Dunkel**★★, a dark lager with a light, chocolatey palate. There are also seasonal specials. Sometimes known as Denison's, after the adjoining restaurant.

Hopps Brau

Two p's because it was the name of the founder of a micro in La Salle, Montreal. **Hopps Brau**★→★★ is a sweetish, golden, lager. The company is also known as Brasserie Allemande, or Brasal.

Horseshoe Bay

The first micro in Canada. It closed when its beers were no longer wanted at the nearby Troller pub, at Horseshoe Bay, on the edge of Vancouver. It has now reopened, and is producing custom ales, unfiltered, for restaurants in the city. Its basic **Horseshoe Bay Ale**★★→★★★ has an amber-red colour and is malty but dry. Available at Leon's, 1630 Albernie St, Vancouver; and Troll's, 6400 Bay St, Horseshoe Bay.

Labatt

Biggest Canadian brewing company until its rivals, Molson and Carling merged. Labatt, controlled by a splinter of the Bronfman (Seagram's whiskey) family, and headquartered in London, Ontario, continues to mount a powerful challenge to its united competitors. Its beers lean toward perfumy sweetness. Its biggest-selling brand is the bland **Labatt's Blue**★, a pale lager. **Labatt's Classic**★→★★ is all-malt and kräusened, but still has relatively little character. **Labatt 50**★ is a lightly aromatic golden ale. The company's golden **IPA**★★ is less distinctive than it was. A relatively new product is a red ale, with a hint of aromatic fruitiness, called **Duffy's**★★. The old-established **Velvet Cream Porter**★→★★ is very sweet and thin, with a hint of roastiness in the finish. Local brands include the sweetish **Schooner**★ (in the Maritimes) and the drier **Kokanee**★→★★ (in the west).

Massawippi

Brewpub-micro in the eastern townships of Quebec. Products include the golden **Massawippi Pale Ale**★★, pleasant, with a clean palate and a fruity, citric, hoppy, finish.

Molson

Founded by John Molson, from Lincolnshire, England, after he emigrated to Montreal. The family heritage – once strongly felt – has been diluted by the merger with Carling. In the past, the Molson products were perhaps slightly more flavourful than their rivals, but today there seems little to choose. The company's basic lager, **Molson Canadian**★, is bland; its principal ale, **Molson Golden**★ only slightly more tasty. Its **Molson Export**★ slightly fruitier. **Molson Stock Ale**★★ has a little more hop character. **Rickard's Red**★★, named after a brewer at Molson, has a deep, copper colour, a malty start and a vanilla-like fruitiness in the finish. **Brador**★★→★★★ (6.25) is an ale-like malt liquor. **Molson Porter**★★ has a welcome dash of fruitiness. **Carling Black Label**★ is a dryish lager; **Old Vienna**★ slightly sweeter; **O'Keefe Ale**★ carbonic and fruity. **Dow**★★, an ale brewed for the Quebec market, seems slightly hoppier. This product portfolio is likely to be slimmed as a result of the merger.

Moosehead

Sizable regional brewer, with plants in Nova Scotia and New Brunswick. Moosehead's beers have a delicate hop character, and firm body, and a grassy yeastiness. Its local brew, **Alpine**★→★★, has a little more character than **Moosehead Canadian Lager**★, which is marketed in the US. **Moosehead Export**★ is a sweetish ale. **Moosehead Pale Ale**★→★★ is drier. **Ten Penny Stock Ale**★★ is slightly more characterful.

Niagara Falls Brewing

In the town of Niagara, on the Canadian side of the Falls. This region grows wine, and a local Italian family with a foot in each industry decided that a micro-brewery would not come amiss.

As several of the vineyards make eiswein, the micro produces as it speciality an eisbock, a style previously not made outside Bavaria. Unlike the Bavarian producers, Niagara does not use the process to make a super-strong beer, though its **Eisbock**★★★→★★★★ is potent enough, at 15.3 Plato (1060-62; 8 percent by volume). This brew is released in late September or early October. For its gravity, it is remarkably delicate, with a peachy colour and palate; a light, soft, maltiness; a smooth body and a dry finish. The brewery has also produced a conventional lager, the hoppy **Trapper Premium**★★ (1048; 5 percent by volume). It also has two more distinctive products with a British (or Belgian?) accent. The tawny, malty, caramelly, fruity, slightly grainy, **Gritstone Premium**★★→★★★ (1050; 5.8 percent by volume) is an assertive brown ale. (The bottled version seems sweeter and fuller than the draught product). The medium-amber, soft, slightly syrupy **Olde Jack**★★→★★★ (1064; 7.2) sounds like an old ale, is billed as an extra-strong bitter, and might best be styled as a barley wine.

Okanagan Spring

Very successful micro in the Okanagan Valley, at Vernon, in the interior of British Columbia. **Spring Premium Lager**★★→★★★ has a sweetish start, a soft body, an aromatic palate and a hoppy finish. **Old Munich**★★→★★★ is a dark wheat beer with a light, fruity, tartness. **Extra Special Pale Ale**★★ has a bronze colour, a malty aroma, a sweet start and a tart finish. **St Patrick Stout**★★ is soft-bodied, creamy and chocolatey. **Old English Porter**★★★ (8.5) is full and rounded, with a depth of fruity-coffeeish flavours.

Ottawa Valley

Micro, originally brewing from extract, but now full grain, in Nepean, Ontario. Products have included **Ottawa Valley Dark Ale**★→★★, thinnish, clean, soft and sweet, with some notes of chocolate; **Bytown Lager**★★, floral, flavourful and dryish; and a bronze, aromatic, sweetish **Bock**★→★★ (6.5), with a rather thin finish.

Pacific Western

Regional brewery in Prince George, British Columbia, with a newer branch plant in St Catherine's, Ontario. Both produce a lower-priced lager called **Pacific Real Draft**★. There is also a bland, reddish ale called **Canterbury**★.

Portneuvoise

Micro in St Casimir, near Quebec City, producing **La Portneuvoise**★★, a fruity, very spicy, distinctive, strong (5.8) ale. Somewhat variable.

Renegade

Former Conner's branch brewery in the college town of Thunder Bay, Ontario. Ownership changes render future plans uncertain.

Rotterdam

Very interesting beers, at a brewpub in downtown Toronto. Regular products have included a very clean, sweetish **Lager**★★, with a mildly dry finish; an aromatically hoppy, Saaz-accented **Pilsener**★★→★★★; and a bronze, soft, malty but dryish

White Cap Ale★★. Specials have ranged through an aromatically malty, chocolatey, buttery, **Scotch Ale★★★**; an earthy **Weiss★★★** (1046), with a lactic fermentation and some matching acidity; and a very hoppy, clean, soft, strong pale lager called **Doppelpils★★★** (1070). At any one time, eight styles are available between the Rotterdam (600 King St. ☎416-868-6882) and its partner establishment the Amsterdam.

St-Ambroise

An outstanding ale from the McAuslan micro-brewery of St Henri, Montreal. The name of the ale is better known than that of the brewery. **St-Ambroise★★★** is amber-red, clean and appetizing, with a very good hop character, from its bouquet to its long finish. Hoppy-fruity and tasty all the way through.

Sculler

So called because its home town, St Catherine's, near Niagara, Ontario, holds a famous regatta, on the Welland Canal. **Sculler Premium Lager★★** has a dense head, a malty aroma and a sweetish, flowery, soft, palate, drying to a firm, hoppy, finish. A winter **Bock★★★** (6.5 percent by volume) had a malty aroma and palate and a depth of hoppy dryness in the finish. More seasonal specials may emerge from this micro, which also produces under licence Grant's Scottish Ale.

Shaftebury

It is meant to be an English name, amended to make it more proprietary. English-style ales, with a smooth, dryish, house character, from a micro in Vancouver. Products include a malty, nutty, dark mild under the curious name of **Cream Ale★★★** (1040-42); an appetizing, light, clean, **Bitter★★→★★★** (same gravity), in a pale bronze colour; and a firmer, fruitier, slightly tart, hoppier, **ESB★★→★★★** (1048-plus), with more of a reddish colour.

Sleeman's

Having brewed in Cornwall, and then in Guelph, Ontario from the mid Nineteenth Century, the Sleeman family lapsed from the industry in 1933, then returned in the 1980s to start this sizable micro in the same town. Products include the dryish **Silver Creek Lager★★**, with some Saaz hop character, and **Sleeman Cream Ale★★**, with a perfumy, sweetish, bouquet and a slightly tart, fruity, flavour development. The **Cream Ale** is to some extent based on an original Sleeman formulation.

Spinnakers

The first brewpub in Canada, known for its outstanding ales, served by hand-pumps, from the conditioning tanks. After a change of ownership, these brews seemed initially to be retaining their quality. It is to be hoped that this is maintained. Products since the change have included the golden, dry, thinnish, **Spinnaker Ale★★** (1032); a chocolatey **Highland Scottish Ale★★→★★★** (1046); the malty, fruity, **Mount Tolmie Dark★★** (1047); the very hoppy, tasty **ESB★★★** (1050-52); and a soft, medium-bodied and dry **Imperial Stout★★→★★★** (1057). **Empress Stout** (1052), is very dry and smooth, but has not been sampled since the change of ownership. Specials have included the whimsical **Dunkel Krieken Weizen★★★** (estimated OG 1062), matured for several months on whole local cherries. This had an excellent sour-cherry character without being astringent, and a great depth of flavour. A Christmas Ale a called **Jameson's**★★→★★★ (1048) seemed to taste of ginger, though its spices were actually nutmeg, cinnamon, cardamom and maple syrup.

Strathcona

Scottish name for a community subsumed into Edmonton, Alberta. The Strathcona Brewing Co, a micro, has endured ups and downs, but has in the meantime managed to produce a good range of beers.

They are: a firm-bodied, fruity, dry, hoppy, best bitter called **Whyte Avenue Amber**★★; the medium-bodied, faintly roasty **Strathcona Ale**★★, loosely in the style of a Northern English brown; a spiced, dry-hopped **King's Ale**★★ for Christmas; an Irish-style stout called **Firkin** (not tasted) for St Patrick's Day; and in late summer and autumn a **County Fair Raspberry Ale**★★→★★★, delightfully fresh and fruity. This was based on a wheat beer, and "fresh frozen" raspberries were added in the kettle, at the end of the boil.

Sunshine Coast

Orca Pilsner and a Lager, brewed from extract by a new micro at Sechelt, BC. (Not tasted).

Swans Hotel/Buckerfield's

New brewpub in Victoria, British Columbia, offering very clean, tasty, products. Some of the lighter ones are presented very cold, but the fuller examples are served on handpump at a more civilized temperature. Products in the latter category include **Pandora Pale Ale**★★, golden, soft and fruity; a **Bitter**★★★, malt-accented, but with a good balance of hoppiness and fruitiness; a very malty, nutty, **Brown**★★→★★★, in the Northern English style; a dry **Stout**★★, with some underlying treacly sweetness; and a sweet, malty, **Bock**★★ (7.5 percent by volume).

Upper Canada

Interesting and well-made brews in a variety of styles from a sizable micro in Toronto. The original product, now styled **Upper Canada Dark Ale**★★→★★★, has a maltier accent than it initially did, but there is still some of the characteristic fruitiness, and a nice dry, hoppy finish. The pleasant, easy to drink **Publican's Bitter**★★ is actually on the sweet side, but with some tartness and hop in the finish, and a full, bronze, colour.

Upper Canada Wheat★★→★★★ is golden and bright, very refreshing and slightly tart. **Upper Canada Lager**★★→★★★ is soft, clean and spritzy, with a good hop character in both the bouquet and the finish. **Rebellion**★★ is a malty, substantial, strong golden lager. **True Bock**★★→★★★ has a good malt character, a warming finish, and a satisfying, full amber colour.

Vancouver Island

Formerly known as Island Pacific. A pioneering microbrewery, near Victoria, on Vancouver Island. Products include a malt-accented **Viking Premium Lager**★★ and a reddish, lightly fruity **Ale**★★. **Hermann's Dark**★★, named after a previous brewer, is on the light side in body, but smooth, with some viscosity and sweetness in the finish.

Wellington County

English-style ales, sometimes cask-conditioned, from a classic micro in the old brewing town of Guelph. **Arkell Best Bitter★★★** (4 percent by volume) has in its cask form an earthy aroma of East Kent Goldings; a deft balance of malty dryness and restrained fruitiness; and a long, hoppy, finish. A good, honest ale. The same beer filtered for the bottle tastes slightly less hoppy. **Wellington SPA★★** (Special Pale Ale), at 4.5, is sweeter and fruitier. **County Ale★★★** (5) is bigger-bodied, complex and well rounded, with a very hoppy finish. **Iron Duke★★★** (6.5) is malt-accented but beautifully balanced, with a great depth of flavour and a dry finish. An experimental Imperial Stout (6.5) was highly promising: roasty, chocolatey, syrupy, peppery and warming. **Wellington Premium Lager★★** (4.5) is clean, rounded and flavourful. Some of the products can be found cask-conditioned in Toronto, at Foster's.

Whistler Brewing

A mountain known as Whistler gives its name to a ski resort about 100km (83 miles) north of Vancouver. Now, the resort has a micro-brewery. Its principal product, **Whistler Premium Lager★★** has a perfumy bouquet; a light but malty body and a gently dry, hoppy, finish. **Black Tusk★★** is a malty, slightly roasty, dryish, tawny ale. **Albino Rhino★★→★★★**, contract brewed for a group of bar-restaurants, is a hoppy, deep bronze ale in the style of the American North-Western micros.

York

New micro in Brampton, Ontario. Its first product, **York Pilsner Lager**, was billed as being brewed according to the Reinheitsgebot and by a decoction mash. An early sample was flowery, dry and somewhat astringent. Too early to rate.

THE UNITED STATES

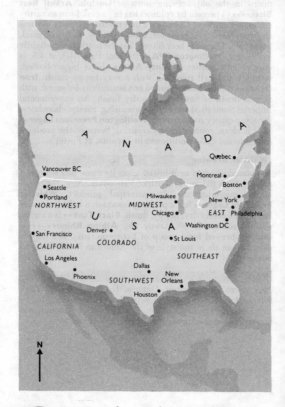

CANADA

Quebec
Montreal
Boston
New York
Philadelphia
Washington DC

Vancouver BC
Seattle
Portland
NORTHWEST

Milwaukee
MIDWEST
Chicago
EAST

U S A

San Francisco
Denver
St Louis
CALIFORNIA
COLORADO
SOUTHEAST
Los Angeles

Dallas
New
Orleans
Phoenix
SOUTHWEST
Houston

N

Contrary to the popular view, both among foreigners and Americans, an astonishingly wide selection of beer-styles is now being produced in the United States: not only are there light lagers, but also truly hoppy Pilseners, malty Vienna types and spicy Munich darks. Bland golden ales are found alongside oak-aged I.P.A.s, rich brown ales and barley wines; and not to mention the beers made with wheat, oats and rye, or seasoned with fruits, herbs and even chilis. The problem lies in finding them.

Ninety-nine percent of speciality beers produced in the United States are made by micros, brewpubs or occasionally contract brewers, most of them relatively new and none much more than a decade old. Many of the states in the North, and some in the South, have at least one micro, but the real concentrations of tiny breweries are in tranches: New England, the area around Chicago and Milwaukee and, especially, the northern part of the West Coast, from San Francisco Bay through Oregon and Washington. If the United States has a speciality beer capital, it is either Portland, Oregon, or Seattle, Washington.

There were fewer than 40 brewing companies in the United States at the beginning of the 1980s, but by the early 1990s the number was more than 200, and still growing fast. The states with the most breweries were also experiencing the greatest growth; as in society, the rich were getting wealthier. Like Czechoslovakia and Germany, Belgium and Britain, the United States is now so rich in beers that its output cannot be considered comprehensively, only selectively. There are many brewpubs that produce very similar ranges, but there are also others that show individuality and flair. The same is true among contract brewers. The churlish will complain that some highly praised beers are hard to find: so are many of life's pleasures. Others will doubt the importance of a brewery that makes only a few thousand barrels a year, but how many bottles does Château Latour produce, as compared to a maker of jug wine? For the consumer, it is the choice on offer that matters, not the volume that is produced. Europe is both an inspiration and a shadow behind American beer. "Can we produce any as good?" is a persistent question. The answer is "yes, definitely".

Czechoslovakia and Germany have countless fine lagers, among which a handful of new American examples could hold their heads high. Belgium and Britain have scores of fine ales, alongside which might be ranged several from the United States. However, this comparison tells only part of the story. European beers like Pilsner Urquell or Duvel are so distinctive that they cannot be compared with anything else. Nor does a European brewer make anything to compare with Samuel Adams' Boston Lager, Anchor Steam or Sierra Nevada Pale Ale. Every nation has its own classics. As elsewhere in the world, the birth of brewpubs, micros and contract brewers has been a reaction to the continued closure of local and regional breweries, and mergers among the nationals. Fewer than 20 old-established local and regional breweries survive. The national breweries, the giants of the industry are (in ascending order): Pabst (which has links with General Brewing and Falstaff); Heileman (which, with Pittsburgh Brewing is, at least for the moment, owned by Bond, of Australia); Coors; Stroh (which also owns Schlitz); Miller; and Anheuser-Busch (Budweiser, Michelob, etc).

The big brewers have in recent years greatly increased their ranges of products, but variations on "Light" and "Dry" brews are unlikely to excite the beer-lover. The giants' essays into true specialities have been several, but less confident. The mainstream beers are themselves very light in both body and palate, and this leads some consumers to believe that they are also unusually weak. That is not so. Some states stipulate that anything labelled "beer" (as opposed to "malt liquor" or "ale") must not exceed 3.2 percent, but that figure represents alcohol by weight. In volume, that amounts to 4 percent, a level not unknown in other parts of the world. A "Light" or low-price beer might be around this level in whatever state it is bought. A standard beer in America has an alcohol content of between 3.2 and 3.9 by weight (4.0-4.8 by volume), from a gravity of 10.25-11.25 Plato (1041-45). That alcohol level is typical in many countries. Most American ales have an alcohol content of around 4.25-4.75 by weight (5.3-5.9), 12.25-12.5 Plato (around 1050). Malt Liquors usually have a similar, or higher, alcohol content, and may go up to around 6.5 (8.0).

The lightness of body and palate is achieved by the use of a high level of adjuncts (sometimes more than 30 percent). One or two premium brands use rice, but corn (maize) is more common, in the form of flakes or grits or (especially in cheap brands) as a syrup. The palate is further lightened by very low hopping rates, with units of bitterness sometimes below ten. That is beneath the level at which hops can be perceived by the palate. Why would brewers seek to make tasteless beer? Only because millions of consumers like it that way.

THE EAST

For every two steps forward, there seems to be one back, but the East is still edging toward a wider appreciation of speciality beers. The hardest road is in New York City, but what's new? New England continues to blossom with boutique breweries, and Catamount, of Vermont, is establishing itself as one of America's best. Samuel Adams now really does have a brewery in Boston, albeit a very small one, producing a new ale rather than the lager. In the past, when the Northeast was America's brewing centre, it was famous for ales, and the revival of this style is presenting some outstanding new products. Pennsylvania's Stoudt brewery, which produces principally lagers, is another Eastern micro with a justifiably national reputation among beer-lovers, and the Allegheny pub is a welcome newcomer in Pittsburgh. Pennsylvania also has more old-established breweries than any other state, narrowly beating Wisconsin. Baltimore, once a great brewing city, is regaining that reputation. Its British Brewing Company makes interesting ales, as does the excellent Sisson's pub, while Baltimore Brewing has outstanding lagers.

Where to drink

Washington, DC, has the pioneering speciality beer-bar of the East, the Brickskeller (1523 22nd St NW, ✆202-293-1885), underneath an hotel, on the fringes of fashionable Georgetown. It stocks hundreds of beers, and admits that the ages of some "endangered species" may render them of less interest to drinkers than can collectors. The same is true in less candid beer-bars. Buffalo stew has been known to feature on the menu. The nation's capital also has one of America's finest beer-shops, Berose Liquors (1711 17th St NW, Dupont Circle. ☎202-667-5010). Pennsylvania boasts 700 beers-plus in an unlikely sounding location, The House of Pasta (East Ross St and New Holland Ave, Route 23, Lancaster). Philadelphia now has a brewpub (see under Boston Brewing).

New York City's oldest-established speciality beer-bar, the Peculier (*sic*) Pub has moved to 145 Bleecker St at W Broadway, near the Village Gate. The new pub is larger, a darkish, barn-like place, with about 200 beers. It opens at 4 o'clock in the afternoon (☎212-353-1327). A newer rival, popular with serious beer-lovers, is Brewsky's (41 E 7th St, at 2nd Ave, East Village), like a small shop with half a dozen tables, and sawdust on the floor. Down the street is McSorley's (15 E 7th), founded in 1854, and worth a visit for its antiquity if not for its lightly fruity house pale and dark beers (brewed by Heileman) or its cheese (no longer Liederkrantz) and onions. Near the Manhattan Brewing Company (see entry) is The Soho Kitchen (103 Greene St), with a large selection of draught beers, wines by the glass, and champagnes. In South Street Seaport, the North Star Pub specializes in British ales, and single malt Scotches (93 South St). Visitors to Brooklyn might enjoy the Waterfront Ale House (136 Atlantic Ave, between Henry and Clinton). Beers are well presented at the fanciest of Manhattan's gourmet food stores, Dean & Deluca (121 Prince St, SoHo).

New England has a growing number of brewpubs (see entries for Cambridge, Commonwealth, Gritty McDuff's and Northampton). As McSorley's is to New York, so Jake Wirth's (founded in 1868) is to Boston. Jake's (31-37 Stuart and Eliot) serves similar house beers, and hearty knuckles of pork. Although the Bull and Finch (84 Beacon St) was the inspiration for the television series "Cheers", an earlier model would have been the area's favourite beer-pub, Doyle's (3484 Washington St, Jamaica Plain; orange line to Green St). Splendidly multi-cultural despite rooms devoted to the Kennedys and Michael Collins.

Abbot Square

New micro (full mash) and restaurant at Lackawanna, Buffalo, New York. German-style beers. Too early to rate. Same owners as Buffalo Brewpub (see entry).

Allegheny Pub

See under Pennsylvania Brewing.

Baltimore Brewing Company

A member of the Grolsch family, Theo de Groen, privately established this welcome addition to Baltimore's wonderfully revived downtown area, adjoining an old brewery-neighbourhood redevelopment. The spectacular copper-clad brewhouse is behind the bar. Beers are served unfiltered but bright: a fresh, malty, wholesome **Helles**★★→★★★, with a gentle hop character; a soft, smooth, very hoppy **Pils**★★★, with a long finish; a medium-bodied, malty-sweet **Dunkles**★★→★★★, with a coffeeish dryness in the finish.

Boston Brewing Company

The new **Samuel Adams Boston Stock Ale★★★** achieves a remarkable balance between its big, firm, malty body and its powerful Goldings hop character. This distinctive, pale amber product is brewed from a gravity of 1052, kraüsened, dry-hopped and cold conditioned. The intention is to revive the American Stock Ale style with its original character. The Stock Ale is made in a considerably upgraded adaptation of the brewhouse used at the former William Newman micro-brewery, in Albany, New York.

The brewhouse has been installed in part of the old Haffenreffer premises, in Jamaica Plain, Massachusetts (near Doyle's pub). Brewery visitors can sample the beer from a pre-Civil War bar (☎617-522-3400). Haffenreffer, founded in 1865, acquired an earlier (founded 1828) Boston Brewing Company in 1957, and the merged enterprise closed in 1965. Jim Koch, from a brewing family, founded this new company in the mid 1980s. His flagship **Samuel Adams Boston Lager★★★** (12.5; 1050; 3.5; 4.4) has already established itself as an American classic. It has a rocky head; a flowery hop aroma, with a definitive Hallertau Mittelfrüh character; a soft, malty palate; and both the taste and dryness of hops in the finish. Among several other products, the dark **Samuel Adams Doppelbock★★★** (21 Plato; 1084; 6; 7.5) is probably the maltiest beer in America, although it still contrives not to be cloying, and has a huge depth of flavour.

The lagers are made under contract in Pittsburgh, and Portland, Oregon. There is also a Samuel Adams Brewpub, at the Sansom St Oyster House, in Philadelphia. This brews a separate range from extract, including a well-made Porter.

British Brewing Company

The English-style **Oxford Ale★★→★★★** was the first product from this Baltimore micro. It is a well-balanced, but malt-accented, honeyish, slightly sticky, top-fermenting ale of 1051-1055. A drier, hoppier, golden, pale ale is planned. There has also been an experimental **Oxford Old Ale★★★** (or barley wine?), rich, malty and slightly vinous. Oxford Ale is available cask-conditioned, at weekends only, at Bertha's Mussels (☎301-327-5795).

Brooklyn Lager

Surely a "designer beer", with a masterful label created by Milton Glaser. **Brooklyn Lager★★** itself is a well-made, firm-bodied, smooth, all-malt, dry-hopped, contract brew, produced at F.X. Matt, in Utica, New York.

Buffalo Brewpub

About 19km (12 miles) from downtown, and eight km (five miles) from the city limit. A handsome, wood-clad building on a franchise strip at 6861 Main St and Transit Rd, Williamsville, New York. (☎716-632-0552). It has a sister establishment, the Market Place Inn, at 800 Jefferson Rd, Rochester. Both use extract, with some whole grains. The Buffalo Brewpub is noteworthy for its light-bodied, smooth, dry **Oatmeal Stout★★**, produced for St Patrick's Day. Its **Buffalo Bitter★→★★** (1050) is fruity and tart; its **Amber Ale★** fruity and soft; and its **Nickel City Dark★→★★** (named after the coin with the American Buffalo) tawny and malty (both 1055). See also Abbot Square.

Cambridge Brewing Company

Not far from downtown Boston, across the river, at 1 Kendall Square, Cambridge. Conservatory-style bar-restaurant, with rotating art exhibits and local folk bands. Beers (top-fermenting) include a sweetish, fruity **Golden**★→★★; a hoppy **Pale**★★; a spicy **Amber**★→★★; and a **Porter**★→★★ that has a hint of treacle toffee.

Catamount

The classic example of a regular golden ale in the East Coast tradition comes from this noted young micro at White River Junction, Vermont. **Catamount Gold**★★★ (1042; 3.6; 4.5) has a good American hop character (the variety being exclusively Willamettes) in both the bouquet and finish. It has a clean, malty body, with its palate becoming fruity toward a well-developed finish. **Catamount Amber**★★→★★★ (1048; 4.0; 5.0) is more assertive all round, with a polite nod toward English pale ale. Catamount also contract-brews the fruity, dry **Post Road Real Ale**★★ (actually, all the products are filtered) and the maltier **Frank Jones Ale**★★. A newer product, **Catamount Porter**★★★ (1052; 4.2; 5.3) is remarkably smooth, creamy, and chocolatey. This is the best Porter produced on the East Coast.

Chapterhouse

A new brewpub, producing ales and stout, at 400 Stewart Ave., Ithaca, New York. Too early to rate. The same company now owns Vernon Valley (see entry).

Commonwealth

Original Burton Union casks decorate the main bar, and the grist hopper and kettle rise through the floor, in this pioneering brewpub. Apart from the fresh, hoppy **Blond**★→★★ (which is served chilled), all of the ales are naturally carbonated and fined, but they are now also filtered before being pulled through handpumps. The **Golden**★★ (1040) is clean, fruity, tart and hoppy; the flagship **Bitter**★★→★★★ (1045), has a bouquet and finish that bears witness to plenty of Goldings, especially in its dry-hopping; the **Amber**★★ soft (1045) and easily drinkable, with a hint of chocolatey sweetness; the unfiltered **Stout**★★→★★★ (1050) is complex, with notes of rum and coffee.

A fruity, faintly medicinal **Porter**★★→★★★ (1050) is produced exclusively in a bottle-conditioned form, and a draught **Winter Warmer**★★→★★★ (1095), which is malty and winey, is retained in bottled form year-round under the label *Special Old Ale*.

The Commonwealth is situated at 138 Portland and Merrimac, between Boston Gardens and Fanueil Hall (☎617-523-8383).

Dock Street

Delicate and fruity (with notes reminiscent of strawberry), **Dock Street Amber Beer**★★ is broadly in the style of an East Coast ale. The beer has a popular following, especially in its home town, Philadelphia. Plans for a brewpub have been announced since Dock Street began its life as a contract brew from F.X. Matt.

Eastern Brewing

Specialist in low-price and supermarket brands. America's most anonymous brewery, in Hammonton, New Jersey.

Elm City

There were once many elms in New Haven, Connecticut; there are now more oaks and maples. **Elm City Connecticut Ale★★★** (1052) is splendidly assertive, with its full, amber-brown colour; its clean malt emphasis in aroma and palate; and its lightly fruity, dry finish. This draught product has a pale, bottled counterpart called **Elm City Golden Ale★★** which is still malt-accented, but much less assertive. A stout is planned.

Elm City is the trademark of New Haven Brewing, an impressive micro, founded in 1989. The beer can be sampled in Richter's Cafe (worth a visit for its 1912 interior), at 990 Chapel St, on New Haven Green.

Geary

There was an English influence in the early American ales, and here it is again in David Geary's well-established new-generation micro. **Geary's Pale Ale★★→★★★** (1047) is a New England (and East Coast) classic: copper-coloured, dry, clean, crisp, with lots of late-hop taste (the emphasis has switched from American Fuggles to Willamettes), in an appetising complex with ale fruitiness (from old Hampshire's Ringwood yeast). A **Hampshire Special Ale★★★** (1070), tawny, bitter-chocolatey, drying to a tremendous hop finish, is produced for winter, and is also vintage-dated. The brewery is in Portland, and its beers are available at Gritty McDuff's (see entry).

Genesee

The name comes from a river. This old-established brewery, America's biggest independent, is in Rochester, New York. Creditably, for a brewery so large, it specializes in ales. Sad to say, neither its **Twelve-Horse Ale★★** (3.8; 4.7) nor its **Genesee Cream Ale★→★★** (3.7; 4.6) has a great deal of character or body. Both have a sweet, creamy palate, balanced by a lightly fruity tartness in the finish. The Cream Ale is the lighter.

Gritty McDuff's

The name is invented. This is a brewpub in the old-town harbour area of Portland, Maine. Products include a hoppy, very fruity **Pale Ale★★** (1042), with a full, amber colour; a well-balanced, soothing, **Bitter★★→★★★** (1050), with a malty start and a dry, hoppy (Whitbread Goldings), finish; a **Brown Ale★★→★★★** (1042), on the light side in palate, but with some maltiness emerging; and a coffeeish **Stout★→★★** (1045). The beers are served unfiltered, under CO_2 and nitrogen.

Heurich

Washington, D.C., once had a brewery called Christian Heurich (pronounced High Rick). Now the proprietor's grandson is trying to revive the city's brewing tradition with a beer called **Olde Heurich★★** (12; 3.52; 4.4). This is a well-made, pale amber lager, with a delicate Saaz bouquet; a soft, sweetish, palate; and a clean, elegant finish. The beer is brewed under contract in Pittsburgh.

Hope

Based on Providence, Rhode Island. Products include **Hope Lager Beer★→★★**, with a hint of new-mown hay; **Hope Bock★→★★**, smooth, with a medium body, and dryish; and **Red Rooster Ale★★**, with a medium amber colour, a smooth, sweetish start, hints of toast or vanilla, and a dryish finish. The beers are produced under contract by Lion, at Wilkes-Barre, Pennsylvania.

Jones

A rock-like Welshman nicknamed "Stoney" Jones founded this brewery in 1907, at the point where coal from the nearby mines was loaded on to the railroad through the Youghiogheny Valley to Pittsburgh. The brewery stands on a sylvan bend in the river, at the hamlet of Smithton. "Stoney's" great grandson is brewmaster, and the company is owned by friends of the family. Beers include the tart **Stoney's★**; the crisp **Esquire Extra Dry★**; and the hoppier **Fort Pitt★★**.

Latrobe

See Rolling Rock.

Lion

Old-established brewery in Wilkes-Barre, Pennsylvania. Products include **Stegmaier 1857★★**, a super-premium lager with a hint of new-mown hay in the nose and a hoppy finish, and **Stegmaier Porter★★→★★★**, once said to contain licorice which it no longer does, but still tastes of it (a small proportion of molasses is used; perhaps that is the tang?). The brewery has also produced a cherry beer, an oatbran lager (for the health-freak market), and a gin-flavoured malt liquor, *Sting Ray*.

Maine Coast Brewing

Portland Lager★→★★ is a Vienna-style lager, with faintly toasty notes and a little balancing hop in the finish. Produced under contract by F.X. Matt.

Manhattan Brewing Company

After a revamp, Manhattan Brewing Company is an even greater asset to New York's limited beer scene. The city's first new-generation brewpub deserves a less grudging appreciation. An ornamental brew-kettle protrudes dramatically from the building, at 40-42 Thompson St and Broome, between 6th Ave and W Broadway, SoHo. Inside, a couple of the ornamental kettles have been removed in the refit, but two survive. The working brewhouse is upstairs. Year-round products include **Manhattan ("Royal") Amber★★★** (1048; 3.9; 4.8), with a beautiful balance of ale fruitiness (perhaps hints of cherry or vanilla?) and hoppy dryness; and the former porter, now re-named **Stout★★→★★★** (1055; 4; 5), is very smooth, gently dry, and has coffeeish notes. The beers are tank-conditioned, fined, held under blanket pressure and served by hand-pump.

Brewer Mark Witty (ex Samuel Smith's) has also produced some interesting seasonal specials, including a wheat beer, a Belgian-style abbey ale and a barley wine. The house lager, **Manhattan Gold★★** began life with a nice hint of Saaz, and has become yet hoppier in recent years. This is produced under contract at F.X. Matt.

Mass Bay

A new lager, a dark Brown Ale, and a nutmeg-spiced Winter Warmer (not tasted) have joined Mass Bay's original product: **Harpoon Ale★★** (1044; 3.7; 4.6), which is fruity, with a cookie-like malt taste and a well-sustained, but gentle, Cascade finish. Draught brews are made by the micro itself, on Boston harbour, Massachusetts Bay. Bottled brews are produced under contract by F.X. Matt.

F.X. Matt

The present Francis Xavier Matt is the third generation of his family to run this handsome independent brewery in Utica, New York. Its own products include **Saranac 1888**★★→★★★ (11.8/9; 3.8; 4.7), a Pilsener type with a good hop character, and **Maximus Super**★★ (4.8-5.2 by weight; 6-6.5 by volume), probably America's best malt liquor...for those with a taste for the style.

F.X. Matt now owns **New Amsterdam Amber**★★→★★★, an aromatic, fruity lager/ale hybrid that was formerly contract-brewed and for a time made in a now-defunct brewpub in the Chelsea neighbourhood of Manhattan. Matt also produces many contract brews.

Mountain Brewers

Near skiing country, at Bridgewater, Vermont. This is a micro producing **Long Trail Ale**★★, reddish in colour; with a a light, soft, body; fruity palate; American hop character, and a good but gentle bitterness.

New England Brewing Company

Micro in Norwalk, Connecticut. The owners plan to move to larger premises, with a brewpub, in Danbury. The original product, **Atlantic Amber**★★→★★★, is a medium-bodied, malt-accented, fruity, brew, modelled on the "steam beers" of the past. A holiday ale spiced with nutmeg (which grows locally) has been produced, and an oatmeal stout for St Patrick's. A Stock Ale is planned.

New Haven Brewing

See Elm City.

Newman

The first micro-brewery in the East, at Albany, New York was ahead of its time, and paid the price. **Albany Amber Beer**★★, a fruity lager/ale hybrid with some hop bitterness, is now produced under contract at F.X. Matt.

Northampton Brewery

Bar and grill making its own all-malt lagers, at Brewster Court, Northampton, Massachusetts. Products have included a fine, Saaz-accented **Gold**★★ (1048); a slightly thin **Amber**→★★ (1048); a dark, smooth **Bock**★★→★★★ (1065); and a fruity, **1055 Steamer** (not tasted).

Pennsylvania Brewing

Spectacular new brewery and beer-restaurant, situated in the old (1880) buildings of the Eberhardt and Ober brewery (closed in 1952), in the Allegheny "Germantown" area, at Troy Hill Rd and Vinial St, to the north of downtown Pittsburgh. Founder Tom Pastorius is a member of a well-known Pittsburgh-German family. The new, solid-copper, brew-kettle is visible from the beer-restaurant. Brews, made by decoction mash, include a clean, malty, Helles, called **Penn Light Lager**★★→★★★ (11.5; 1042); a hoppy **Kaiser Pils**★★★ (12; 1048; 35 units of bitterness); a chocolatey, slightly roasty **Penn Dark**★★ (12; 1048); an aromatically malty, smooth, dryish

Märzen Fest★★★ (14.5; 1058); and a very malty, delicious Bock★★→★★★ (18; 1072). The brewery also has a **Penn Pilsner★★**, quite full in colour for the style, soft and smooth, with a late, hoppy finish. This is the brewpub counterpart to the prototype Pennsylvania Pilsner, made under contract at Jones. These two beers might better be described as being in the Dortmunder style.

Pittsburgh Brewing

Best known for its **Iron City Beer★→★★**, once a hefty brew, still firm in body, but scarcely exceptional. **Iron City Dark★→★★** is one of the better examples of a dark lager, but that is not to say a lot. Pittsburgh is owned by Bond.

Rolling Rock

Cult beer, although its status may owe as much to its evocative name and silk-screened bottle (bearing the mysterious number 33, which even the brewery cannot adequately explain) as to its slender character (hint of new-mown hay in the bouquet, very light palate indeed, crisp). **Rolling Rock★→★★** is the long-established beer of the old monastery town of Latrobe, near Pittsburgh, Pennsylvania. The brewery is now owned by Labatt, of Canada.

Sissons/South Baltimore Brewing

Beer-lovers have long enjoyed the selection at this chatty, pubby bar and restaurant, opposite Baltimore's Cross Street Market; now Hugh Sisson is additionally offering his own ales. Both a refreshing, aromatic, golden **Marble Ale★★→★★★** (1040) and a less distinctive, amber **Stockade Ale★★** (1052) are heartily dry-hopped. Even the **Stout★★** (1046) has a lot of hop aroma before it moves from licorice sweetness to spicy dryness. Rotating specialities have also included a tasty, tart, but smooth **Dunkel Weizen★★★**. The beers have been filtered, but Sisson hopes to cask-condition.

Stoudt

Despite the name, this is a lager brewery, and one of the best on the East Coast. Ed Stoudt, who founded the brewery in 1987, traces his family name back to 1733 in the US and 1535 in Germany. His products include a Saaz-accented **Pilsener★★**; a Munich-style **Gold★★→★★★**; a creamy, malty **Adamstown Amber★★→★★★** and some excellent rotating specialities, which have included a Dortmunder, a Vienna-style lager, a Kulmbacher Dark and a *Rauchbier*. The brewery is found at Adamstown, Pennsylvania, on route 272, between Reading and Lancaster, and adjoins the Black Angus restaurant, with a beer garden and a Sunday antiques market.

Straub

Smallest of the old-established breweries in the US. Family owned and a part of the local folklore in St Mary's, in the Allegheny Mountains, about 160km (100 miles) north of Pittsburgh. **Straub Beer★→★★** has a sweet aroma and palate, a light body and a dry finish.

Vermont Pub and Brewery

Respected beer-maker Greg Noonan (author of "Brewing Lager Beer") now has his own establishment. It is a vaguely Irish pub in an Italianate restaurant (144 College St) in downtown Burlington (a college town and tourist spot on the American side of Lake Champlain, in Vermont). Products include a full-bodied but dry **Kellerbier**★★→★★★ (1050-52); the sweetish, perfumy, but slightly thin (despite its name) **Burly Irish Ale**★★ (1046); a hoppy **Winter Ale**★★ (1045); a **Smoked Porter**★★★ (1048-50), not intense but quite clear in its flavour profile; and a rich **Maybock**★★→★★★ (1056), with plenty of depth. Noonan works with three or four yeasts, has made the occasional tart "sour mash" beer, and has been known to use a lactobacillus to produce a wheat beer in the North German style.

Vernon Valley

Will the outstandingly traditional, German-style beers from this micro survive the takeover by Chapterhouse (see entry)? With its lightly smoked malt, its double boiling system, its wooden fermenters and lagering vessels, its unfiltered **Pilsner**★★→★★★, its outstandingly well-balanced, malt-accented **Dark**★★★→★★★★ and its rich **Bock**★★★ (16.5; 1066), Vernon Valley began with a great contribution to American brewing. Its problem has been its unsuitable location: in a family oriented ski resort and amusement park, two hours from New York City, at Vernon Valley, New Jersey. The brewery is definitely worth a visit, but call first (☎201-827-0034).

Wild Goose

The geese that give their name to this micro-brewery visit its home turf each October, and take their chances with hunters. The Wild Goose Brewery is at the small port of Cambridge on the peninsula that forms the eastern shore of Maryland. Its flagship **Wild Goose Amber Beer**★★ (1051; 4.04; 5.05) is a reddish bronze ale, light-bodied for its gravity, malty but dry, with a dash of hop in the finish. The company also contract-brews the lighter-coloured, softer, sweeter, aromatic **Samuel Middleton's Pale Ale**★→★★, and produces **Thomas Point Light**★, a mainstream golden ale.

Yuengling

The oldest brewery in the United States. Yuengling, founded in 1829 and still family owned, is best known for its **"Celebrated Pottsville Porter"**★★, which has a soft, medium body and a dash of roasty dryness. The brewery is at Pottsville, in the Delaware Valley of Pennsylvania. It other products include **Lord Chesterfield Ale**★→★★, English-sounding but American in style, with a flowery hop character. Both are actually bottom-fermented.

THE SOUTHEAST

Despite hot weather that favours the coldest beer in town, religious fundamentalists who prefer their counties dry, and social attitudes that deem anything but Budweiser or Schlitz a Communist plot, the South is beginning to gain one or two more interesting brews. It is to be hoped that they survive where some worthwhile predecessors have failed.

At the Virginia Brewing Company, Wolfgang Roth is making his classic *Bock*, now under the name Dark Horse. In North Carolina, the Durham branch of Weeping Radish has produced an outstanding dark lager. In Tennessee, Bohannon

Brewing has made an ambitious start. In Georgia, the curiously German town of Helen appears to be getting its own brewery.

Where to drink

In states where they are permitted, brewpubs are popping up, many belonging to chains. Charlotte, North Carolina and Savannah, Georgia, both have branches of the Mill Bakery, Brewery and Eatery, with its original establishment and headquarters at Huntsville, Alabama (2003 Whitesburg Drive; ☎205-533-7029). The Mill is very much a chain operation, but it is sufficiently beer-sensitive to have begun switching from malt extract to full-mash. Its brews include both lagers and ales. Its early branches included three locations in Florida at Tallahassee, Gainesville and Winter Park as well as one in Baton Rouge, Louisiana.

Florida has sprouted with about ten brewpubs. Among those attracting attention in the early days are McGuire's Irish Pub (600 E Gregory St, Pensacola) and the Sarasota Brewing Company, in the town whose name it bears (6607 Gateway Ave). Sarasota has won praise for its Pilsener, Amber Ale and occasional Honey Mead Ale, produced by Gisele Budele, an ethnically German Venezuelan. Louisiana has the pioneering Abita micro-brewery, and New Orleans (the home town of cocktails) has two pubs that specialize in beer. Cooter Brown's (509 S Carrollton) is most notable for the sheer size of its selection. Nearby, Carrollton Station (8140 Willow, at Dublin) is more of a place for the devotee. In a region with few such pubs, two in one city is a luxury.

Abita

The sulphur spring at Abita was once thought to offer protection against yellow fever. Today the town of Abita Springs is little more than crossroads in swampy country, wooded with pecans, magnolias and sweet gum trees, across Lake Ponchartrain from New Orleans. Its modern-day claim to fame is an isolated micro-brewery, producing a dry, malty, **Golden**✲✲ (1040), with some Saaz hop character, a sweeter **Amber**✲✲ (1040) and seasonal specialities. The beers, both lagers, do not taste of sulphur.

Blue Ridge

Brewpub at Charlottesville, in the horse country of the Shenandoah Valley. Produces lagers, ales, a stout and seasonal specials, from a full mash. (Beers not tasted.)

Bohannon

Lindsay Bohannon's family were in the tobacco business, but he prefers beer. His micro-brewery is in the elegant former offices and warehouse of the long-defunct Green Briar whiskey distillery, backing on to the Cumberland river, at Nashville. The brewery is on Second Ave, formerly Market St, which gives its name to the beers. **Market Street Pilsener**✲✲→✲✲✲ is smooth and dry, with a spicy hop finish. Among seasonal specialities, **Market Street Oktoberfest**✲✲✲ (15 Plato; 1060; 4.5; 5.6) has a beautifully sustained aromatic malt character.

Dilworth

New brewpub producing lagers and ales (not tasted), in Charlotte, North Carolina.

Dixie

Much-loved brewery that clung to survival as its two seemingly stronger local rivals in New Orleans went under. Its 1907 building, domed and handsome behind its great iron gates, but run down, retains the original copper as a souvenir and some working cypress vessels. **Dixie Beer★★** is a light lager with some pleasing malt character. **Dixie Amber Light★→★★** is what it says.

Duncan

Produces "own-brand" beers for supermarkets, etc. In Auburndale, Florida.

Federal Hill

This brewery is found in the town of Forest, Virginia. First product is the garrulous **Jefferson Blue Ridge Mountain Traditional Amber Lager Beer★★**, very malty, with a hint of citric fruitiness. Produced under contract by Schell, at New Ulm, Minn.

Greenshields

Brewpub making variety of ales and porter (not tasted) in an old food market at Raleigh, North Carolina.

Helenboch

Helen is in the north of Georgia. It was a logging town until the industry took a downturn, at which point it was converted into an "Alpine" tourist resort (it is at the base of the Appalachians). **Helenboch★★** (not "bock") is a soft, sweetish malty beer of 11 Plato (1044), in broadly the Munich Helles type. A faintly roasty and very pleasant dark lager of the same (1044) gravity is produced under the misnomer **Oktoberfest★★**, and made available in Helen during festive weekends in September and October.

There has also been a hoppy, experimental Pilsener. The beers were contract-brewed by Schell, of Minnesota, while the Helen brewery was under construction.

Hops

Brewpub in Clearwater, east of Tampa, Florida. Very light, sweetish **Golden★** and malty, well-balanced, **Hammerhead Red Ale★★** (13; 1052; 4.6; 5.7). There is an unrelated brewpub called Hops in Scottsdale, Arizona (see Southwest).

Loggerhead

New brewpub making lagers and ales at Greensboro, North Carolina. Too early to rate.

Oldenberg

A Southern brewery by virtue of its location in Fort Mitchell, Kentucky, but just across the river from the Midwestern city of Cincinnati. It looks authentically like a German brewery of the 1880s, but was built in the 1980s, with its own entertainment hall and pub-restaurant. Its principal product is a soft, aromatically malty pale lager **Premium Verum★★→★★★** (11.5; 1042; 3.8; 4.7). Seasonal specialities have included a tawny, smoky **Bock★★** (15.3; 1061; 4.8; 6.0); a faintly medicinal **Stout★★**; and a sour-mash **Summer Beer★★→★★★**. The fruity **Vail Ale★★** is brewed under contract for a company in Colorado.

Tampa Bay Brewing

Hearty beers at a brewpub owned by an enthusiast. Products have included a medium-dry **Pilsner**★★ hopped with Saaz blossoms; a sweetish, sedimented **Wheat Beer**★→★★; a dry **British Red**★★→★★★ (12.75; 1051; 4.5; 5.6), hopped with Fuggles and Kent Goldings; and a dry but chocolatey **Porter**★★ (13; 1052; 5; 6.25). Address: 10330 N Dale, ☏813-264-6669.

Virginia Brewing Company

New company making new beers at the former Chesbay brewery in Virginia Beach, near Norfolk. Its unmemorable brand-name, Gold Cup, is intended to have Virginian horse-racing associations. **Classic Light**★→★★ is hoppy for the style; **Export Beer**★★ (12.4; 1050; 4.1; 5.2) smooth and firm, with a dryish, flowery finish; **Dark Horse**★★★ (16.3; 1065; 5.8; 7.2) an excellent malty *Bock*, again with a flowery finish. This beer is available unfiltered, under the name *Virginia Native*, at the Union St Public House, in Alexandria, Virginia.

Weeping Radish

Large, black-skinned radishes accompany every beer-snack in Bavaria. They are peeled and salted, and must begin to "weep" before they are eaten. Bavarian Uli Bennewitz has brewpubs called the Weeping Radish at Durham and Manteo (Roanoke Island), North Carolina, and a third called the International Fest House, at Virginia Beach. The latter two each produce a sweetish, unfiltered, easily drinkable, **Lager**★★. Durham has filtered beers, with a notably clean palate, including a malty **Helles**★★→★★★; a smooth, toffeeish, **Fest**★★→★★★ (13.5; 1054; 4.4; 5.5); and an outstanding dark lager called **Black Radish**★★★, soft, with a malty start and a dryish finish. Each pub has had several changes of brewer, so beers may vary.

Wild Boar

Based in Atlanta, Georgia, but contract-brewing at Schell. **Wild Boar Special Amber**★★ has a reddish colour, hoppy aroma and malty-fruity palate.

THE MIDWEST

It may no longer be America's brewing capital in volume, or even variety, but the Midwest is fighting back. When the people in the Midwestern cities such as Milwaukee boast of their brewing tradition, they are usually unaware even of its decline at the hands of the giants, let alone its revival in the care of the micros. Schlitz no longer brews in the city it "made famous"; Pabst sounds like a name from the past; Miller is best known for Lite, whatever that means. The good news is that Milwaukee and other Midwestern cities now have micros making more interesting beers; that Chicago, briefly without a brewery, now has six (two micros and four brewpubs); and that there is, more than ever, a distinct flavour to the region's beers. The Midwestern giants made lager the American national style. Now, many of the micros are also specializing in lagers while their counterparts elsewhere in America tend to favour ales.

Where to drink

Every beer-loving visitor to Chicago should make sure they have a glass or two of beer at the Goose Island brewpub (see entry; also for Sieben, Tap and Growler and Weinkeller). It would equally be a shame to miss the Berghoff (17 W Adams and State St, in the downtown "Loop"). Several American cities have famous beer taverns dating from the 1800s, but none quite manages the balancing act achieved by the Berghoff, which is owned by an old brewing family. Somehow, this establishment retains its tradition and integrity (keeping a carefully chosen small selection of well-kept beers) while also thriving as a crowded, stand-up lunch counter (famous for its halibut sandwiches) and an evening oyster bar for today's business people. For a far larger beer selection seek out Quencher's, originally a neighbourhood bar, at Fullerton Ave and Western. For German beers and nationalism try Resi's, on Irving Park Road, west of Lincoln. Chicago also has a remarkably well-stocked retail store for speciality beers and other drinks: Sam's Wine Warehouse (1000 W North, at Clybourn).

Milwaukee has several famous old German restaurants. These include the grand, vaulted dining rooms of Maders (1037-41 N 3rd Ave Tel 414-271-3377), with a long list of beers and a museum of steins. Drinking vessels also form a part of the lavish decor at Karl Ratsch's (320 E Mason). The less elaborate Kalt's (2858 N Oakland, on the east side) has a good selection of beers and a collection of breweriana, including bar-trays of the post-war period. There is a long beer-list and a splendid 1930s interior at the former Schlitz Brewery Tap: the Brown Bottle (221 W Galena Court). There are also good lists at Zur Krone (839 S 2nd St); Gasthaus Nurnberg (3450 E Layton Ave, Cudahy); Gaslight Square, a neighbourhood bar at 4500 W Garfield; and the Port of Hamburg, opposite the airport. Excellent retail stores in Milwaukee are Keller's (5500 W Capitol Drive) and Heiden's (8510 West Lisbon Ave).

Madison, Wisconsin, has two well-known beer bars: Ein Prosit (106 King St) and Essen Haus (514 Wilson St). The Minneapolis/St Paul area has two micros and a couple of brewpubs (see entries for Summit, Page, Sherlock's Home and Taps). Iowa has the Millstream Brewing Company (see entry). See also entries for Indianapolis Brewing, Columbus, Hoster's and Great Lakes, among others. Visitors to Cincinnati should pop over the river to Oldenberg.

Ambier

Good, malty, amber, Vienna-style lager. **Ambier★★★** has been produced under contract by a variety of Midwestern breweries.

Anheuser-Busch

The world's biggest brewing company, headquartered in St Louis, Missouri, and producing almost 90 million barrels a year, shared between a dozen plants across the nation. Anheuser and Busch were related by marriage, and the company – dating from 1860 – is still controlled by the family. The beer called simply **Busch★** was once the most traditional of the company's principal products, but is now the lightest-tasting. Bohemia's royal court brewing town, Budweis, inspired the name of the first beer in the world to be consciously mass-marketed. America's **Budweiser★**, launched in 1876, is the world's biggest selling beer. Budweiser is very light in both body and palate, and sweetish. It has lost some of its already delicate hop character in recent years. A careful blend of famous hop varieties is used, but in such small quantities that their influence is barely perceptible. The beer also has a characteristic hint of apple-like, estery fruitiness. A Bohemian brewing town also inspired the name of the "super-premium" **Michelob**★★, which is fractionally fuller-bodied (a higher malt-to-rice ratio) and better balanced. **Michelob Classic Dark**★→★★ is a pleasant enough beer, but has less character than it promises. **Anheuser**★★ is a new, relatively pale, Märzenbier, with a good, firm, malty body and a dash of hop character. The flagship beers are fined by maturation over beechwood chips, a very old Bavarian technique. Anheuser-Busch also produces a wide variety of "Light" and "Dry" products.

Adler of Appleton

Revival of an old local beer-name by a brewpub in Appleton, near Lake Winnebago, Wisconsin. Among early brews, the sweetish, fruity **Amber**★★; dry, chocolatey, **Porter**★→★★; and rich **Bock**★→★★; have shown the most character.

Blatz

A famous old name now used on a low-price beer by Heileman. The revivalist Val Blatz micro-brewery, in Milwaukee, was opened in the late 1980s to produce speciality beers for Heileman. It made the odd interesting beer, then ceased production after Heileman was acquired by Bond.

Boulevard

New micro-brewery in Kansas City, Missouri. Products have so far included an amber beer and a Scottish ale. Too early to rate.

Brewmasters Pub

In a former monastery building in Kenosha, an industrial port on Lake Michigan, between Milwaukee and Chicago. **Kenosha Gold**★ is a soft, sweetish, lager; **Royal Dark**★★ is malty and pruny; while **Maibock**★★ is rich and malty; and **Nort's Cream Ale**★→★★ has the appropriate tartness. This brewpub has also made specials with cocoa and coffee flavours.

Capital

Capital's beer-garden gave the title Garten Brau to this excellent micro in Middleton, which adjoins Madison, state capital of Wisconsin. Products include a dry, malty, clean-tasting **Lager**★★ in broadly the Munich Helles style; a Pilsener called **Special**★★→★★★ that has lots of hop taste; a light, clean, faintly nutty lager called **Wild Rice**★★ (it contains 15 percent of that raw material); a malty, coffeeish, **Dark**★★; a malty, toasty, **Märzen**★★→★★★; a rich, dark, **Bock**★★→★★★ (14; 1056; 4.5; 5.6); a golden, smooth, malty **Maibock**★★★ (15.25 Plato; 1061; 5 by weight; 6.25 by volume); and an enjoyably spicy **Weizen**★★★ (served with a yeast sediment).

Cherryland

This is a brewpub that uses malt extract in its brews, and is situated in a pizza restaurant at resort of Sturgeon Bay, Wisconsin. Too early to rate.

Chicago Brewing

New micro, producing the aromatic, pale amber, **Legacy Lager**. Too early to rate.

Chiefs Brewing Company

Brewpub, using malt extract, in the college town of Champaign, Illinois. Plans a range. Too early to rate.

Cleveland Brewing Company

Contract-brewer whose principal product is the award-winning **Erin Brew★★**, which might loosely be classified as a cream ale. It has a full, gold, colour and a hoppy, fruity, palate. The beer is made in Pittsburgh. Not to be confused with Great Lakes, which brews in Cleveland at its own pub (see entry).

Cold Spring

Very old plant in Cold Spring, Minnesota. Its **Cold Spring Export★** originally had some Dortmunder character, but that is long gone.

Columbus Brewing Company

Promising ales, made with a mix of whole grain and malt extract, at a very small micro in an old brewery complex in Columbus, state capital of Ohio. Products include a perfumy, hoppy **Gold★★** (9.2; 1037), reminiscent of a Kölsch; a **Pale Ale★★★** (11; 1044) in very much the British style; a **Nutbrown Ale★★→★★★** (13; 1052) with a malty palate and a "winter warmer" character; and a sweetish **Black Forest Porter★★**. The beers are available at Gibby's Tavern, Pete's (a steak restaurant) and Dom's (an oyster bar) all near the brewery.

Detroit Brewery Inc

Brewery planned to service Traffic Jam restaurant, sausage shop, cheese dairy and bakery, near Wayne State University.

Frankenmuth Brewery Inc

Lutheran settlers from Franconia gave their name to Frankenmuth, which has become a tourist town, promoting itself as Michigan's "Little Bavaria". The town's local brewery, founded in 1862, closed in a very run-down condition in the mid 1980s, but soon afterwards a new company built afresh on the same site. Company president Fred Schumacher is a member of the Düsseldorf brewing family. He recruited another German, Fred Scheer, who was already a respected brewmaster in America. A brew-house was imported from Franconia. Products, under the title "Old German", include: a lightly dry **Pilsener★★**; a smooth **Dark★★→★★★**; a buttery-malty, warming **Bock★★★** (1056; 4.8; 6.0); a refreshing and distinctive **Weisse★★★**, lightly sedimented and with a sweet-apple fruitiness; and a well-balanced amber ale, **Old Detroit★★→★★★**, that is reminiscent of Franconia's Maisel Dampfbier. Old Detroit is brewed under contract for a company in the nearby city whose name it bears.

Free State

Well-regarded brewpub at Lawrence, 24km (40 miles) west of Kansas City. Produces a Kölsch-type beer called **Wheat State Golden**, a **Pale Ale**, and seasonal brews that include an Oatmeal Stout for St Patrick's, fruit beers, and a popular **Bock**. Not tasted.

Goose Island

Excellent beers, constantly changing through a well-polished repertoire, at a brewpub in Chicago's Clybourn/Halsted nightlife area. Their products include a clean, lightly hoppy **Golden Goose Pilsener**★★→★★★, with lots of Saaz aroma; something between a Vienna and a Munich Dark called **Lincoln Park**★★★, with a distinctively aromatic, toasty, malt character; the fruity, clean, smooth, **Honker's Ale**★★→★★★, with a faintly buttery Irish character; **Hopscotch**★★, which is dry-hopped and has a distinctively herbal note; a beautifully malty, rounded amber **Maibock**★★★ (17.5; 1070; 5.6; 7.0); and a fruity, spicy, sedimented wheat beer, **Chicago Vice**★★★ (as opposed to Miami Weiss). Knowledgeable staff and good, inventive, food.

Great Lakes

In an 1860s saloon (complete with genuine bullet holes), extending into the former premises of a feed-and-seed store, Jungian academic Patrick Conway and his brother Dan have installed Cleveland's first brewpub, with a modestly serious restaurant downstairs. Hearty products include a soft, perfumy, dryish, Dortmunder named after footballer **John Heisman**★★→★★★; a rounder, deeper, Vienna-style named after local gangbuster **Eliot Ness**★★→★★★; a tawny, malty **Maibock**★★; and specials that have stretched from a strong, aromatic, honey-flavoured **Pils**★★ (5.5; 6.6), with a sweet start and a dry finish, to a ginger-and-honey Christmas beer.

Growlers

Suburban brewpub in Columbus, Ohio, with a brother establishment in Dayton. Friendly and enthusiastic, but beers unambitious. The most interesting are a **Gaelic Ale** and a **Wheat Beer**. Too early to rate.

Heileman

Wisconsin brewer, headquartered in La Crosse, that became national through acquisitions (see Blitz, Rainier and Pearl), then fell into the hands of Bond before that company's troubles. Heileman's Wisconsin products include **Old Style**★, a rather limp beer with a lot of corn in the palate; and **Special Export**★→★★, which has a hint of hop and bears better witness to the company's much-vaunted kräusening.

Hoster

Revival of an old brewery name, near to its original premises, in Columbus, Ohio. The new Hoster's is an excellent brewpub, in an old trolley barn (tramshed). The delicate hop character in the **Double X**★★→★★★ is reminiscent of that in some Pilseners from the Rhineland; the Export-style **Gold Top**★★★ (13.1; 1052-3; 4.3; 5.4) is firm-bodied and well balanced, with a malt accent; **Amber Lager**★★ has a nicely malty finish. Bologna sandwiches are recommended.

Huber

Well-regarded, old-established brewery, back in family hands after a period under another owner. The brewery is in Monroe, Wisconsin, but its products include beers originally made for the Berghoff tavern, in Chicago. **Berghoff Beer**★★→★★★ is firm-bodied and dry, with a nice dash of hop character (reminiscent of Augsburger when it was made by Huber). **Berghoff Dark**★★ has a chocolatey malt character. **Berghoff Bock**★★, with a prune-like sweetness, is one of the better examples of this style from an established brewer. **Dempsey's**★

is a lightly fruity ale originally licensed from a now-defunct micro-brewery in Ireland.

Hudepohl-Schoenling

Merger of the last two old-established breweries in Cincinnati (a town that once had 30). Hudepohl brought into the partnership its super-premium **Christian Moerlein★★**, a creamy, sweetish lager in broadly the Munich Helles style, and brewed according to the Reinheitsgebot, but still not quite as characterful as it might be. **Christian Moerlein Double Dark★★→★★★**, with a good dose of black malt, has more character. The Schoenling speciality is **Little Kings Cream Ale★★→★★★**, a classic example of this hybrid American style. Little Kings is made by a conventional bottom fermentation, and gains some of its distinctive character from the use of Belgian-grown Hallertau hops. The company has over the years produced some good seasonal and anniversary beers.

Indianapolis Brewing Company

Revival of an old name by a new micro. Sad to say, the city's German brewing heritage is not widely remembered, so the company has settled for the brand Main Street (more "American"?). Products include a well-rounded, relatively malty, **Golden Pilsener★★**; a bigger-bodied, and definitely malty, **Premium Lager★★→★★★** (which also has a good, hoppy, finish); and a toffeeish, dark **Bock★★→★★★** (1065; 5.2; 6.5). These well-made, enjoyable, beers are available at the Corner Wine Bar (6331 Guilford Ave, Indianapolis).

Kalamazoo Brewing Company

Talented brewer Larry Bell makes a varying portfolio of tasty, fruity, brews, all top-fermenting, at his tiny micro in Kalamazoo, Michigan. These include the peachy, soft **Great Lakes Amber Ale★★★**; the drier, more aromatic, hoppier, golden **Bell's Beer★★**; and the remarkably warming **Third Coast Old Ale★★★**, starting malty and finishing dry. Specialities have included a cherry stout.

Lakefront

Weekends-only micro run by enthusiasts in Milwaukee. Products include the creamy, clean, well-balanced but hop-accented **Klisch Lager Beer★★→★★★** (named after one of the partners); **River West Stein Beer★★→★★★**, a strong (1065), firm-bodied, hoppy, amber lager; and the smooth, spicy **East Side Dark★★★**. Specialities have included a **Cherry Beer★★★** with a beautiful colour, aroma and fresh fruit character. Made in August, cherries from Door County, Wisconsin. Available at local bars, including Tracks (1020 E Locust).

Leinenkugel

An old-established small brewery, still operating in Chippewa Falls, Wisconsin, although it is now owned by Miller. The flowery, dry, clean beer known simply as **Leinenkugel★★** (or, by devotees, as "Leiny") has something of a cult following. **Limited★→★★** is slightly fuller-bodied, spritzy, with some tartness. **Bock★→★★** is tawny and pleasantly sweet.

Melbourne's

Vaguely "Australian theme" brewpub at Strongsville, south of Cleveland, Ohio. Products include the malty, dry **Bondi Beach**

Blonde★, a lager; the unfortunately named **Wombat Wheat★★→★★★**, which tastes better than it sounds (smooth and, in the unfiltered version, peachy); the sweetish **Perth Pale Ale★→★★**; the darker, chocolatey, **Down Under Ale★★**; and seasonal specials. Australian hops are used.

Miller

Owned by Philip Morris, and very market-oriented. **Miller Lite★**, a pioneer in its segment, is America's second biggest-selling beer. It has been described as "wet air" and "the nearest thing to nothing in a glass". **High Life★** is a dryish premium beer. **Genuine Draft★** (which is sterile-filtered) has a fresh start, smooth body, and watery finish. Miller frequently test-markets beers that sound more characterful, but they rarely are. **Miller Reserve★**, firm-bodied and fruity, with the faintest hint of hop, is a recent example.

Millstream

By a mill stream in the main village of the Amana Church colonies of Iowa. These villages are better known for fruit wines, but this micro adds beer to their offerings. **Millstream Lager★→★★** is sweetish. soft and light; **Schildbrau★★** is a malty, amber lager in broadly the Vienna style; **Millstream Wheat★→★★**, is lightly tart, and filtered.

Pabst

Pabst Blue Ribbon★ was once the blue-collar beer of America, but that slightly chewy brew has lost sales over the years. The Milwaukee brewer now also produces another item of American nostalgia, **Ballantine Ale★→★★**, with its characteristic hint of geranial hop character. Likewise the relatively hoppy **Ballantine IPA★★**.

James Page

Young micro in the old brewery quarter of Minneapolis. **James Page Private Stock★★→★★★** is a hearty, American-accented Vienna-style lager, with plenty of both the malt and the hop in its palate. Page pioneered the use of wild rice in beer, which is native to the Minnesota lake country. He has two products in this style, both taking their name from a natural park on the borders of Minnesota and Canada. **Boundary Waters Wild Rice Beer★★★** is light, clean and dry, but with plenty of flavour. It contains ten percent wild rice. **Boundary Waters Bock★★** also with wild rice, is amber with a clean, sweetish, palate.

Pavichevich

New micro in Chicago, making a Czech-style Pilsener beer, with the odd name of **Baderbrau★★★**, that is outstanding when served fresh on draught, more variable in the bottle. One taster simply exclaimed, "real hops!" when he nosed a (fresh) bottle. This beer has a delightfully flowery bouquet of hops, and some malty sweetness; and both characteristics are sustained through the soft palate to a gentle, elegant, finish. Early brews had a hearty 40 units of bitterness, and it is to be hoped that this standard is maintained.

Point

This brewery has remained independent while other old-established Wisconsin breweries have been bought and sold, and is rightly held in affectionate regard for that. **Point**

Special★→★★ has a sweetish palate, drying toward the finish. The super-premium **Special Edition**★★ is notably maltier, and with more hop character. **Point Genuine Bock**★★ is malty and smooth, with a dryish finish.

August Schell

Not only the prettiest location of any brewery in the United States, but also some interesting beers. Schell, founded in 1860, in New Ulm, Minnesota, has a deer park and gardens open to the public. Products include a good, hoppy **Pils**★★★; a lightly malty **Export**★★; a tawny, rummy **Bock**★★; and a **Weizen**★★→★★★ with a good apple-pie fruitiness. Schell, still owned by the founding family, also produces a wide range of interesting contract-brews (see Pete's among others).

Sherlock's Home

Despite the dreadful pun, this brewpub, in a suburb of Minneapolis, is well worth a visit. Although its lagers – and one ale – are chilled in the American fashion, several of its other products are fined and served (under blanket pressure) at 52°F (11°C), from handpumps. These include **Bishop's Bitter**★★★ (1041), well hopped with Fuggles and Kent Goldings, and with a British-style acidity in the finish; **Piper's Pride**★★→★★★ (1048), a malty but well-balanced Scottish ale; **Palace Porter**★★ (1040), more on the lines of a strong Mild; and **Stag's Head Stout**★★★, dry and faintly medicinal. The *Bishop's* is perhaps as close to an English Bitter as any made in the US. Some seasonal specials, including a hoppy *Old Ale* and a *Winter Warmer* (1080), have been served from wooden "pin"-sized casks.

The owner, Bill Burdick, is distantly related to the late Peter Maxwell Stuart, of the Traquair House brewery, in Scotland. The pub also keeps a good selection of Single Malt Scotches.

Sieben

The name previously belonged to a famous Chicago brewery that closed in 1967. It was revived in 1987, when a new brewpub opened at a former water-bottling plant (436 W Ontario St), in the gentrified inner-city area called River North. The progress of the new Sieben's has been interrupted by frequent management changes, but it is definitely worth a visit. Products have varied considerably. At the most recent tasting, they included a pleasant **Lager**★→★★ with a sweetish start and a dry finish; a sweetish, fruity-hoppy **Amber Ale**★→★★; a fruity-malty, but well-balanced, **Irish Ale**★★→★★★; a relatively thin, coffeeish, **Bock**★→★★; and a tart, light, but firm-bodied **Weiss**★★.

Sprecher

Hearty beers, evoking the traditions that Milwaukee almost forgot. Randy Sprecher worked at Pabst before launching his micro-brewery, across the railroad tracks, down by the riverside, in an old packing plant. Products include: **Special Amber**★★ (13; 1052; 4.3; 5.3), a tasty, malty brew in broadly the Vienna style but with a notably dry finish; **Black Bavarian**★★★ (15; 1060; 4.8; 6.0), smooth and intense, with hints of treacle toffee, but dryish, with a huge finish (worthy of Kulmbach any day); **Irish Stout**★★→★★★ (15; 1060; 4.8; 6.0), hoppy, roasty fruity and enwrapping; **Milwaukee Weiss**★★→★★★ (11.5; 1046; 3.6; 4.5), a lovely pale amber colour, with both acidity and sweetness in the aroma, then an apple-pie character; and **Hefe-Weiss⋆⋆⋆** an unfiltered version, that is full of flavour.

Sterling

Former Heileman brewery in Evansville, Indiana, making budget brands.

Stroh

Based in Detroit (where it no longer brews), Stroh attempted to go national by acquiring Schaefer and Schlitz, then abortively sought a merger with Coors. Although still a national, with several breweries, Stroh is suffering an identity crisis. The beer called simply **Stroh's⋆** is slightly sweeter and fuller-tasting than its rivals. This is due in part to the use of kettles fired by direct flame. The celebrated "fire-brewing" creates hot spots in the kettle, and thus a very faint caramelization. The super-premium **Signature⋆**, slightly fuller-bodied, also has this character. Stroh's has acquired **Augsburger⋆⋆**, which has lost some character in the process.

Summit

Successful micro in St Paul, twin city to Minneapolis. A new, summertime **Sparkling Ale⋆→⋆⋆⋆** (11; 1044; 3.4; 4.3) is light, clean and dry, with a faintly yeasty finish. The well-established **Extra Pale Ale⋆⋆** (12; 1048; 3.9; 4.8), with a malty middle, a good development of perfumy fruitiness and a dry finish, is a more interesting product, though it has lost a little of its attack. **Great Northern Porter⋆⋆⋆** (13.4; 1053-4) is smooth, dry, and slightly herbal at first, but chocolatey in the finish. Summit has produced an excellent malty, strong **Brown Ale** for Christmas. The beers can be found opposite the brewery, at Johnny's and at the micro-brew specialist Shelly's Wood Roast.

Tap and Growler

Brasserie-ish brewpub serving interestingly Mexican-accented food in the Greektown area of Chicago. To add to this cosmopolitan insouciance, its beers include **Eagan's Irish Ale⋆⋆**, creamy, nutty and fruity, and **Northumbrian Ale⋆⋆**, smooth and very dark. There is also a dryish **Amber⋆→⋆⋆** and a sweetish **Lager⋆→⋆⋆**. The beers, brewed from malt extract, are somewhat variable. Address: 901 W Jackson, at Peoria.

Taps

In a former livery stables, adjoining the Riverfront development in Minneapolis, this is a brewpub with live comedy upstairs. Early products, still being perfected, included a **Pilsner⋆⋆** with a malty start and a hoppy finish; a malty **Marzen⋆→⋆⋆** at the low gravity of 11.5 (1046); the golden, fruity, tart, **Nicollet Island Ale⋆⋆**; and a sweetish **ESB⋆→⋆⋆**, again at a relatively low gravity (1050). Address: 25 Main St, SE, ☎612-378-1337.

Water Street

Milwaukee brewpub, at 1101 N Water St, near the old Blatz brewery and the Fine Arts Center. Brews from extract, but beers are well regarded.

Weinkeller

It was meant to be a German Weinstube, and has a good list, but somehow it went on the beer. Its many Bohemian neighbours in the Chicago suburb of Berwyn probably helped. The Weinkeller stocks at least 500 beers, and makes its own. Products include a lightly hoppy **Pilsner★★**; the oddly named **Aberdeen Amber★★→★★★**, which might better be called Düsseldorfer Alt; the dry, fruity **Dublin Stout★★→★★★**, at a hefty 1082, made with yeast from Cooper's of Adelaide; a very malty, faintly phenolic, **Düsseldorfer Doppelbock★→★★** (1086); a plummy, sweetish, **Bavarian Weiss★★** (1042); and a nicely tart but well-balanced **Berliner Weisse★★★** (1042), which the brewery claims to make with a lactic culture. There are also seasonal specials. Address: 6417 W Roosevelt, Berwyn, ☎708-749-2276. Nearest station: Austin (Congress Line).

Zele

Silly name bestowed by the marketing man who acquired the handsome old brewery variously known as Rhomberg, Dubuque Star and Pickett's. Zele is the brand name of a range of fruit-flavoured beers. Perhaps it is churlish to complain: thanks to the new owner, the brewery – on the banks of the Mississippi, at Dubuque, Iowa – is still working. Its more traditional products include an amber version of **Rhömberg★★→★★★** (12; 1048; 3.95; 5.0), a lightly malty, Vienna-style beer; **Erlanger★★**, a paler beer at the same strength, also malt-accented, and described as a Märzen; and the firm-bodied, drier, all-malt **Dubuque Star Private Reserve★→★★**.

COLORADO AND THE SOUTHWEST

Few Americans would nominate Colorado as the nation's biggest brewing state but, in volume, it is. The state's best-known brewery, Coors, is perceived by many consumers as some folksy place in the mountains, but it makes more beer on one site (at Golden, near Denver) than any other in the world: between 15 and 20 million barrels a year. Other states have more breweries, but Colorado's volume of output became the greatest when it gained another large brewery, opened by Anheuser-Busch at Fort Collins, in the north of the state. It is a curiosity that this small town now has four breweries: Anheuser-Busch, a micro and two brewpubs.

From Fort Collins in the north of Colorado to Park City, Utah, to Virginia City, in the far west of Nevada; from Bisbee, Arizona, to Shiner, Texas, the most unlikely towns have breweries. In its broadest sweep, this might be regarded as the Southwest. California, of course, is another country.

Where to drink

Denver has in recent years been the location of the Great American Beer Festival, by far the biggest public tasting of US beers. The date varies, but can be checked with the Association of Brewers (Box 287, Boulder, CO 80306-0287, ☎303-447-0816). Colorado is lucky to have the Old Chicago chain of pizza restaurants, which always have a good beer selection (headquarters: 1102 Pearl St Mall, Boulder, ☎303-443-5031).

Apart from the brewpubs discussed below, there are few well-established and reliable speciality beer-bars in the Southwest. The pickings are especially slim in Nevada and Utah. In Arizona, The Shanty (4th Ave and 9th St, Tucson) looks like a concrete bunker (apart from its copper canopy and door) and serves its beer in frosted glasses, but it does have a loyal following. At the other end of the region, Texas has several worthwhile spots. Austin is a good beer town, especially along 6th St, with Maggie May's (323-325 6th St) a favourite. Dallas has an excellent selection of beers in a cosy little bar called Mimi's (5111 Greenville Ave). At the lower end of Greenville (No. 1520), Flip's has 20 draughts, good food, a rotating exhibition of art, and a high-tech interior. Houston has The Gingerman (5607 Morningside), one of the best beer-bars in America.

Albuquerque Brewing

There are plans to expand, move to full-mash brewing, and open a pub on its present site. In its early years, this was a tiny brewery, even by micro standards, working from malt extract. Despite those limitations, **Michael's Golden Ale**★★→★★★ (1043; 3.4; 4.25) is a clean, crisp, very refreshing brew, with a good hop character. An experimental *Stout*, brewed with triticale (a cross of wheat and rye) was smooth and delicious.

Bandersnatch

A good, English-style Bitter, called **Premium**★★→★★★ (12.8; 1048-51), is sweetish at first, with a hoppy finish; a pleasant **Milk Stout**★★; and a lightly fruity **Cream Ale**★★; all produced from extract. These products are naturally conditioned but served under pressure, or packaged in champagne bottles, at the Bandersnatch brewpub, in a suburb that accommodates the Phoenix Cardinals football team and the Arizona State University. It is linked with a brewpub called Barley's.

Black Mountain

See Crazy Ed.

Boulder

Pioneering micro. Although its beer is available nationally, it is not as well known in its own local market as it should be. The brewery has a tasting bar and lunch room (2880 Wilderness Pl, off Valmont, Boulder ☎303-444-8448). Regular products are a fruity, dry **Extra Pale Ale**★★; a sweeter **Amber**★→★★★; and a roasty, complex **Porter**★★→★★★. Seasonal specials include a tart **Tanker Ale**★★; a **Black Cherry Porter** (not tasted); and an intense, characterful, sweetish **Stout**★★★.

Breckenridge

The Continental Divide provides a backdrop for this ski-resort (3,200m/9,600ft) brewpub, at the old gold-mining town of Breckenridge, Colorado. Products include the pale amber **Avalanche Ale**★→★★, fruity, tart and refreshing; the fuller-coloured **End of Trail Ale**★★, which is drier; a chocolatey, creamy, **Oatmeal Stout**★★→★★★; and a soft, fruity, **Wheat Beer**★★. The brewery also produces the odd *India Pale Ale*.

Cooper Smith's

Smart brewpub in former bakery in Fort Collins. Well-made beers are served under blanket pressure through hand-pumps. Products include: an appropriately dry **Bitter**★★→★★★, with a typically English thinness of body but an American hop character; a malty, very authentic, **Scottish Ale**★★; a smooth, fruity, **Nutbrown**★★→★★★; a burnt-tasting **Stout**★★★; a sherberty **Wheat Beer**★★→★★★; and a chocolatey **Bock**★★.

Coors

The cleanest-tasting mainstream American brew is the one simply called **Coors★★**. It also has enough maltiness, just, to remind the drinker that it is not pure Rocky Mountain Spring Water. Indeed, some of its rivals currently seem lighter in body. Coors also makes a **Light★**; a faintly fruitier **Extra Gold★**; a faintly hoppier **Herman Joseph's★→★★**; a distinctively malty, seasonal **Winterfest★★→★★★** (4.5; 5.6) in broadly the Vienna style; and **George Killian's★★**, an amber lager that is intended to evoke an Irish Red Ale. The company also has "popular price" brands under the Keystone brand. Coors is famously particular about the quality of its barley, and pioneered the use of sterile-filtration as an alternative to pasteurization. Its care is reflected in the clean taste of its products. Their fashionability in some markets has been damaged by the political views of members of the Coors family.

Crazy Ed's Black Mountain

This brewery is situated in the fake Wild West town of Cave Creek, near Phoenix, Arizona. **Black Mountain Gold★★** has a malty start and a hoppy finish, with a hint of Saaz. It is occasionally available unfiltered. **Frog Light★** is on the sweet side. Black Mountain is a micro, but the beers are featured at the adjoining Crazy Ed's Satisfied Frog saloon, where they are served too cold to taste, in Mason jars.

Dallas Brewing Company

Unusually elaborate extract micro-brewery, once called West End. Brands have included **Outback**, **Bluebonnet** and **Texas Cowboy**. Products unambitious, and variable.

Electric Dave

A strange, although colourful, location. The brewery is reached by a road that runs through a culvert into a crater created by copper mining, in Bisbee, Arizona. Electrician-turned-brewer Dave Harvan always offers one golden beer and one dark. Different styles of golden beer are made according to the time of year. The Pilsener version of the neatly named **Electric Light★★** is soft, clean, smooth and malty. **Electric Dark★★** (1050) is a clean, chocolatey, Munich-style (or Kulmbach?) lager.

Hops

Cafe-style brewpub, with good food and wine, in fashionable Scottsdale, a suburb of Phoenix. Products include a dryish **Pilsner★→★★**; a spicy **Weizen★★**; a fruity **Pale Ale★★** (1054); a malty **Amber★★→★★★**; and a rather stout-like **Bock★→★★**. With the exception of the Amber, all are on the light side in flavour profile.

Lone Star

Chauvinistic Texans swear by **Lone Star★→★★**, a dryish beer with a slight sharpness in the finish, but not exceptional. The brewery, in San Antonio, is owned by Heileman.

Manzano Mountain

Garage-based ale brewery in Tijeras. Products include the dry **Duke City Wheat★→★★**; the soft, fruity, bronze-coloured **Sandia Peak★→★★**; and the smooth, hoppy, reddish **Class Axe Classic★★**. Linked with Class Axe rock band.

Odell

Decorated with sun signs and terracotta, this micro-brewery is in a former Mexican tile shop underneath a grain elevator in Fort Collins. Products include a perfumy, dry-hopped (with Saaz) **Wheat Beer**★★→★★★ (1045; 3.8; 4.7); a malty-fruity **Golden Ale**★★ (1050; 4.2; 5.3); and a smooth, nutty, Scottish-style **Ninety Shilling**★★★ (1056; 4.8; 6.0).

Old Colorado

In a grandiose old hotel that fell upon hard times before closing (the lobby is now a second-hand bookstore). Old Colorado, in Fort Collins, is a brewpub. Idiosyncratic brews include a Pilsner that needs more work; a very fruity, hoppy, reddish-amber ale called **Fort Collins Pride**★★; **Poudre River Porter**★→★★, with notes of apple-ester and chocolate; and a light-bodied but smooth, sweetish **Oatmeal Stout**★★→★★★.

Pearl

The light, sweetish **Pearl**★ and the similar **Jax**★ are made in San Antonio, Texas, at a brewery owned by the Pabst group.

Pendleton

Brewpub that operated for a short time in Paradise Valley, Arizona. Its brewers later sought to contract an ale/lager hybrid called **Desert Red**. Possibility of reopening.

Preston

Smallest brewery in America, making half-barrel batches in the old railroad station at Embudo, where the "Chili Line" ran between Santa Fe and Taos, New Mexico (state highway 68). The speciality is a wonderfully aromatic, dry, peppery **Taos Green Chili Beer**★★★. This golden brew is "dry-hopped" with roasted chilis. Other products have included a dry **Wheat**★★; a well-balanced **Mesa Pale Ale**★★; an aromatic, malty, fruity **ESB**★★→★★★ (4.4; 5.5); a honey-flavoured **Stout**★★→★★★ that is nonetheless very dry; a hoppy **Wee Heavy**★★→★★★ that is more of a barley wine; and a dark brown **Gingered Ale**★★. The beers are served at the adjoining Embudo Station restaurant (mainly summer months: ☎505-852-4704), with a terrace on the banks of the Rio Grande.

Reinheitsgebot

The name is an allusion to the German Beer Purity Law, which inspired this micro-brewery at Plano, in Collin County, on the edge of Dallas. **Collin County Pure Gold**★★★ is a Pilsener-style beer with a firm body and a herbal hop aroma. **Collin County Black Gold**★★→★★★ is dark, and relatively light-bodied, with some coffeeish dryness.

San Francisco

Brewpub in Tucson using extract and some grain. Produces a sweetish **Wildcat Ale**★→★★ and other products. Has undergone changes of ownership.

Santa Fe Brewing Company

On a horse ranch at Galisteo, in the High Mountain Desert of New Mexico, about 32km (20 miles) southeast of Santa Fe. This micro produces just one brew: the bottle-conditioned **Santa Fe Pale Ale**★★→★★★ (12.2; 1049; 4; 5), soft and smooth, malt accented, with some fruit and a long, gentle, hoppy dryness in the finish. The company also has a beer-bread mix and a beer jelly. The ale is widely available in New Mexico.

Schirf

In unlikely Utah, a micro and brewpub producing **Wasatch Premium**★★, a hoppy but well-balanced ale, and **Wasatch Gold**★★, a flavoursome wheat beer. The great-granddaughter of the founder of Schlitz is the brewer. The brewery is in Park City, a ski resort 40km (25 miles) east of Salt Lake. There is also an unrelated brewpub, Squatter's, in Salt Lake City.

Shiner

Spanish mission-style building in a tiny town about 112km (70 miles) south of Austin and slightly farther from San Antonio. Originally brewed for a scatter of incongruous Bohemian and Bavarian settlements, which vestigially survive. Today, **Shiner Premium**★ is a light, undistinguished, American lager. **Shiner Bock**★→★★ is a dark counterpart. Shiner contract brews a tastier, ale-like, bronze-coloured beer called **Pecan Street**★★, which is soft and fruity, with a pleasantly hoppy finish.

Southwest Brewing

Tiny micro in Tucson, brewing from extract and some grain. An early product was **Catalina Cream Ale**★★ (1042). It is, in fact a reddish ale, malty, with a hint of sweet sherry. Available at Blue J's (University and Euclid).

Telluride Beer

The Colorado ski resort gives its name to **Telluride Beer**★→★★, a light, dryish lager brewed under contract elsewhere.

Union Brewery

At the Union Saloon, in Virginia City, formerly a gold and silver-mining town, in the Comstock area, south of Reno, Nevada. Because a brewery operated there from 1864 until the late 1890s, the present owners were permitted to restore one in 1987. There are no other breweries in Nevada and, since Prohibition, the state has had a law forbidding any new ones. **Union Beer**★→★★ is a hearty, amber lager in broadly the Vienna style, served very cold.

Vail Ale

Colorado ski resort brew. **Vail Ale**★★ (12.5; 1050; 4.2; 5.25), fruity and sweetish, is produced under contract at Oldenberg (see Southeast).

Walnut Brewing

An early 1900s post-and-beam building on Walnut St, in the downtown area of Boulder, Colorado. This brewpub makes a lightly tart **Swiss Trail Wheat Ale**★★; a soft, full-textured, dry, hoppy **Big Horn Bitter**★★★ (1052); a smooth, clean **Old Elk Brown Ale**★★→★★★ (1056); and a creamy, roasty **Devil's Thumb Stout**★★→★★★ (1064-6).

Wynkoop

A busy brewpub in the revived old warehouse district of Denver. Good food, and live jazz most nights. While some beers are served cold, others are only lightly chilled, held under blanket pressure, and dispensed from handpumps. Products include: **Wilderness Wheat★★→★★★**, lightly plummy; **Mär-zen★★→★★★**, golden, malty and sweetish (lagered for a minimum of four weeks); **India Pale Ale★★→★★★** 1044-48), soft, fruity and dry (aged on oak chips); **Extra Special Bitter★★→★★★** (1048), good and hoppy; **Special Old Bitter★★★** (1048), hoppier still (Tuesday nights only); **Quinn's Scottish Ale★★** (1052), malty and chocolatey, with some bitterness in the finish; **Sagebrush Stout★★** (1055), soft, dry and herbal-tasting. The **IPA**, **ESB** and **SOB** are dry hopped, the latter for three or four weeks.

HAWAII

Despite its superficially glitzy image, Hawaii is not the most sophisticated of regions gastronomically, and is therefore not very beer-aware. It has in recent years gained two local micros, but both have experienced a tough time in their local market. One, the Honolulu Brewing Company, produces the all-malt **Ko'olau Lager Beer★★**, well balanced, with a nicely hoppy finish. Its other products include the slightly fruity **Diamond Head Dry★** and the sweetish **Pali★**.

The other micro makes the faintly malty **Maui Lager★→★★**, on the island of the same name.

Both the Ko'olau and Maui lagers seem to have lost some of their attack since they were launched. Ko'olau (pronounced with a glottal stop) refers to the mountains whence the brewery's water flows. Hawaii veterans will remember **Primo**, an undistinguished local beer that was taken over by Schlitz.

CALIFORNIA

There are more breweries, by far, in California than in any other state, but this is a very recent phenonemon. There were just four national giants, plus Anchor Steam, when America's first micro-brewery, New Albion, fired its kettle in Sonoma, California, in the late 1970s. New Albion did not survive (although its crew and its yeast went on to make Red Tail Ale in Mendocino County), and by the early 1990s there were between 60 and 70 breweries in the state. Among them are Anchor and Sierra Nevada, two of the world's great speciality breweries. Southern California was much slower to develop micro-breweries than the Northern part of the state. This may be in part due to Southern California's hotter climate, which does not favour speciality beers. Perhaps Southern California, more transient and faddish, did not have the attention span to grasp such an idea easily. Speciality beers have been especially successful in the San Francisco Bay area and the wine country, where a serious interest in the characteristics of food and drink is never far from view. No doubt the micro-brewery movement, having established its first America foothold among the vines in Sonoma, benefitted from the precedent set by the boutique wineries.

Anchor Steam's principal, Fritz Maytag, grows famous Cabernets (and olives, and has a share in his family's cheese business); the founders of the Santa Cruz Brewing Company were originally wine-growers; the brewer at Butterfield formerly made wine at Heitz; there are many other similar examples. The University of California at Davis, which is oriented toward agriculture and winemaking, even has a department dealing with brewing.

Where to drink

California is the land of brewpubs, although many of them offer very similar selections ("We have our Gold, our Amber, our Dark..."). Apart from its many brewpubs, California has one of the best beer-bars in America, specializing in West Coast micro ales on draught: Father's Office (1018 Montana Ave, Santa Monica, ☎213-393-1337). For a large selection of bottled imports, try Barney's Beanery (8447 Santa Monica Boulevard, W Hollywood). Both are in the Greater Los Angeles area. In the middle of the state, the town of San Luis Obispo has an outstanding speciality beer-bar called Spike's (570 Higuera St. ☎805-544-7157). Check Spike's for information on the California Festival of Beers, which usually takes place in San Luis Obispo around Memorial Day Weekend, in May.

The largest combined festival of American and imported beers to be held anywhere takes place in San Francisco on a weekend in early to mid July under the auspices of the local public television and radio station (For information: KQED, 500 8th St, ☎415-553-2230). Both of these events are fundraisers, as is the Celebrator Summerfest, which takes place in San Francisco in late August. This is organized by the *Celebrator*, a bi-monthly newspaper for beer-lovers, which has listings of breweries, bars, and stores all over the state (Box 9001 No 52, Pleasanton, CA 94566, ☎415 447 7727). In the East Bay area, Lyon's Brewery (7294 San Ramon Rd, Dublin) is actually a pub, renowned for its draught selection. Lovers of Belgian beer should take a trip to Mrs Coffee and Bistro (Nob Hill Shopping Center, 3004 Pacific Ave, Livermore. ☎415-449-1988). Among the many beer-aware establishments in San Francisco, Le Petit Cafe is recommended (2164 Larkin. ☎415-776-5356). Several New Wave nightspots in Haight St, notably Toronado (547 Haight St), offer an odd environment for speciality brews.

There are very good beer selections at the Cannery Wine Cellars (2801 Leavenworth) in San Francisco, and the Wine Exchange (452 1st St E) on the town square at Sonoma.

Alpine Village

With Disneyland nearby, visitors might easily be confused. The Alpine village may be a fake, but the brewery is genuine, making a light, sweetish, malty **Lager**★★ and a very good, hoppy, dry, **Pilsner**★★→★★★. These products have developed well in the hands of Bavarian brewer Ludwig Erl. The brewery (☎213-329-8881), its adjoining beer-hall, a wedding chapel and the "20 unique European shops" of Alpine Village serve an unlikely German community among the oil refineries of industrial Los Angeles (833 W Torrance Boulevard).

Anchor

The renown of this small San Francisco brewery has gradually spread across the nation, although its greatest claim to fame is not always understood. The point is that its principal product, **Anchor Steam Beer**★★★★ is made by a process unique to the United States (and, for more than 60 years, to this brewery). Anchor Steam Beer is not only a (protected) brand but also a style. Before refrigeration reached the West, pioneering brewers used lager yeasts at natural temperatures, in unusually shallow vessels that resemble coolers as much as fermenters. Anchor Steam is still made in this way, albeit with more control, and in the distinctive style of vessels. The result is a beer that has some of the roundness of a lager but the fruitiness of an ale, with a characteristically high natural carbonation. It is also an all-malt beer, with a very good hoppy dryness (the varietal accent being clearly Northern Brewer). The brewery also makes a rich, creamy, faintly herbal, **Porter**★★→★★★ that might better be described as a bottom-fermenting medium Stout. Anchor's intensely aromatic, hoppy-tasting (Cascade accent), dry, top-fermenting **Liberty Ale**★★★→★★★★ is an American classic, widely copied. Its **Old Foghorn Barley Wine**★★★→★★★★ (1100), matured for 9 to 18 months) is beautifully rounded, soothing and warming. Its **Wheat Beer**★★, the first in America since Prohibition, is very light, clean and delicate, with a hint of honey and apple. From Thanksgiving through Christmas to New Year, a different **Holiday Ale**, is available each year. A particular field of barley is earmarked, so to speak, for this brew. In 1989, Anchor made a beer from bread, according to Sumerian practice, and called it **Ninkasi**. This special brew was aromatized with dates and honey, and had a nutty, spicy, sherryish, character. Anchor was founded in 1896, and given a new life by its present owner, Fritz Maytag, in the late 1960s. Its products are of impeccable quality, and it has been an inspiration to the new generation of speciality brewers that began to spring up in the late 1970s.

Anderson Valley

Well-regarded ales which are smooth, clean, complex and beautifully balanced, in the bottle or from the brewpub, at Boonville. Brand-names are derived from the patois allegedly once used by hop-growers, and now by cultivators of marijuana, in this backwoods valley in Mendocino County. **Poleeko Gold**★★ is soft, lightly citric and dry; **Boont Amber**★★★ has a wonderful complex of fruit and hop, starting sweet and finishing dry; **Deep Enders Dark**★★ is a chocolatey but dry porter; **Barney Flats Oatmeal Stout**★★★ is beautifully silky; **High Rollers Wheat Beer**★★ is very fruity. Seasonal specials have included a fruity, aromatic *Wild Blackberry Ale*.

Angeles

British-accented ales from a brewery in suburban Chatsworth. **Angeles Amber Ale**★★→★★★ has a full copper colour, a medium body, a malt accent, and pleasing hop dryness in the finish. A similar, perhaps more assertive ale, called **Rhino Chasers**★★→★★★, is produced for a marketing company in LA.

Back Alley

Student-oriented brewpub in Davis. Early products included a golden, malty **Pale Ale**★; a fruity **Amber**★→★★; and a sweetish **Porter**★.

Belmont

Beach brewpub. At the beginning of the pier, at Belmont Shore, Long Beach. Early products included the tart, dry-hopped **Marathon Ale**★★ and the sweeter, fruitier, amber-red **Full Sail Ale**★→★★, not to be confused with a product of the same name from Oregon. A Brown Ale and a Porter, to be called Long Beach Crude, were planned.

Biersch

See Gordon Biersch.

Bison

Offbeat beers, in a constantly changing repertoire, from a brewpub with distinctively Post Modernist interior, in the student town of Berkeley. Early examples have included a **Honey Basil Ale**, which defied rating, but tasted robustly of both ingredients; a sweetish **Nutbrown Ale** with carob; and a sharp, dry **IPA** with wormwood, matured over oak chips. This *is* California.

Brewpub on the Green

Golf-course brewpub at Fremont. Early products included the lightly fruity **Hole in One Lager★** and the coffeeish **Mission Peak Porter★★**.

Brown St

A Ginseng Beer, pale, light and dry, tasting of the herb, and surprisingly more-ish, is one of the specialities of this engaging brewpub in the wine capital, Napa. A Ginseng porter is also promised. Other products include a Chili Beer, with a splendidly long, peppery, finish, and some notably smooth brews in more conventional styles. These include a fruity **Wheat Beer★★**; a rich, chocolatey **Brown Ale★★→★★★**; and a faintly medicinal, strong **Stout★★**.

Buffalo Bill

Pioneering brewpub established by Bill Owens, a feisty propagandist for the movement, on the East Bay at Hayward. His everyday beers are characteristically rough-and-ready, unfiltered lagers, but there is always a surprise, for example his seasonal pumpkin ale, with a cinnamon spiciness. Owens has written books on brewpub operation, maps and guides. He also owns the lively *American Brewer* magazine.

Butterfield

Hearty products from a brewpub in the Central Valley city of Fresno. **Bridal Veil Ale★★** (named after a waterfall) is reddish-amber, soft, slightly chewy, with a balance of aromatic hop and fruitiness. **Tower Dark★★→★★★** is hoppy and dry, but with a malty mouth-feel. Somewhere between a strong dark bitter and a porter.

Calistoga Inn

Italianate chalet-style bed-and-breakfast, restaurant, brewpub and beer-garden at Calistoga, in the Napa Valley. A delightful spot, although its beers are less consistent since a change of ownership. Products include a dryish, hoppy **Lager★→★★** and a rich, spicy **Red Ale★★→★★★**. Also known as the Napa Valley Brewing Company.

Callahan's

Brewpub in a suburb of San Diego. Early products included a sweetish **Shamrock Gold★→★★** and a nutty **Callahan Red★★**.

Crown City

In the old winter resort of Pasadena, part of the Los Angeles metro area. Crown City is a brewpub in a renovated china factory, now a small mall. Products include a sweetish, fruity **Amber★** and a **Porter★→★★** with a hint of blackcurrant. After a hesitant start, Crown's products continue to develop. The pub has a wide range of American and imported beers.

Dead Cat Alley

Not quite a biker brewpub, but with tendencies in that direction. Established by micro veteran Jim Schlueter. Products, also available in the bottle, include: a lightly hoppy **Lager**★→★★; a malty, fruity, dry, reddish **Ale**★→★★; and a dry, smooth **Porter**★→★★.

Devil Mountain

This well-regarded brewery has now moved to Benicia, where it operates as a micro, but it still supplies the Devil Mountain Pub at Walnut Creek (850 S Broadway. ☎415- 935-2337). Products include the golden, well-balanced, tasty **Gayle's Pale Ale**★★ (1045); the malty, Scottish-accented **Railroad Ale**★★→★★★ (1066); and the smooth, coffeeish, gentle **Devil's Brew Porter**★★→★★★ (1052). The much-loved, malty **Iron Horse Alt**★★→★★★ (1048) re-named Devil Mountain Draught.

Emery

Visitors to San Francisco might want to take in this pleasant brewpub, with very drinkable beers, at Emeryville, near Oakland and Berkeley. Products include the golden, fresh, fruity, dryish **Christie Pale Ale**★★; **Emery Amber Ale**★★→★★★, with an appetizingly hoppy finish; and **Powell Street Porter**★★→★★★, chocolatey and dry. Seasonal specials have included a clean, fruity, sedimented **Wheat Beer**★★.

Etna

Revival of an 1870s brewery (closed at Prohibition), on the site of its bottling hall, by Andrew Hurlimann, the stepson of the founding family (who came from Alsace-Lorraine). Etna (population: 770) was a gold-mining (and hop-growing) town. It is north of Mount Shasta, and south of Yreka. The first product, **Etna Light Ale**★→★★ is clean, soft, fruity and dry. The local blackberries may feature in a future beer.

Eureka

Star chef Wolfgang Puck is one of the partners in this sizable micro, which shares premises with the stylish Eureka restaurant. The brewery stresses that its beer is brewed according to the Reinheitsgebot. Its initial product, a Pilsener, has a firm, malty, body and plenty of hop in the finish. It is to be hoped that this hop character is maintained. **Eureka California Lager**★★→★★★ expresses its aromatic, dry, character very well in the unfiltered version offered in the restaurant.

Firestone and Fletcher

Produces a non-alcoholic beer.

Golden Pacific

See Thousand Oaks.

Gordon Biersch

This is a classic brewpub in Palo Alto, home town of Stanford University. It has serious beers, in German styles; an inventive menu, of a high standard; and good service. Generally, the same applies at a new branch in San Jose, although some of the beer has been served a little young.

Products include a malty but firm **Export**★★★; a classic **Marzen**★★★, slightly dry for the style; and a tasty, slightly roasty, **Dunkles**★★→★★★.

Gorky's

Arty, cafeteria-style, with Russian food and its own beer. Open round the clock at weekends. Early brews included: **Baltic Light★**; **Gorky's Russian★★**, a hoppy Pilsener-type; **Gorky's Red★★**, a dry-hopped ale; and a **Russian Imperial** (not tasted). Recent reports vary.

Grapevine

In "Grapes of Wrath" country. The Grapevine is the name of a stretch of Interstate 5 that threads through mountains northwest of Los Angeles, in the direction of Bakersfield. From downtown Los Angeles, it is about 128km (80 miles) to the Frazier Park exit, which leads to the Grapevine brewpub, built in the style of an 1890s saloon, in the middle of nowhere, a mile or two from Lebec. Early products, all very clean-tasting, included a malty **Special Lager★★**; a hoppy, well-balanced, **ESB★★★**; and a chocolatey **Dry Stout★★**.

Heritage

At a new beach development and para-sailing resort called Dana Point, about half way between San Diego and Newport, Orange County. Despite the location, it is an unpretentious bar-restaurant. Products, all top-fermenting, include the malty, perfumy **Lantern Bay Blonde★★** (1056); the fruity, smooth **Sail Ale★★** (1060); a tart, hoppy **IPA★★→★★★** (1060); a rich **Nutbrown★★★** (1060) and a slightly chewy, chocolatey, **Porter★★** (1062).

Hogshead

In the Old Town area of Sacramento. Cellar bar founded by micro pioneer Jim Schlueter, now under new ownership. Early product was a malty, sweetish, **Hogshead Lager★★** (1050).

Hübsch

The spectacular, copper-clad vessels of Privatebrauerei Hübsch are the dominant feature of Sudwerk, an impressive pub in Davis. (20001 2nd St, ☎916-758-8700). The brewhouse makes the house beer, **Hübsch-Brau Lager★★→★★★**, which is soft, malty, and served unfiltered. It is also available in the bottle, where it will "fine" in the fridge. Once the yeast has settled, the malt accent emerges loud and clear. Hübsch, which means "pretty" in German, is the surname of the mother of one of the owners. Sudwerks means "brewhouse".

Humboldt

Situated in the far north, on Humboldt Bay, at Arcata, this is a "Frontier" brewpub whose founders include Mario Celotto (former linebacker with the Oakland Raiders). Products, all top-fermented, include **Gold Rush★→★★**, soft, fruity and dry; **Red Nectar★★**, smooth, slightly buttery, very tasty; **Appleton Brew★★**, hearty, with a sweetish start and a roasty finish; **Storm Cellar Porter★★**, with an espresso-chocolate character; the smooth **Harvest Stout★★**; and the firm, hefty, **Oatmeal Stout★★→★★★** (1060).

Huttenheim

Jack London lived in Benicia, Gentleman Jim Corbett fought there, and now the Huttenheim brothers, veterans of the Californian wine industry, have started a brewpub at 321 First St, overlooking the Carquinnez Straits. Their products include a flowery, slightly tart **Lager**; a gently fruity, sedimented **Waterfront Weiss**; a malty, fruity **Sunset Amber**; and a dry **Shipyard Stout**. Too early to rate.

J. and L.

Jim and Lee are the partners in this new micro, in San Raphael, but it needs a more memorable name. Early products include a tart, dry, **Traditional Pale Ale**. Too early to rate.

Kelmer's

Sports-accented brewpub in Santa Rosa, a college town in the county of Sonoma. Products, all top-fermenting, have included the soft, lemony **Big 100 Wheat Beer★→★★**; the golden **Krystal★→★★**, smooth and dryish; the copper **Klassic★★** has a good balance of malt and hop; the chocolatey **Klout Stout★★→★★★**; and seasonal specials. Beers have been quite variable, and are served very cold. Also worth a visit in Santa Rosa: the Wild Hare Pub, with about 30 draughts.

Karl Strauss

See Old Columbia.

Lind

A veteran of the movement, Roger Lind, now has his own micro at San Leandro. Products include: **Drake's Gold★★→★★★** (1050), a wheat accent, and evident dry-hopping; **Drake's Ale★★→★★★** (1054), smooth and hoppy; **Captain Porter★★→★★★** (1058), chocolatey but dry; and **Sir Francis Stout★★→★★★** (1064), spicy, with a big, rounded finish.

Lost Coast

Brewpub in the town of Eureka (617 4th St), on Humboldt Bay. Mammoth Lakes. There is also a brewpub in a ski resort of same name which uses extract and some whole grain. Early products are somewhat astringent. Too early to rate.

Marin

A ferry ride from San Francisco, at 1809 Larkspur Landing Circle (☎415-461-4677). Products have included the deep golden **Mount Tam Pale Ale★★→★★★** (1058), with a fruity start and a very hoppy finish; the sweetish **Albion Amber★★** (1054); the malty **St Brendan's Irish Red★★→★★★** (1068); an aromatic Imperial-style **Stout★★→★★★** (1072-76); the herbal-tasting, dry-hopped, **Old Dipsea Barley Wine★★★** (1072-76); and a soft, perfumy **Raspberry★★★** wheat beer.

Mendocino

The New Albion yeast, and two of the brewers, went to Hopland. So America's original micro begat one of the country's first brewpubs, in the 100-year-old Hop Vine Saloon. This establishment, with a decorative kiln added, is in the town of Hopland, which constitutes a few hundred yards of Highway 101, about 144km (90 miles) north of San Francisco. This was originally hop country, but now grows wine grapes.

The brewery still grows hops in its beer-garden. Its brews include the golden, lightly fruity, sweetish **Peregrine Pale Ale★→★★** (1044); the bronze, fuller-bodied and much hoppier **Blue Heron Pale Ale★★** (1054); the justifiably renowned **Red Tail Ale★★★** (1054), copper-coloured and beautifully balanced; seasonal specialities like **Eye of the Hawk★★→★★★** (1062), a strong, malty ale; and **Black Hawk Stout**★★ (1054), medium-dry, fruity and chocolatey. Visitors who are staying in the area can book a room at the Thatcher Hotel, next door. Mendocino's beers are available in the bottle.

Mission

The original Mission Brewery, which opened in San Diego in 1913, closed four years later, and failed to reopen after Prohibition. The site is now being renovated to house a new micro-brewery and restaurant. Initial plans are for a range of ales and a porter.

Monterey

Brewpub at Monterey.

Napa Valley

See Calistoga. Also Brown St and Willet's.

Nevada City

Despite its name, Nevada City is in California, albeit on the way to Reno. With its location in the Sierras, it has become a retreat for writers and artists, who can also enjoy local micro-brewed beers. **Nevada City Light**★→★★ is malty and fruity. **Nevada City Dark**★★ is a Vienna-style lager with a clean, sweetish, palate.

North Coast

Excellent beers from a smartly fitted brewpub and micro in a former chapel of rest at the old port of Fort Bragg, in Mendocino County. Its flagship product, named after one of the founders, is **Ruedrich's Red Seal Ale**★★→★★★ (1057), fresh, fruity, and soft, with an appetizingly dry finish. **Old No 38 Stout**★★★ is creamy, chocolatey, fruity, with lots of aromatics in its flavour development, and a dry finish.

Obispo

German-style lagers planned by a prospective micro in the town of San Luis Obispo.

Old Columbia

The full name of this brewery is Karl Strauss' Old Columbia Brewery and Grill. Strauss, a German-born veteran of American brewing, has consulted for many micros, but has family links with this one. Products include **Gaslight Gold**★★, a firm-bodied, mild interpretation of the Dortmunder style; **Columbia Amber Lager**★→★★, lightly malty, with some hop in the finish; **Downtown After Dark**★→★★, vaguely in the style of a British ale; **Black's Beach**★→★★, dryish and Porter-like; and **Red Trolley**★★→★★★, a fruity strong (4.4; 5.5) ale.

Pacific Coast

Outstanding ales, from a rather reticent brewpub in Oakland. Products include: a remarkable English-style dark **Mariners' Mild**★★★ (1040), with a reddish-brown colour, and a light, smooth, fruity, refreshing palate; the very hoppy **Gray Whale Ale**★★→★★★ (1052); the rounded, assertive, very big, dry-hopped **Blue Whale Ale**★★★, matured over oak chips; and **Killer Whale Stout**★→★★★ (1050), smooth, dry and herbal. Pacific Coast is opposite the Oakland Convention Center. No visitor to the San Francisco Bay area should miss it.

Pasa Robles

Commercial home-brewery. The reddish Dry Land Lager has been variable in character.

Pete's

California-based contract brewer whose beers are produced by Schell, far away in Minnesota. **Pete's Wicked Ale★★→★★★** has a dark, reddish colour and is splendidly assertive, with a strong winey character. There are several other products.

Rubicon

Well-regarded brewpub in Sacramento. Products include a dry **Pilsener★★→★★★**; a **Summer Wheat★★** with a lot of hop in the finish; an **Amber★★→★★★** that is again well-hopped; an intensely hoppy **IPA★★★** (16.2 Plato; 1065); a malty springtime doppelbock called **Legislator★★** (Sacramento is the state capital); the coffeeish, burnt-tasting **Ol' Moe's Porter★★→★★★**; and a spectacular **Winter Wheat Wine★★★** (28 Plato; 1120), fruity, smooth and warming, but not at all cloying. There have been several other excellent products. The brews are naturally carbonated but usually filtered.

San Andreas

On the fault line, in the small country town of Hollister. This brewpub suffered only minor damage in the 1989 quake, but one or two of its immediate neighbours were less lucky. Some blamed the brewery for tempting providence with its **Earthquake Pale Ale★★→★★★** (1036), golden and extremely dry but hardly vengeful. **Kit Fox Amber★★** (1044), named after an endangered species, is maltier but still dryish. **Earthquake Porter★★** (1042) is chocolatey, dry and fruity. **Survivor Stout★★** (1048) is coffeeish and dry. On occasion the brewery has "dry-hopped" its beers with woodruff. This produces a minty, aromatc, complex product that is worthy of further exploration. Despite its eccentricities, San Andreas is a family oriented brewpub, in a former milk bar. The beers are available in the bottle.

St Stan's

See Stanislaus.

San Francisco

In the heart of San Francisco, at the beginning of the North Beach restaurant neighbourhood, a 1907 saloon now houses a brewpub that is definitely worth a visit. Products, good at their best but somewhat variable, have included a Pilsener-style **Lager★→★★** (upper 1040s), dry and spritzy; **Emperor Norton★★** (upper 1050s), amber, soft, and broadly in the Vienna style; **Gold Rush Ale★★**, amber, fruity and tart; and a chocolatey, medium-dry **Porter★★**.

Santa Cruz

This seaside resort in Northern California gives its name to a brewing company based in a popular pub (516 Front St, ☎408-429-8838). Its products have included a rare brewpub **Dry★→★★**, which dares to have a hint of taste; a **Lighthouse Lager★→★★**, clean and lightly hoppy; **Lighthouse Amber★★**, which is well-rounded, with a very hoppy finish; a **Dark Lager★★**, roasty, with a slightly medicinal finish; **Pacific Porter★★→★★★**, very dry and assertive, with coffeeish notes.

Seasonal specialities have included a smooth, chocolatey **Pacific Stout**★★→★★★, served in the pub at room temperature; a rich but hoppy **Beacon Barley Wine**★★→★★★; and an outstanding, intensely aromatic, Christmas beer called **Hoppy Holidays**★★★. The owners have backgrounds in the wine business.

Seabright

Santa Cruz's second brewpub, in a "desert deco" building, with a terrace (519 Seabright Ave, ☎408-426-2739). Early products have included **Pelican Pale**★★ (1055), slightly syrupy, with a dry finish; **Seabright Amber**★★→★★★ (1054), fruity and hoppy, with a long finish; the fruity, chocolatey, reddish-brown **Portola Dark**★★ (1056); and the assertive, chocolatey, well rounded, Imperial-style **Seabright Stout**★★→★★★ (1064).

Sherwood

The name derives from a classic film version of Robin Hood which was shot in the town of Chico, California. This brewpub, at 319 Main St, has undergone changes of ownership, and its future product policy may vary. It was formerly associated with the Saxton micro-brewery, which suspended trading in 1990.

Shields

Between Los Angeles and Santa Barbara, in Ventura, this family run brewpub produces the dryish **Gold Coast Beer**★→★★; the creamier, maltier, amber **Channel Islands Ale**★★ (the allusion is to a nearby group of islands, not those in the English Channel); and a dry **Shields Stout**★★.

Sierra Nevada

The Château Latour among American micro-breweries. Sierra Nevada was one of the earliest micros in the United States, and its products would win a "first-growth" rating anywhere in the world of brewing. **Sierra Nevada Draught Ale**★★★ (1048) is very slightly sweeter in palate than its companion bottled **Pale Ale**★★★→★★★★ (1052). This American classic has an irresistibly teasing balance between a huge floweriness of Cascade hops and the fruitiness of a top-fermenting yeast in its fresh bouquet and complex palate. The **Porter**★★★ (1050-52) is among the best brewed anywhere in the world: firmly dry, but with a gentle, coffee-toffee finish. The strong **Stout**★★★ (1064) is very smooth, with a powerful roastiness in the finish. A **Celebration Ale** is brewed for the winter holiday period, to a different specification each year, sometimes with experimental new varieties of hops. In late winter and early spring, Sierra Nevada has its **Big Foot Barley Wine**★★★→★★★★, with a huge hoppiness in its earthy aroma and chewy palate, and is one of the strongest beers in the United States (1095; 24.5 Plato; 8.48 alcohol by weight; 11.06 by volume). This beer is bottle-conditioned for four weeks at the brewery, and begins to become winier if it is kept for a further three months. It remains in good condition for a maximum of one to two years. In April, May and early June, the brewery has a springtime **Pale Bock**★★★ (1066), bright gold, very clean, soft, and dry, with a real punch of hops in the finish. In late June, this is replaced by a light, but hoppy, new lager called **Summerfest** (too early to rate). The brewery now has a taproom, with good food, a terrace and a family atmosphere.

San Luis

This micro, in San Luis Obispo, has undergone changes of ownership. Its product is **San Luis Lager**, and its makers are variously identified as Braun Breweries or Central Coast. The brew has a full amber colour and a fruity, tart, slightly astringent character. Too early to rate.

SLO

The town of San Luis Obispo gives its initials, and a location, to this brewpub. Products include a golden **Pale Ale★**, with a dry maltiness and some fruit; a smooth, definitely fruity **Amber Ale★★**; a fruity, chocolatey, sweetish **Porter★★** (1056); and very distinctive **IPA★★★**, matured over oak chips.

Stanislaus

This micro-brewery produces altbiers in broadly the Dussel-dorf style, originating from what seems an unlikely location amid the almond orchards of the Central Valley, and is owned by an American and his German wife, whose influence offers a clue to the style. Stanislaus County has a German history, but most of it is abstemiously Baptist. St Stan's is moving from its original ranch home to a more congruous pub and restaurant in Modesto. The original products are the full-coloured **Amber Alt★★→★★★** (1048), with a malty accent in its bouquet and soft palate, and some underlying fruitiness; and more assertively malty, sweeter, and faintly roasty, ruby-coloured **Dark Alt★★** (1056). St Stan's has a lighter, very dry, summer special called **Graffiti Alt** (too early to rate) - the name is a reference to the movie "American Graffiti".

Thousand Oaks

This tiny but respected lager brewery was originally operated in the cellar of his private house in a smart neighbourhood of Berkeley by enthusiast Charles Rixford. He has now taken his expertise as a consultant, and his products, to a re-structured version of the micro Golden Pacific, in Emeryville. Products include **Thousand Oaks★→★★**, an aromatic and well-balanced but slightly fruity lager broadly in the style of a Munich *Helles*; **Cable Car★★→★★★**, broadly in the Dortmunder style, with lots of hop aroma and a firm, malty texture; **Golden Gate★★**, in the Vienna style, sweetish, clean and very pleasant; and **Golden Bear★★→★★★**, somewhere between a Munich *Dark* and a *Bock* (5.5; 6.6), with lots of malty fullness and a balancing dryness. **Golden Pacific Bittersweet Ale★★** has a full, copper colour, some malty chewiness, and lots of balancing dryness. Golden Pacific also has a **California Pale Ale** (not tasted). These products are still evolving.

Tied House

The name whimsically indicates the intention to start a chain of "tied houses" on the British pattern. The first is in Silicon Valley, at the town of Mountain View. The original beers are a lightly fruity **Pale★**, very low in hop character; a fruity, lightly tart, pleasant **Amber★→★★**; and a maltier, hoppier **Dark★★**, reminiscent of a fairly soft English Bitter. The style is less of a pub than a cafe, with a flower garden.

Triple Rock

Well-established, down-to-earth, studenty brewpub on the main street of Berkeley (1920 Shattuck Ave. ☎415-843-2739).

Products include the golden **Pinnacle Pale Ale**★→★★, dry, lightly hoppy and fruity; **Red Rock Ale**★★, sweeter, still fruity, with more hop in a late finish; and **Black Rock Porter**★★, light-to-medium in body, but dry and quite complex. Many periodical specials. A Triple Rock is planned in San Francisco, at 316 11th St. The company also owns Big Time, in Seattle (see Northwest).

Truckee Brewing

High in the Sierras, between Sacramento and Reno. Parts of the brewery and bar are in a Southern Pacific boxcar and caboose, attached to a 1950s diner that has been given a new life as Pizza Junction. Since its establishment in 1985, the brewery has been upgraded. A prototype of a new Pilsener, called **Truckee Light**, was slightly fruity and very hoppy. The brewery has since added a **Dark** (not tasted).

Willett's

Charles Willett Ankeny is a member of the family that once owned the Hamm's breweries, of San Francisco and St Paul, Minnesota. In the late 1980s, he quit the wine industry to restore the family tradition. In the town of Napa he established a brewpub serving good food with a river-side terrace. Products have included the golden **Full Moon Light Ale**★★→★★★, very hoppy and appetizing; the extremely hoppy **Golden Thistle Bitter**★★→★★★; the tawny, fruity **Victory Ale**★★; the smooth, rich, dryish, cosmopolitan **Nelson's Black Beer**★★★ (dedicated to Nelson Mandela, but modelled on a Kulmbach-Japanese Black Beer); the very creamy, chocolatey, dry **Old Magnolia Stout**★★→★★★ and the smooth, malty, dryish pale **Maibock**★★. The selection is constantly varied.

Winchester

A house once owned by the Winchester gun family is a tourist attraction in San Jose. Hence the name of this brewpub. Products have included a hoppy, golden **Pale Ale**★★; a slightly syrupy, fruity, **Red Amber**★★; and a coffeeish **Special Porter**★★. Many seasonal specials.

THE NORTHWEST

For connoisseurs of beer, no American cities can approach Portland, Oregon, and Seattle, Washington.

Portland has more breweries than any other city (eight or nine in the metro area, subject to frequent openings: one regional brewery, three micros and four or five brewpubs. There are at least a further half-dozen micros or brewpubs elsewhere in Oregon.

Seattle also has one regional brewery, two micros, a third micro in the suburbs and a fourth on the edge of the metro area, and three brewpubs at the last count. There are another five or six breweries elsewhere in the state of Washington, and more in the adjoining parts of British Columbia, Canada.

In no other American cities are micro-brewed beers so widely served in bars and restaurants. Portland is perhaps the more chauvinistic about its local brews, but Seattle has more speciality beer bars. Both cities are small enough to have a local pride in their products, but are sufficiently large enough to offer a worthwhile market to their brewers. With their relatively cool weather, both states favour indoor drinking, in taverns, and draught beer is more widely marketed here than elsewhere in the US, which has helped the micros. Some establishments even serve cask-conditioned beer. The climate also favours the fuller-flavoured speciality brews, as opposed to light quenchers.

Seattle is known for its interest in quality drinks and food, and Portland quietly shares the same enthusiasm for civilized living. In both cities, the local daily newspapers run beer columns in rotation with their wine features. Seattle has America's most adventurous beer importer, Merchant du Vin. Portland has one of the more innovative regional brewers, Blitz Weinhard. Both cities are near wine-growing areas and, it must be whispered, share much culturally with the more northerly parts of California, where the micro-brewery movement began.

Where to drink

Portland has the biggest regional beer festival in the United States, usually the third weekend in July. Information can be obtained from any of the city's three micros (see entries for BridgePort, Portland and Widmer).

In Portland, its suburbs and neighbouring towns, Grateful Deadhead Mike McMenamin has a growing chain of pubs producing their own, offbeat beers. A good example is the Hillsdale (1505 SW Sunset Boulevard, ☎503-246-3938).

The best-known speciality beer pubs in Portland are the Horse Brass (4534 Belmont St) and Produce Row (204 SE Oak). Others include the Leaky Roof (1538 SW Jefferson), the Laurelthirst (30th and E Glisan), Coyotes (NE 28th and Sandy), and the Dublin Pub (6821 SW Beaverton and Hillside Highway). The Dublin pub has 102 draught taps, which may be a record – but can that many beers be in good condition? The Burlingame Grocery (8502 SW Terwilliger) claims to carry all the speciality and imported beers available in the state.

The elegant Heathman Hotel (SW Broadway and Salmon, ☎503-241-4100) is the place for the well-heeled beer-lover. Its two bars offer differing selections of micro and imported beers, and the hotel also owns the nearby B. Moloch bistro, which has its own associated brewery (see entry for Widmer).

In Seattle, recommended beer-bars include the Red Door (3401 Fremont Ave N, ☎206-547-7521), the Latona (6423 Latona Ave) and Murphy's (2110 N 45th, near the university). Coopers (8065 Lake City Way NE) is noted for its large selection of micro brews. The Blue Moon, famous as a picaresque and vaguely literary tavern, also has a good selection of beers. F.X. McRory, a bar-restaurant near the Kingdome (419 Occidental Ave S) has a large selection of micro brews on draught, and many of the city's restaurants offer micro brews. Cask-conditioned Redhook ESB is a surprise feature amid the apparent decadence of the Italian-tasting, Spanish-sounding Palomino restaurant.

The monthly *Cascade Beer News* (PO Box 12247, Portland, Oregon 97212) or the *Northwest Beer Journal* (2626 Lodge-pole Drive SE, Port Orchard, Washington 98366) and the Microbrew Appreciation Society (12345 Lake City Way NE, Seattle, Washington 98125), provide up-to-date information.

Alaskan Brewing

This is the most Northwesterly brewery in the United States (or even the American continent) and is to be found in Juneau, the state capital. It is renowned for its Christmas seasonal **Smoked**

Porter★★★→★★★★ (1055). The malt is smoked over alder twigs, across the street from the brewery, at an establishment that normally gives its attention to Alaskan salmon. The end product, which is top-fermented, has a powerful smokiness, a mellow woodiness, a faint hint of fruit, and an oily finish. The Smoked Porter is part of a changing repertoire of seasonal brews, also including an aromatic, hoppy, tawny **Autumn Ale**★★→★★★, and a wheat beer (not tasted). Regular products include a notably soft-bodied, fruity **Pale Ale**★★; and a remarkably smooth and malty altbier, **Alaskan Amber**★★★. The brewery was formerly called Chinook, but remains under the same ownership.

Bay Front

In the coastal resort of Newport, Oregon. This brewpub shares a range of products with Rogue (see entry), in Ashland.

Bayern

The name is German for "Bavaria", but this "Gasthaus Brauerei" is in Missoula, Montana. Initial products (not tasted) have included **Bayern Amber**, a Marzenbier of 13.5 Plato, hopped with Saaz as well as Cascades; and a **Wheat Beer**. The brewery uses a single decoction mash.

Big Time

This Seattle brewpub is an offshoot of Triple Rock, in Berkeley, California. Products have included a golden **Pale Ale**★★ with a good hoppy finish; a smooth, fruity, dryish **Amber**★★ (1058); a **Cask-Conditioned Amber**★★★ that is manifestly dry-hopped; a smooth, dry **Porter**★★ (1060); a **Rye Beer**★★★ that combines the spicy, minty notes of that grain with a refreshing sharpness (gravity has varied); and a barley wine called **Old Woolly**★★ that is very malty indeed.

Blitz Weinhard

Best known for its super-premium **Henry Weinhard's Private Reserve**★★→★★★. When this product was launched, in the 1970s, the brewery took what was then the revolutionary step of letting the hops proclaim themselves. Such extrovert behaviour is less noticeable in today's climate, but Henry's is still one of the more aromatic examples of a light, American-style Pilsener. **Henry Weinhard's Dark**→★★ is light and dry. **Blue Boar Ale**★→★★ is gently fruity and popcorn-sweet. Its claims to being of an Irish style are nonsense. The brewery, in Portland, is owned by Heileman.

BridgePort

There is the rare opportunity to compare a range of conventionally served draught ales against their cask-conditioned counterparts at the tap-room of this micro-brewery. The **Golden Ale**★→★★, light, firm and dry, is not available cask-conditioned. The following products are rated at their best – in cask form. The ruby-coloured **BridgePort Ale**★★★ (1048) is soft, malty, fruity, and Scottish-accented. The amber-red (despite its name) **Blue Heron**★★★ (1052) is creamy, again quite malty, but with much more aromatic hop coming through in the cask version. It appears to be a genuine coincidence that both BridgePort and Mendocino County in California, have ales called Blue Heron. BridgePort's **Double Stout**★★ is smooth, toffeeish, fruity and dry, with a good length. The bottled **Old Knucklehead**★★→★★★ is a malty, fruity, well-rounded, very alcoholic-tasting barley wine. The brewery's founders are the winemaking family Ponzi.

Coeur d'Alene

A resort in Idaho. The Coeur d'Alene brewery is attached to the T.W. Fisher brewpub (204 N 2nd St. ☎208-664-2739). An early product has been a light, fruity **Pale Ale**★★.

Columbia River

Now re-named BridgePort.

Deschutes

The name emerges from rapids near the town of Bend, Oregon. The town in turn takes its name from a bend on the Deschutes river. The Deschutes Brewery and Pub has produced a hoppy **Festival Pils**★★; a soft, sweetish **Cascade Golden Ale**★★, with an appropriate dash of hops in the finish; a slightly chewy, malty **Bachelor Bitter**★★→★★★, satisfying and distinctive; a fruity, dry-hopped **Mirror Pond Pale Ale**★★→★★★ (1050); a smooth, soft **Anniversary Alt**★★★, with a malty start, a fruity middle and a hoppy finish; a dry, oily **Black Butte Porter**★★→★★★ (1054); a fruitier, sweeter **Obsidian Stout**★★→★★★ (1068); and a malty, creamy **Weissbock** (tasted out of season – not rated). All of the brews have a very good head, and there is some butteriness in the house character.

Fort Spokane

In the eastern Washington city of Spokane, this brewpub has made a smoked beer, among other products (not tasted).

Grant's

Hop country micro-brewery and pub, known for its distinctive products, and making liberal use of the Yakima Valley crop. The beers are created by the equally characterful Scottish-born brewer, hop expert Bert Grant. The fruity **Celtic Ale**★★★ has the gravity (1034) and appearance of a dark Mild (less Irish than Middle English), but with far more hop. The medium-amber **Grant's Ale**★★★ (1052), smooth and malty, is billed as being Scottish in style, but again has more hop than that suggests. The golden **IPA**★★★ takes full advantage of that description and permits itself to be very dry indeed, with a powerful, lingering, hop finish. The **Imperial Stout**★★★ (1068) is fruity and honeyish, but still dry. The oddly-spelled **Weis**★★, made with 30 percent wheat, is light, smooth, dry and tart (1044). The brewery is in the old opera house at Yakima, Washington. Its associated pub has now moved across the street to the baggage room of the old railroad station, whence trains still depart on tours through the valley. **Grant's Scottish Ale** is served cask-conditioned and is softer and sweeter. The taproom also has its own small brewhouse, making one-off specials.

Hale's

Two-branch micro-brewery. The more accessible branch is the newer one, in a Seattle suburb, Kirkland. The brewery adjoins a restaurant called the Kirkland Roaster. Products have included the very pale and light, hoppy **Cascade Mist**★→★★; the thinnish, lightly fruity, hoppy **American Pale Ale**★★; the fruitier, pleasant **Moss Bay Amber**★★; the fruity, tart, hoppy

Moss Bay Extra★★; a maltier, rounder, softer **Special Bitter**★★→★★★, which has a good aromatic hop character in the finish; a fruity, roasty, dry **Porter**★★→★★★; and a sedimented, light, dry, appleish **Wheat**★★. A **Stout** has also been produced (not tasted) and a **Wee Heavy** for Christmas. The products seem slightly drier, firmer, and fuller in flavour at the original brewery, in distant Colville, in eastern Washington.

Hart

See Pyramid.

Hood River

From Mount Hood, the river of the same name flows towards Columbia. At Hood River, Oregon, the smaller waterway flows into the larger one. Now, there is a brewery and pub: the Hood River Brewing Company and White Cap Pub have grown very quickly on the popularity of their Full Sail Ales. These include **Golden**★★, hoppy in its bouquet and palate; **Amber**★★★, malty-buttery, fruity, smooth and rounded, with a depth of flavour and an aromatically hoppy finish (it was inspired by Samuel Smith's Pale Ale); **Brown**★★→★★★, northern English in style but almost mahogany in colour, chocolatey, with an underlying fruitiness; **Porter**★★, fruity, almost raisiny, with a hint of oloroso sherry; **Stout**★★→★★★, chocolatey, fruity, very dry and assertive; **Barley Wine**★★→★★★, tawny, with lots of hop taste; and other seasonal specials. Pubs opening varies according to season.

Kemper

Much-improved products from one of the few Northwestern micros to specialize in lager. There remains a nostalgic hint of the famously inappropriate "blueberry" fruitiness in the **Helles**★→★★, but a different yeast is used for the hoppy, dry, clean, soft, **Pilsener**★★→★★★ and the malty, slightly toffeeish, **Dunkel**★★. Seasonal specialities include a **Maytime Bock**, an autumn **Festbier** and a heavy, sweetish, dark **Winterbrau**. The brewery now has a taproom and garden.

Kessler

A local brewery name revived by a micro in the unlikely location of Last Chance Gulch, Helena, Montana. Early products included an excellent, wide range of German styles. More recently, Kessler seems to have been devoting a lot of attention to making contract-brews for other companies.

Noggins

Cafe-style brewpub on the third floor of a shopping development, the Westlake Center, in Seattle. Early products included a **Best Bitter**★→★★ (1052), with a full copper colour, a thinnish palate and a hint of apple in the fruity palate; a blackcurranty **Porter**★→★★ (1056), dry-hopped with East Kent Goldings; a golden **IPA**★→★★ (1060), with some hop in the finish; and a **Weizenbrau**★★ (1047) with both tartness and sweetness. A sister establishment in the University district closed. Neither had beers of a quality to match those of their parent, Spinnakers, in Victoria, Canada.

Olympia

Light-tasting mainstream beers from a brewery owned by Pabst. At Olympia, state capital of Washington.

Oregon Trail

Hop country micro in Corvallis, Oregon. Sporadic production of ale, porter and stout.

Pacific Northwest

The word "Pacific" has featured in more names of beers and breweries than anyone cares to remember. This is a brewpub in the heart of downtown Seattle. Its founder, Richard Wrigley, also launched the Manhattan and Commonwealth brewpubs, on the East Coast, but is no longer involved with either. Pacific Northwest produces a tasty range of brews, all with a good hop bouquet. These have included a **Blonde★★** (1040), with Saaz as the finishing hop, and a fuller-coloured **Gold★★** (1045), with more of an American Northwestern accent. At the same gravity are an English-accented **Bitter★★→★★★**, with Goldings in the aroma but Tettnang in the copper; a fruity, tasty, well-balanced **Amber★★→★★★**; and a very fruity, dry, **Stout★★**. Seasonal specials have included an amber-red **Winter Warmer★★★** (1100), very malty in both bouquet and palate. House specialities include *Strawberry Blonde* – laced with Cointreau and Grenadine. The British-style beers in the range are fined, kept under blanket pressure, and served at 12°C + (55°F +).

Pike Place

High-quality, truly hand-made beers from a tiny, four-barrel micro, with a solid copper kettle, in the Liberty Malt home-brew and bookshop at Seattle's famous retail produce market (1432 Western Ave, ☎206-622-1880). The brewery is on the site of the La Salle Hotel, once a house of ill repute. **Pike Place Pale Ale★★★** (1052-54) is nutty, with a creamy complex of malt and hop; **5X Stout★★★** (1068) is very soft, smooth, toasty, dryish and even more delicious.

Pizza Deli and Brewery

New brewpub in an old-established restaurant at Cave Junction, Oregon.

Portland Brewing

The name belongs to a brewing capital, but blends too easily into the beery cityscape. The American-accented ales of Portland Brewing should not be overlooked. The soft, easily drinkable, **Oregon Dry★★** (1042-45), primed with honey, is something of an oddity; **Timberline★★** (1046-47) is a quench-ing, golden ale, sweetish but with a good hop note in both bouquet and finish; **Portland Ale★★→★★★**, at around the same gravity and still on the light side, is very hoppy all the way through; **Portland Porter★★→★★★**, again at 1048, is light and dry – a good example of the style. Portland also brews, under licence, very well-made examples of the Grant's products. Portland Brewing is a micro and pub.

Pyramid

Is there a pyramid among the peaks of the Cascade mountains? The whimsical say it is true. This brewery, formerly known as Hart, is not far from Portland, across the Washington state line in Kalama. Pyramid's products may evolve in new premises, but it is to be hoped that they retain their considerable individuality. The oddly named **Wheaten Ale★★→★★★** (1042) is golden and bright, slightly perfumy, well attenuated, smooth, dry, tart and refreshing. **Pyramid Pale Ale★★★** (1046)

has a reddish-amber colour, a very hoppy-fruity bouquet, a hint of sweet, almost chocolatey, malt in the well-rounded palate, and a lingering, dry finish. **Pacific Crest★★** (1052) is a pale amber, smooth and malt-accented, with a hoppy balance in the finish. **Sphinx Stout★★→★★★** has an appetizing coffee-chocolate aroma, a good flavour development, and a dry finish. This product is unfiltered. **Snow Cap★★★** (1066-72) is a vintage-dated barley wine, with a beautiful balance of malt, aromatic hop (sustained all the way through) and fruit.

Rainier

It was once dubbed "The Green Death", but **Rainier Ale★★** today seems a shadow of its former sins. Even the regular **Rainier Beer★** seems sweeter and less firm-bodied than it was. Rainier, in Seattle, is owned by Heileman.

Redhook

One of the first micros in the Northwest and now by far the biggest, in new premises with its own taproom in a former streetcar barn (Redhook Brewery and Trolleyman Pub). The original product, the full-coloured **Red Hook Ale★★** (1050) now makes only occasional appearances, like an aging star of showbiz. When it does appear, its intense fruitiness is whimsically alluded to by a drawing of a banana on the neck label. The year-round **Red Hook ESB★★** (1054) has a paler amber colour, is more conventionally fruity and medium-dry, and expresses itself at its best in cask-conditioned form. **Ballard Bitter★★** (1044), named after the site of the original brewery, is pale, fruity and dry. **Blackhook Porter★★** (1047) is smooth and dryish, with a hint of treacle-toffee. **Wheat Hook★★**, available in spring and summer, is fruity, hoppy, crisp, firm and clean. It can occasionally be found unfiltered. In the fall, a tawny, nutty **Winterhook** is available (not tasted). The Redhook brews remain interesting, but the principal products have lost a tad of character since the early days. The founders of Redhook have backgrounds in coffee and wine.

Rogue

Tasty brews made at related micro/brewpubs in Oregon, at Ashland and Newport. Products have included the soft but very dry **Microlite Wheat★★**; the pink, tart, aromatic, **Boysenberry Wheat★★**; the clean and fruity **Rogue Golden★★**; the aromatic, slighty caramel-like, faintly oily **Ashland Amber★★**; the similar **Rogue Red★★**, with a dry finish; the smooth, substantial, coffeeish, dry **Royal Shakespeare Stout★★→★★★** (named after the theater festival in Ashland); and a light-tasting but smooth, silky **Oatmeal Stout★★→★★★**.

Roslyn

The old coal-mining town of Roslyn, about 120km (75 miles) east of Seattle, in the direction of Yakima, now has a micro-brewery, with tasting room. Its first product, called simply **Roslyn Beer★★→★★★**, is a reddish-brown ale, with an assertive palate that combines some chocolatey sweetness with a good belt of Northern Brewer hops in the finish.

Smith and Reilly

Broadly in the Pilsener style, **Smith and Reilly Honest Beer★★** has a grassy hoppiness and a little more firmness than most American pale lagers. The company is based in

Vancouver (Washington state, not Canada), and the beer is contract-brewed at Olympia.

Snake River

A hop-farming family owns this micro at Caldwell, west of Boise, Idaho. A hop garden surrounds the brewery, and the family also grows its own malting barley. Surprisingly, there is only a light hop character – and a proportion of rice adjunct – in **Snake River Premium Lager**★→★★, which is on the sweet side. There is also a very sweet **Amber Lager**★→★★.

Sun Valley

White **Cloud Ale**★★, with a full, amber colour, a toasty-malty aroma and palate, and some balancing dryness, is the first product from this company, in Sun Valley, Idaho. This hearty brew used to be produced under contract by Kessler, in Montana.

Widmer

German-style beers from a family run micro in Portland. The family is of German origin. Products have included a very dry **Weizenbier**★★; a yeasty **Hefe-Weizen**★★→★★★; the flagship **Alt**★★★, with a malty start and an splendidly hoppy palate and finish; a full-coloured, malty **Marzen**★★→★★★; a slightly paler, malty-fruity **Oktoberfest**★★; a bronze, malty **Bock**★→★★ for the spring; and other specialities. Widmer is moving from the northwest of the city to the east side of the river, where its new brewery will also have a saloon. In the downtown area, some of the Widmer beers are also produced (and all are available) at a brewpub and "bakery" (it serves light meals), called B. Moloch (which is associated with the Heathman Hotel).

THE CARIBBEAN

Emigrants from the Caribbean have helped spread the popularity of several beers from the region. The best-known internationally is **Red Stripe**★→★★, light-tasting, soft-bodied lager from Jamaica. Other examples include the maltier and fruiter **Banks Lager**★→★★ from Barbados; and the malty, but drier **Carib Lager**★★ from Trinidad. Gravities are typically in the classical Pilsener range of 11.5-12 Plato (1046-48); units of bitterness low (15-19); and lagering times short (two weeks is common). In Caribbean ethnic markets in Britain, Red Stripe has an extra-strong lager called **Crucial Brew**★. Several Caribbean breweries also have sweet or medium-dry stouts, often bottom-fermented, and usually at "tropical" gravities; in the range of 15-20 Plato (1060-1080), with alcohol contents of between 4.5 and 6 percent by weight; 5.75-7.75 by volume. Some of these are produced in unlikely places, Haiti, for example, has the dry, fruity, **Prestige Stout**★★.

St Thomas, on the US Virgin Islands, has the world's biggest malt-extract brewery, capable of producing 13,000 barrels a year of Spinnaker Lager.

LATIN AMERICA

All the countries of Latin America have brewing industries, some very large. All produce beers distantly derived from the Germanic tradition, including the occasional dark speciality. A good example is Brazil's tasty **Xingu**★★→★★★, the US with a spurious story linking it to the Indians of the Amazon.

Outside Latin America, the sub-continent's best-known beers are those from Mexico, many of which are exported to the US. The success in the US of a product called **Corona** (see entry, under Modelo) has done a disservice to Mexican beer. Corona is a cheaply made, watery, sweetish, beer, originally intended simply as a thirst-quencher for manual workers in Mexico. Each of the brewers in Mexico has such a product, usually bottled in plain glass, with an enamelled name instead of a label. By a freak of fashion, and initially with very little promotion, Corona became a cult beer among sub-Yuppies in the southwest of the US. This has encouraged Mexican brewers to concentrate on such products, at the expense of their several more interesting beers. It has also encouraged Americans to believe that all Mexican beer is light and bland. The way things are going, that will soon be true.

Cuauhtémoc

Second-largest of the Mexican brewing companies. Also owns Cruz Blanca. (And is itself owned by the same holding company as Moctezuma.) The Cuauhtémoc products are lightened by a high proportion of corn, and tend to have a dry, slightly tannic, finish. The company has a typically Mexican range. The "clear-glass" brand is **Chihuahua**★. The dry, crisp, quencher **Tecate**★ began as a regional brand. **Carta Blanca**★ and (in the US market) the smooth **Carta Blanca Dark**★→★★ are mainstream brands. **Bohemia**★★ is a pleasantly hoppy Pilsener with a high gravity for the style (13; 1052; 4.2; 5.4). **Indio Oscura**★→★★ is a reddish lager, broadly of the Vienna type but a little thin and dry for the style. **Commemorativa**★★→★★★ (14.3; 1057; 4.3; 5.6) is a medium-dark Christmas beer.

Moctezuma

Biggest exporter, but smallest in the Mexican market. Uses a lower proportion of adjuncts and makes a point that they include rice. Its beers tend to be relatively smooth, with a spritzy finish: kräusening is another point of policy. **Sol**★ is its is a newcomer to the range; **Superior**★→★★ is a lightly fragrant, spritzy, Pilsener-type (11.5; 1046; 3.6; 4.5). Then comes the rather confusing Equis range. **Tres Equis**★→★★ is a marginally fuller Pilsener-type. **Dos Equis Lager Especial**★→★★ is fractionally fuller again (12; 1048- 3.7; 4.6). The best-known version, simply called **Dos Equis**★★, is amber-red in colour, and broadly in the Vienna style. It, too, has a gravity of 12 Plato. The dark brown **Noche Buena**★★★ Christmas Beer

(15; 1060; 4.2; 5.4) is very full-bodied, with both malt and hop in its long finish, but there are doubts about its continued existence. **Tres Equis Oscura** has been discontinued, because the company has more faith in its less interesting beers.

Modelo

Biggest of the Mexican brewing companies, also owning Yucatan. Its most noteworthy product is the **Negra Modelo★★★**, on the dark side for a Vienna-style beer, creamy in body, with a hint of chocolate (just the thing with chicken molé). The Yucatan brands include a similar beer, the tasty, hoppier, **Negra Leon★★**.

ASIA

When the United States sent Commodore Perry to "open up" Japan in 1835, the idea of beer-brewing was seeded, and soon grew. Outside the United States, the biggest brewing company in a domestic market is Kirin, of Japan.

The basic **Kirin Lager Beer★→★★** has the fullest body among the Japanese Pilseners, with Hallertau and Saaz hops in both aroma and flavour. Among several excellent specialities is **Kirin Stout★★★** (18 Plato; 1072; 6.4; 8) which is especially notable. It is bottom-fermenting, but full of "burnt treacle toffee" flavour.

Sapporo Black Beer★★★ represents a Japanese speciality (which seems originally to have been based on the Kulmbach beers). This dry, dark lager, with licorice tones, can best be tasted in the beer garden in the Victorian part of the brewery in Sapporo. This company also has an unpasteurized (micro-filtered), all-malt premium Pilsener called **Yebisu★★**, very fruity, with some hop bitterness in the finish. It has also experimented with a very mild wheat beer. Asahi's beers tend to be dry and fruity, but with a weak finish. Suntory produces unpasteurized beers that are notably clean and mild, though dry. This company's speciality is a sweetish beer called **Malt's★★**.

No brewing country is as innovative as Japan, nor as susceptible to marketing fashions. Asahi pioneered "Dry" beers, contributing much to its own business success and to marketing mythology. This is not a style that need greatly detain serious beer-lovers, though the Japanese versions do have a tad more taste than their American disciples.

When Germany enjoyed a colonial "concession" in Shantung, China, a brewery was established in the resort town of Tsingtao. This is now one of China's major exporters, and **Tsingtao Beer★→★★**, a hoppy

Pilsener, is a popular accompaniment to its national cuisine in New York and San Francisco. The very sweet **Tsingtao Porter**★ is harder to find the West. Many Chinese beers have made brief appearances in the US, sometimes under Anglicized names invented by importers. Meanwhile, China now has a British-style micro-brewery, producing ale, at Changsha, in Hunan province.

German technical help was used in 1934 to set up the Boon Rawd Brewery, which produces the outstandingly hoppy **Singha Lager**★★★ (13.8 Plato; 1055; 4.8; 6; and a hearty 40 units of bitterness) in Thailand. The local rival **Amarit**★→★★ is milder.

While the Singha is a mythical creature resembling a lion, Tiger Beer is a legend in its own lunch-time, perhaps because it entered literature through the pen of Anthony Burgess. **Tiger Lager Beer**★→★★ is a hoppier cousin to Heineken. The same brewery has in its range the creamy, roasty, medium-dry **ABC Extra Stout**★★→★★★ (18.2; 1073; 6.5; 8.1). These products are made in Singapore and Malaysia.

India had 14 breweries in Colonial days, four by Independence, and now has no fewer than 32. United Breweries, of Bangalore, is active in export markets with its flowery **Kingfisher**★ lager and a slightly hoppier, and smoother, premium Pilsener variously called **Jubilee** and **Flying Horse**★→★★. Kingfisher is brewed under licence in Britain, by Shepherd Neame. In Sri Lanka, McCallum makes an all-malt **Three Coins Pilsener**★★ and a smooth, chocolatey, bottom-fermenting **Sando Stout**★★→★★★ (15; 1060). The rival Ceylon Breweries has the fruitier, top-fermenting (in wood) **Lion Stout**★★★, also all-malt, at a similar gravity, producing 5 percent alcohol by weight; 6.3 by volume. Astonishingly, Ceylon Breweries' lager and stout are available, unpasteurized, from wooden casks, drawn by hand-pump, at The Beer Shop, in the brewery's home town of Nuwara Eliya, and at U.K.D. Silva, in the holy city of Kandy.

Except in fundamentalist Muslim countries, almost every corner of Asia has breweries. In a reversal of Colonial roles, Spain's San Miguel breweries have their parent company in The Philippines. In addition to the light, smooth, dry **San Miguel**★→★★, a pale Pilsener, the Filipinos also enjoy **Gold Eagle**★→★★, lower in gravity but fuller in colour, and the stronger (14; 1056; 5.5; 6.8) **Red Horse**★→★★, soft-bodied, with some fruity notes. **San Miguel Dark Beer**★★ also has an above-average gravity (13.5; 1054; 4.1; 5.2) and a good toasted-malt character.

AUSTRALIA

Australia's Big Two, Elders (with its brewing interests now re-grouped under the banner of Foster's, its principal brand) and Bond (Castlemaine/Swan) have both proven to be over-ambitious. Their Byzantine empires have encountered difficulties at home, and plans to conquer the world have been further hindered by a fading of the fashion for everything Australian.

At home, Foster's has now acquired Matilda Bay, the leader of the Australian micro-brewery and brewpub movement (if you can't beat 'em. buy 'em). The micro phenomenon began in the early 1980s, and a decade later there are about 30 new breweries in Australia and several more in New Zealand.

Where to drink

Brewpubs in Sydney include The Lord Nelson, Argyle and York Streets, The Rocks (ale, stout and wheat beer); Craig's, on the Ultimo side of Darling Harbour; and the Pumphouse, Little Pier St, Darling Harbour (a wheat beer). The Pumphouse also has beers from Brittens brewery. South of Sydney, at Picton, is Scharer's Little Brewery, producing a lager and a dark Burragorang Bock (6.8 percent by volume), both all-malt, unfiltered and noted for their fullness of flavour.

Melbourne's first brewpub, The Loaded Dog (324 St George's Rd, North Fitzroy) now has a small Burton Union brewing system. Other brewpubs include The Geebung Polo Club (Auburn Rd, Hawthorn), making ales and stouts; Bill Bell's (Moray St, South Melbourne), with bitter, porter and ginger ale; and The Station Tavern (96 Greville St, Prahan) producing ale and stout. There is a tiny Redback branch brewery at the Royal Hotel, 75 Flemington Rd. North of Melbourne, at Bendigo (137 View St), a country pub called the Rifle Brigade produces lagers.

South Australia has the most interesting old-established brewery in the country: Cooper's. There is also a view that Cooper's local rival, South Australian, makes the tastiest beers of any mainstream brewer. This is, of course, relative.

In Tasmania, the St Ives Hotel (Sandy Bay Road, Hobart) has brewed on occasion. North of Launceston, the Rosevears Hotel makes a mild, a bitter, a porter and a stout.

In Western Australia, The Sail and Anchor, in Fremantle (64 South Terrace), was the first brewpub in Australia. The same owners founded the first micro-brewery, Matilda Bay. The Sail and Anchor specializes in top-fermenting ales, served on hand-pump. Its flagship ale is now known as Ironbrew. The earlier name, Dogbolter, has been appended to a dark lager produced by Matilda Bay.

In Brisbane, Kelly's Brewery and Cafe (521 Stanley St) produces a mainstream, Australian-style bitter and a dark lager. The Sanctuary Cove brewery makes a lager, served in its own beer garden.

Cascade

This Tasmanian concern is the oldest-established brewery in Australia, founded in 1824. Its **Cascade Draught**★→★★ has a marginally lower gravity and alcohol content, but a fuller colour and more flavour, than its **Special Lager**★→★★. The crisp **Cascade Premium Lager**★★ is popular on the mainland. A bottom-fermenting **Sparkling Pale Ale**★★ has a little more hop character. **Cascade's Export Stout**★★ is slightly paler, but higher in gravity and bitterness than that from the island's other brewery, Boag's, which is under the same ownership. Boag's, in Launceston, has a fairly full-bodied and dry **Lager**★★.

Castlemaine

Bond-owned brewery producing the firm-bodied **Castlemaine XXXX**★★. Products also include the tasty, bottom-fermenting **Carbine Stout**★★→★★★.

Cooper's

Classic brewery, founded 1862, still run by the Cooper family, producing ale and stout fermented and wood and bottle-conditioned. **Cooper's Sparkling Ale**★★★→★★★★ (1046; 4.6; 5.75) is, in fact, heavily sedimented. It is full of fruitiness, with a good dash of hop bitterness, though it has lost some of its colour over the years. **Cooper's Extra Stout**★★★→★★★★ (1054; 5.4; 6.8) is splendidly earthy and dry. Newer products include a **Pale Ale** (4.5v) and a dark, malty, heavily-sedimented **Scotch Ale**, which shows promise.

Eagle Hawk Hill

English-accented ales from a brewery with its own bar, in a motel and convention complex at Sutton, in Canberra.

Eumundi

Lager brewery adjacent to the Imperial Hotel, Eumundi. Too early to rate.

Foster's

One of half a dozen breweries that combined to form Carlton and United in Melbourne in 1907. It is only in recent years that Foster's became a national brand in Australia (and Britain). **Foster's Lager**★ is sweetish and full-bodied. **Carlton Draught**★→★★ is dryish and slightly fuller in colour. **Victoria Bitter**★ is a lager. In Australia, the term Bitter implies a lager with some hop character. There is also a **Melbourne Bitter**★→★★, with perhaps a dash more hop. The company also makes a couple of similar stouts.

Hahn

Well-made, tasty, lagers from a substantial new brewery at Camperdown, Sydney.

Kent Town

Historic maltings that now has a tiny brewery producing ales in a similar style to those made by Cooper's.

Kiewa

Spring water is brought by tank to this micro in Bayswater North to help produce the all-malt **Wattle Lager**. Specials have included a honey beer called **Kiewa Gold**.

Matilda Bay

Now in new premises in Fremantle, with a brewhouse that first saw service in Northern France. Flagship product is **Red-Back★★★**, a wheat beer. RedBack is made from locally grown wheat, which comprises 65 percent of the mash. It has a gravity of 1045 and an alcohol content of 3.7; 4.8. RedBack is an interesting brew, slightly reminiscent of Belgian "white" beers. It has a very pale golden color, a light, firm body, and a faintly acidic, honey-apple aroma and palate. RedBack is now a "bright" beer, though there is talk of re-launching the original unfiltered version as RedBack Classic (or some similar name). In the meantime, the integrity of the brand-name has not been helped by the launch of RedBack Light. The brewery also has a very hoppy Pilsener-style beer, a dark lager, and seasonal specials for winter, Christmas and Easter.

Old Lion

Micro adjacent to the Lion Hotel (Melbourne St, North Adelaide), but a separate business. Produces a **Pilsener**, a **Light Ale**, a **Dark Lager**, a **Strong Ale** (with the traditional name *Stingo*) and promises a Wheat Beer.

Power's

Very aggressive new brewery producing a mainstream, Australian-style **Bitter** to compete with Castlemaine (especially) and the local Elders branch brewery.

South Australian Brewing

Independent (though some equity is held by Foster's) brewery in Adelaide that has diversified into other businesses. Products include the dryish **West End Draught★→★★**; the perfumy, but maltier, **Southwark Premium★★**; the sweetish **Old Southwark Stout★★→★★★**; and a moderately hoppy, spritzy, **Broken Hill Lager★→★★**.

Sovereign

Substantial micro in Ballarat, making "European-style" lager and stout.

Swan

Bond's first brewery. Its beers, under the Swan and Emu brands, are – by Australian standards – dryish and fairly light-bodied.

Toohey's

Bond-owned breweries in Sydney. Noted for **Hunter Old★★→★★★** (1040), a dark, top-fermenting ale with some aromatic, estery, fruitiness and roasted barley notes. **Tall Ships★★★** was launched in the late 1980s as a super-premium brew in a similar style.

Tooth's

Elders-owned producer of **Kent Old Brown★★** and the dryish **Carlton Stout★★★** (formerly Sheaf). Its **K.B.★→★★** is a dryish lager.

NEW ZEALAND

The country's first brewpub was the Shakespeare Tavern and Ale-House, at 61 Albert St, Auckland. The area now has two micros in Henderson (Waitakere and Stockan) and a third at Onehunga. This is called Newbegin, and produces a hoppy Pilsener called **Silver Fern** and a malty, dark lager under the name **Old Thumper**. At New Plymouth, the tiny White Cliffs brewery sells beer at the cellar-door. The Anchor brewery, of Porrirua, Wellington, produces a range of sweetish ales, including the assertive Coaster Blotto (6.5v). In Petone, the Strongcroft brewery makes a sweetish Directors' Ale and a Best Bitter (both 4v) and Owd Jim (5v). Further brewpubs include three in Christchurch: the Brewer's Arms (Merivale); Dux Delux (Arts Centre, City) and Hororata Hotel; and one each in Gisborne, Hamilton and Tauranga.

As in other countries, one stimulus to open a new brewery is a minority's dissatisfaction with the blandness of the mainstream products (which in New Zealand tend also to be very sweet). Equally, the widespread popularity of those products can make life difficult for the micro-brewers, especially in a country with few big-city markets.

Lion

Sweetish products under the Lion brand, a lager in the Heineken style under the name **Leopard**$\star\to\star\star$, and the mildly dry, award-winning **Steinlager**$\star\star$.

Mac's

The first micro-brewery in New Zealand, near Nelson, at Stoke. Founder Terry McCashin buys hops and barley grown in the locality, and has his own maltings. **Mac's Real Ale**$\star\star$ is actually produced with a lager yeast and, in its bottled form, pasteurized. It is intended to have ale characteristics but is really a malty, full-flavoured, bronze lager. **Black Mac**$\star\star$ is a dark lager. **Mac's Gold**$\star\star\to\star\star\star$ is a pale lager, well-hopped and smooth. **Southop**$\star\to\star\star$ is a sweet lager in the style typical of New Zealand.

Maxim

Formerly known as Dominion. The dubious achievement of having developed the continuous-fermentation method is accorded to this company. **Dominion Bitter**$\star$ is its main product. **Kiwi Lager**$\star\to\star\star$ has a little more character.

AFRICA

The continent of Africa might claim to have had some of the first brewers, as the ancient Egyptians produced beer in at least 3000BC.

These beers were brewed from barley that was "malted" by a process of being germinated and then baked into a bread-like condition. This was then fermented, and must have produced something like the *kvass* that is still widely consumed in Russia. The unfiltered beer may have resembled the turbid, porridge-like traditional brews that are still made in Africa, from millet, cassava flour, plantains, or whatever is locally available.

However, all except the most fundamentalist Muslim countries of Africa have their own breweries producing modern beers. Most of these beers are of the Pilsener type, though the odd *bock* can occasionally be found – and there are one or two ales (in South Africa) and stouts (in several countries, notably Nigeria). The stouts are usually dry, and sometimes of considerable strength (the tropical version of Guinness, at more than 18 Plato and 1070; around 8 percent alcohol by volume is typical).

Household names in most western European nations have established in Africa, or contracted or licensed their products to be made there. Or they have acted as consultants or partners to local breweries, often with participation from national governments. In all, there are about 175 breweries in Africa, in at least 45 countries. By far the most heavily-breweried country is Nigeria, with more than 50, most of them built in the last two decades. Zaire and South Africa are also significant brewing nations in terms of volume. However, some very well-made beers are brewed in very small countries, like Gambia, Togo and the Seychelles. Several African breweries have at times exported. A super-premium version of Kenya's **Tusker**★★ lager, much more aromatic and hoppy than the usual domestic products, has attracted some attention.

Africa's first micro-brewery went into operation in 1984, in Knysna, Cape Province. The brewery began with an all-malt draught lager, then began to experiment with seasonal ales and stouts, cask-conditioned. Knysna is on the south coast, between Cape Town and Port Elizabeth. A second micro, called simply Our Brewery, has since opened at St. George's St, Johannesburg. Produces a filtered but unpasteurized ale. There have also been tentative attempts to start a wheat-beer brewery in South Africa. Such are the ambitions of the beer renaissance.

INDEX

Main entries are indicated by figures in **bold**